The Magic of Lewis Carroll

Also by John Fisher:

John Fisher's Magic Book
Funny Way to be a Hero

The Magic of Lewis Carroll

EDITED BY
John Fisher

Simon and Schuster New York

SBN 671–21604–X
Library of Congress Catalog Card Number: 73–3973
Manufactured in Great Britain

The Magic of Lewis Carroll
has been set in 11/13 point and
10 point Monophoto Apollo

Line illustrations by Sir John Tenniel,
Henry Holiday, Arthur B. Frost,
Harry Furniss and Lewis Carroll;
diagrams by Laura Potter.
The book has been designed by
John Lewis

Printed in Great Britain by
Butler and Tanner Ltd Frome and London

Contents

For Susanna

Introduction

On March 1, 1875, the following entry appeared in Lewis Carroll's diary:

> Wrote to Tenniel on the subject of an idea which I first entered in my memorandum book, Jan: 8th, of printing a little book of original puzzles etc., which I think of calling *Alice's Puzzle-Book*.

Ten years later the idea had grown. In his diary entry for March 29, 1885, Carroll admits that 'never before have I had so many literary projects on hand at once.' He then proceeds 'for curiosity' to list fifteen separate projects from dryasdust mathematical treatises with titles like *Supplement to Euclid and Modern Rivals* and *Plain Facts for Circle-Squarers* under his real name of C. L. Dodgson to a projected bowdlerised edition of Shakespeare for young girls. More promising, however, at No. 8 in the list, are details of 'A collection of Games and Puzzles of my devising, with fairy pictures by Miss E. G. Thomson. This might also contain my "Memoria Technica" for dates, etc., my "cipher-writing", scheme for Letter-registration, etc. etc.' Sadly, the book never appeared. It was advertised with rash prematurity under the title *Original Games and Puzzles* in the preface to *Sylvie and Bruno Concluded* at Christmas, 1893, but had not materialised by the time of his death on January 14, 1898. To understand fully, however, the complement such a volume would have made to his life's work, one must sketch a fuller portrait of Carroll himself.

The Reverend Charles Lutwidge Dodgson (January 27, 1832–January 14, 1898) was a dull, mediocre lecturer in mathematics at the Oxford college of Christ Church, his own alma mater, from 1855 until the end of Michaelmas Term, 1881, when he resigned to devote his life to writing – 'partly in the cause of mathematical education, partly in the cause of innocent recreations for children, and partly, I hope (though so utterly unworthy of being allowed to take up such work) in the cause of religious thought.' He had gone up to Oxford in May, 1850 and resided there in college quarters in Tom Quad leading a bachelor existence – the condition of his fellowship being that he remain celibate and proceed to holy orders – until his death thirteen days before his sixty-sixth birthday. But to focus upon the author who wrote insignificant, unexciting treatises on plane trigonometry and algebraic determinants, the tutor whose students once signed a round-robin to the head of the College asking to be transferred to other hands, is to do injustice to a genius of fantasy and imaginative whimsy. In 1856, while completing the studies for his Master's degree, he was even then spinning words magically for a short-lived publication, *The Train*, using for the first time the immortal pseudonym which set the seal on his escape into a more comforting, exciting world.

Dodgson had, however, found the basic key that would release him from the disappointments of conformity long before he revealed himself as Lewis Carroll. As a boy, amid the sheltered innocence and prim propriety of a childhood which presents its own parallels to the academic and emotional seclusion of the Oxford of his later years, he had stumbled, surprisingly for the son of an archdeacon with principled objections to the stage, across the secrets of the conjuror's craft, a fascination that persisted throughout his life. His nephew and authorised biographer, Stuart Dodgson Collingwood, describes how a favourite fantasy as a child entailed dressing up for exotic effect in astrological nightshirt and flowing brown wig in order to entertain his brothers and sisters at special performances of sleight of hand, displays sometimes supplemented by his equally deft manipulation of the toy theatre and 'penny plain, tuppence coloured' marionettes of cardboard on wood built by his agile fingers with the help of the village carpenter. A born entertainer, he wrote his own plays for the latter, the most popular of which were *The Tragedy of King John* and *La Guida di Bragia*, an operatic burlesque of *Bradshaw's Railway Guide*. He was in his element conjuring up voices and effects out of nowhere from behind a discreet screen, 'just like a conjuring-trick', and always requiring, at a White Knight's insistence, 'plenty of practice!' At the age of twenty-three he was still organising these performances and finding cause to complain in his diary on April 11, 1855 of the lack of suitable plays for puppet theatres: 'All existing plays for such objects seem to me to have one of two faults – either (1) they are meant for real theatres, and are therefore not fitted for children, or (2) they are overpoweringly dull – no idea of fun in them.'

The itch to baffle and mystify, and to entertain into the bargain, remained with him until his death. And yet the reciprocal rewards for Carroll himself were far greater than for his average wand-wielding contemporary. With a magician's instinct for tracking down the impossible, he was able to apply something more than the straightforward academic approach to his studies in mathematics and logic, sources of mystification no conventional magician had ever tapped. He did not need long to realise that not only did mathematics present an infinite means of bewilderment in stark contrast to the stereotyped repertoire of the drawing-room entertainer, but even more remarkably often displayed a baffling aspect which he, the magician himself, could not account for. Logic professed fallacies which when decked out with entertaining characters were far more spellbinding than the contrived red-herring patter used to misdirect an audience's awareness away from a more tangible secret. Here was as near as he would ever come to discovering real magic.

Nothing serves more effectively than this discovery to underline the futility of the habitual critical practice of assigning separate identities to the literary wizard and writer of fantasy on the one hand and the dull if conscientious teacher of mathematics on the other. There was a vast area where the two worlds overlapped, far wider than that suggested by the now familiar part played by logic in the Alice books. When Dodgson kept his head he was barely moderately successful; only when he allowed the tedious routine of his day-to-day studies to come under the distorted perspective of his magician's approach did he disclose the full range of his subtlety and invention in his chosen professional sphere. An author much influenced by Carroll is Vladimir Nabokov. In the Russian's novel, *The Defence*, the central, chess-addicted character has as a boy been a poor student in mathematics, while at the same time 'extraordinarily engrossed in a collection of problems entitled *Merry Mathematics*, in the fantastical misbehaviour of numbers and the wayward frolic of geometric lines, in everything that the schoolbook lacked'. It is not difficult to surmise at least one individual who could have written both academic text and mathematical fun book.

The full extent of Carroll's mathematical hocus-pocus coupled with his quiet sense of showmanship was not confined to the numerical tricks and puzzles which comprise a major part of the following pages. In 1868, in *The Offer of the Clarendon Trustees*, Carroll made the priceless suggestion that the University should provide 'A narrow strip of ground, railed off and carefully levelled, for investigating the properties of Asymptotes, and testing practically whether Parallel Lines meet or not: for this purpose it should reach, to use the expressive language of Euclid, "ever so far".

This last process, of "continually producing the Lines", may require centuries or more: but such a period, though long in the life of an individual, is as nothing in the life of the University.'

In the introduction to *Dynamics of a Parti-cle*, a small pamphlet of political satire first published three years earlier in 1865, he anticipated by nineteen years the *Flatland* of Edwin Abbott where two-dimensional, one-eyed creatures with luminous edges and of infinitesimal height glide over a surface approximating to a map, themselves not too distant relations of the obvious inhabitants for such a world, the playing-card characters of Wonderland, 'oblong and flat, with their hands and feet at the corners', and as incapable of imagining a three-dimensional interior to the flower-pot where Alice successfully hides the gardeners as we ourselves are of thinking four-dimensionally:

> It was a lovely Autumn evening, and the glorious effects of chromatic aberration were beginning to show themselves in the atmosphere as the earth revolved away from the great western luminary, when two lines might have been observed wending their weary way across a plane super-ficies. The elder of the two had by long practice acquired the art, so painful to young and impulsive loci, of lying evenly between his extreme points; but the younger, in her girlish impetuosity, was ever longing to diverge and become an hyperbola or some such romantic and boundless curve. They had lived and loved: fate and the intervening superficies had hitherto kept them asunder, but this was no longer to be: a line had intersected them, making the two interior angles together less than two right angles. It was a moment never to be forgotten, and, as they journeyed on, a whisper thrilled along the superficies in isochronous waves of sound, 'Yes! We shall at length meet if continually produced!'

The same publication shows the high point of his skill in mathematical punning. The following are the 'definitions' specified at the opening of the first chapter:

> 1. PLAIN SUPERFICIALITY is the character of a speech, in which any two points being taken, the speaker is found to lie wholly with regard to those two points.

> 2. PLAIN ANGER is the inclination of two voters to one another, who meet together, but whose views are not in the same direction.

> 3. When a Proctor, meeting another Proctor, makes the votes on one side equal to those on the other, the feeling entertained by each side is called RIGHT ANGER.

> 4. When two parties, coming together, feel a Right Anger, each is *said* to

be COMPLEMENTARY to the other (though, strictly speaking, this is very seldom the case).

5. OBTUSE ANGER is that which is greater than Right Anger.

Equally relevant is his parody of Euclid's third 'postulate', transformed by Carroll from 'let it be granted that a circle can be described about any centre at any distance from that centre' to 'let it be granted that a controversy may be raised about any question, and at any distance from that question.'

In the above instances the mathematics, while seen through a tricksy squint, are of course wedded to an unmistakable literary style, reminding one that the child who began life as a wizard eventually found his greatest fame as a writer. To emphasise this is not to bypass his magical flair. One could be forgiven for seeing in his literary, as distinct from mathematically orientated, writings the peak of Victorian drawing-room entertainment. As early as 1850 Carroll, realising even then that the pen can be more potent than the wand in conjuring up the impossible, had been practising how to convey in narrative form the special aura of a successful magical performance with its own individual blend of mystery, suspense and tongue-in-cheek humour. 'The Walking Stick of Destiny', first published in *The Rectory Umbrella*, one of the household magazines which he wrote for his brothers and sisters, features a magician at work in his laboratory with a comprehensive retinue of two ebony cats, glaring owl, deadly viper, and a whole sprawl of spiders. By the time he came to write his two masterpieces, however, he had adopted a more subtle approach, despising the paraphernalia that can only embarrass, the contrived mechanism implied by shiny metallic tubes and sturdy cabinets which appear outside twice the size to which they admit within. Like all great magicians he needed only simple, everyday objects such as a ball of wool, a kitten and some chessmen, together with the almost obligatory mirror and the assistance of a little girl to produce a spectacle unrivalled in later years by Houdini or Disney. He had another 'assistant', Alice's White Rabbit, an unexceptional rabbit perhaps until one considers its props – a watch, a fan, a pair of gloves – and then infallibly a magician's rabbit. Moreover, if the world of the impossible is the world of dreams, no magician ever conjured up the latter with greater ease, or, to quote Walter De La Mare instancing the fluidity of the repeated transitions in the 'Wool and Water' episode, in such 'serene seductive discontinuity'. But no quality is more apposite to this consideration of Carroll than the sheer sense of wonder instilled by him into his very special audience of one, that sense of wonder on a level with the intense curiosity which animates great scientists, poets, inventors, and magicians. Whatever Carroll's own magic word, 'curious' is Alice's repeated response to the endless succession of weird escapades and eccentrics he produces on her behalf. As Harry Levin has remarked, no novelist ever identified more intimately with the point of view of his heroine. Certainly no magician ever won over an audience without embarking upon his act with the same sense of wonder he hoped to arouse in the serried rows before him.

It is no secret that Carroll modelled his White Knight upon himself. They shared the same shaggy hair, gentle face, mild blue eyes, the same topsy-turvy outlook on the world. As important from our point of view is their mutual fondness for tricks and gadgets. Like his much-practised character, Carroll was not merely a 'great hand at inventing things' but took immense delight in showing off the results to a captive audience. It does not require too exhausting a stretch of the imagination to equate the White Knight's 'queer-shaped little deal box' with Carroll's own ubiquitous black bag, the special travelling arcana of baffling means into which he would delve to produce mystification on railway journeys or at the seashore. Carroll's own inventions included the prototype of the miniature travelling chess set with holes to prevent the pegged pieces from tumbling over and the original double-sided adhesive tape: 'June 18, 1896: Invented a substitute for gum, for fastening envelopes (as used to be done with wafers), mounting small things in books, etc. – viz: paper with gum on *both* sides. It should be supplied in sheets, and also in discs.' There was also the prototype of what one may assume to have evolved into the game of 'Scrabble': 'December 19, 1880: The idea occurred to me that a game might be made of letters, to be moved about on a chess-board till they form words'; an erratic system, to ensure the secrecy he demanded with regard to forthcoming literary projects, of cutting finished letters into strips and posting them indiscriminately in large envelopes to be read with the aid of a cipher; a cardboard liqueur scale for placing alongside a glass to ensure that a fair measure is given for differently priced drinks, a device symptomatic of the pernickety care with which he discharged his duties as curator of Christ Church Common Room. He made endless suggestions for improving things, including a streamlined steering gear for the velociman, an early, rather cumbersome form of tricycle guided by means of a curved rail at your back; a plan for controlling the traffic at Covent Garden; an improved method for assigning prizes in Lawn Tennis Tournaments, together with 'a proof that the present method is, except in the case of the first prize, entirely unmeaning', and a similar reappraisal of voting procedure: 'June 3, 1884: Concocted a new "Proportional Representation" scheme, far the best I have yet devised. The chief novelty in it is the giving to each candidate the power of transferring to any other candidate, the votes given for him.'

Ideas for games and puzzles, riddles and charades besieged his mind at all hours, sustaining his own sense of wonder and providing a constant source of entertainment for his child-friends who, if not treated extempore to the surprises of his black bag on special excursions, were fêted in his rooms at Christ Church where Carroll was able to exhibit his vast collection of toys and gadgets. These included a distorting mirror; a minute pair of ivory binoculars which contained two photographs of the original Alice and showed them enlarged when held to the eye; a Zoetrope or 'Wheel of Life' depicting a juggler tossing balls into the air; solitaire; mechanical animals and music boxes which he often played backwards for perverse amusement. Among the automata, pride of place was shared between a walking bear and 'Bob the Bat', an ingenious construction of gauze, wire and elastic which when wound up would fly round the room for about half a minute. Isa Bowman recounts how this 'had many adventures. There was no way of controlling the direction of its flight, and one morning, a hot summer's morning, when the window was wide open, Bob flew out into the garden and alighted in a bowl of salad which a scout was taking to someone's rooms. The poor fellow was so startled by the sudden flapping apparition that he dropped the bowl, and it was broken into a thousand pieces.'

There was one further source of spellbinding activity – photography. It is highly probable that Carroll himself invented the first self-photographing device. What is certain is that he eventually acquired prominence as one of the leading portrait photographers of his time, what had begun as a hobby becoming an integral part of his life, winning him acceptance into the company of other celebrities and further little girls who not surprisingly were among his most successful subjects. It is hard to believe, though, that he wasn't first attracted to what was initially an almost unknown and exclusive, because expensive, pastime by the sheer fantasy in the idea of being able to produce magic pictures out of a simple, hooded rosewood box.

By the end of Carroll's life the number of his child-friends had snowballed into hundreds, and of his customary audience he wrote: 'I am fond of children (except boys).' In this most sensitive area of Carrollian controversy Martin Gardner has pointed out that there is certainly no indication that he was aware of anything but the purest innocence in his relationships with young girls. The editor of *The Annotated Alice* makes the distinction between Carroll and Humbert Humbert, the narrator of Nabokov's *Lolita*: 'Humbert Humbert's "nymphets" were creatures to be used carnally. Carroll's little girls appealed to him precisely because he felt sexually safe with them.' For our purposes they were a captive audience for much of the material that appears in this volume. They acted upon the prim, fussy, stammering bachelor as an irresistible stimulus, causing his speech impediment and shyness to fade away in their presence and igniting his enthusiasm to amuse and entertain, providing him at last with a happy outlet whereby he could communicate even the most abstruse scientific ideas, cunningly arrayed in harlequin guise to arrest the attention of a mere child. But physical presence was not essential. The actual lengths to which he would go to tease and to please in absentia can be seen from his letters, excerpts from several of which are reproduced later.

Frequently his young friends would be fortunate enough to accompany him on his visits to the theatre, often of particular relevance to our magical theme. On June 24, 1876 he indulged his passion for automata and 'Went to Maskelyne and Cooke and saw Psycho (which I have no doubt has a dwarf inside), and the spiritualist seance, which is very astonishing. Lord Westmorland was the volunteer to be shut up in the cabinet.' Psycho was the first of several ingenious mechanical figures to be presented at the Egyptian Hall in Piccadilly by John Nevil Maskelyne and George A. Cooke, the forerunners of a great tradition of British stage illusionists in the grand manner. Dressed in Hindu costume, Psycho rested on a box which in turn stood upon a transparent glass cylinder.

After examination by the members of the audience, the figure would indicate the answers to simple mathematical problems by moving its arm to pick out the relevant cards in a rack attached to the box. It could communicate also by striking a bell a specific number of times, as well as meet all comers at whist, lifting the playing card required at each successive play from the rack with finger and thumb and then turning it over to show the audience. Within time Psycho even learned to smoke. Its secret still intact, it now lives in dignified retirement in the theatre collection of the London Museum. Greville MacDonald, the physician and one of the minority of Carroll's male child-friends, recalls in his *George MacDonald and his Wife* how in the sixties 'one annual treat was Uncle Dodgson taking us to the Polytechnic for the entrancing "dissolving views" of fairy tales, or to go down in the diving-bell or watch the mechanical athlete *Leotard*. There was also the Coliseum in Albany Street, with its storms by land and sea on a wonderful stage, and its great panorama of London. And there was Cremer's toy shop in Regent Street – not to mention bath-buns and ginger-beer – all associated in my memory with the adorable writer of *Alice*.' Twenty years later Carroll himself was still keen:

> September 20, 1884: Took Margie and Ruth Dymes and Marion Richards to Brighton. We picked up Gracie Smith and all went to the Aquarium, where we saw Dr. Lynn's *Thauma* (a very clever illusion, looking like the upper half of a female, cut off just above the waist, resting on a shelf which could be swung from side to side). We also saw some clever conjuring and acrobatism: then by Electric Railway, and reached Mrs. Smith's about 5.

As Carrollian scholar Roger Lancelyn Green has indicated, the most significant reference in the entire *Diaries* to his attendance at a magic show is contained in the entry for April 6, 1863, during his visit to Charlton Kings, near Cheltenham: 'April 6, 1863: Rain all day. Spent most of the time at Hetton Lawn, in the schoolroom with the children, showing them photographs, etc. Went with the party in the evening to see Herr Dobler, a conjurer.'

The children were Alice, the daughter of Henry George Liddell, the Dean of Christ Church, herself the original inspiration for the Alice of Wonderland, together with her sisters Lorina and Edith. In 'Looking-Glass Reflections', an article in the Autumn, 1971 edition of *Jabberwocky*, Green provides a convincing argument for supposing that the Hetton

Lawn mansion was the original Looking-Glass House; that Miss Prickett, the governess accompanying Alice, was the prototype of the Red Queen, 'the concentrated essence of all governesses'; that Leckhampton Hill nearby – 'Principal mountains – I'm on the only one' – provided the ideal vantage point from which the Gloucestershire plain itself would appear 'marked out just like a large chess-board'; that the four days Carroll spent at Cheltenham from April 3 to April 7, 1863 were as crucial to the inception of *Through the Looking-Glass* as the river excursion to Godstow on that 'golden afternoon' in 1862 had been to *Alice's Adventures in Wonderland*. If that is so, then the repertoire of Herr Dobler could well have played its own part in a story which contains, as we shall see, a plethora of conjuring motifs.

Histories of magic and magicians tell us that a Herr Ludwig Leopold Döbler was born in Vienna in 1801 and graduated from being a favourite of Viennese society to universal acclaim, whereby he eventually came to England in 1842. An artistic as well as box-office success, he caused a sensation with his varied feats – igniting with a single pistol shot every one of the two hundred candles which made up his stage setting; his version of the inexhaustible bottle yielding not merely an overflow of wine but a spectator's marked handkerchief borrowed earlier in the performance; and his 'Distribution of Flora's Gifts' from a small twisted felt hat to the ladies in the audience. He retired in 1848 and died on April 17, 1864. It is feasible that he may have ventured to England during the last months of his life, but if he did so no record of the visit other than Carroll's can be traced. Scheduled to give a public performance, he would surely have attracted press billing, if not the publicity worthy of a magician who was the first in history to have a street named after him, the Döblergasse in Vienna. Neither the weekly *Cheltenham Chronicle* nor the daily *Cheltenham Journal* carry a report or prior announcement of a performance by a Herr Döbler around the time in question. They do, however, go out of their way to record another magical performance that took place in the Cheltenham Assembly Rooms on April 6, 1863, namely the controversial ghost lecture of Professor Pepper, who the Christmas before had caused his own sensation at the Royal Polytechnic in London with his materialisation of a ghost-like presence on a fully lit stage. The *Cheltenham Journal* described the event: 'It's a lecture illustrated by a large number of attractive electrical experiments and the exhibition of a spectral figure produced by the aid of an instrument called the photo-drome which was as good an imitation of what we should imagine a ghost ought to be like as anything that can be conceived.' Could Carroll have possibly confused the names? Could Herr Dobler have been a joke name among the children and himself for Professor Pepper, its own pun on the 'seeing double' the phenomenon implied? Is there any significance in Carroll's omitting the umlaut from Döbler's name in the diary entry? Was a small town like Cheltenham ever likely to sustain two shows by two master professional magicians on the same evening?

The remarkable coincidence is that of all other magicians it should be Pepper's name that presents itself in this context. Had the illusion with which he made his name not been presented to the public until 1872 there would have been reason for supposing that Pepper himself had been inspired by *Through the Looking-Glass*. As it is, to know that the illusion involved the uncanny mingling of live action with what amounted to mirror reflected forms is to find it difficult to see how Pepper could have sent Carroll back to Hetton Lawn the following day without the framework for what would prove to be his own most ingenious creation. But whether on that day Carroll saw Professor Pepper, the authentic Herr Döbler, or an impostor, he must have been familiar with Pepper's phenomenon. As we have seen, he was a regular visitor to the Royal Polytechnic where eventually, after Pepper had moved his own spectacle to the Egyptian Hall, another Carrollian haunt, the first dramatic presentation of 'Alice' tableaux using 'dissolving views' and dumb show took place in April, 1876.

This book is its own definition of the sense of wonder first evident in the activities of the boy wizard and later providing the protective cloak essential as refuge from an adult life that came to encompass loneliness and left-handedness, stutter and seemingly unconquerable shyness. In amassing for this purpose as comprehensive a collection of Carroll's original games and puzzles as possible, one trusts that he would not have objected to the inclusion in the cause of ambience of several of the various magical tricks and gambits which, while not originated by himself, would certainly have been familiar and therefore of some influence on him, manifestations of that same basic desire to fascinate and intrigue, whether his audience be young friend or high-table colleague. Throughout, an attempt has been made to place the items featured in a chronological sequence parallel to Carroll's own life span, the introductory quotation to a section itself providing an arbitrary peg for material which it is impossible to pinpoint specifically in time. Fortunately one can at least raise the lid of the box of tricks that follows confident in the knowledge that no magician was more fascinated by erratic time schemes or ever played more fanciful tricks with time than Carroll himself.

Carroll died at the age of 65 on January 14, 1898, the sudden victim of bronchial influenza, at his sisters' home in Guildford, Surrey. Throughout his life he was moving towards creating a more realistic literary Wonderland than that conjured up for Alice, but although his mind was active until the end he sadly failed to complete the one work intended for this purpose. However unsatisfactory a substitute this book may be, it will hopefully provide the same sort of fascination for all those who have ever taken delight in imagining themselves in Alice's shoes. No one wore them more happily than the shy Oxford don whose adopted name became a synonym for a very special magic.

J.F.

Mazes and labyrinths

'I was thinking,' Alice said very politely, 'which is the best way out of this wood: it's getting so dark. Would you tell me, please?'

Through the Looking-Glass

As a boy the young Lewis Carroll once traced a maze on the snow-covered lawn of the Rectory garden at Croft, in Yorkshire, where his father had accepted the living in 1843. This was possibly the earliest of his mathematical puzzle-games and set the stage for a theme to which he would return several times in later years. He drew the following in his early twenties for his family magazine *Mischmasch*, the object being to find one's way out of the central reservation. One is presumably allowed to cross over and under paths as illustrated, but not to go beyond the strategically placed single-line barriers.

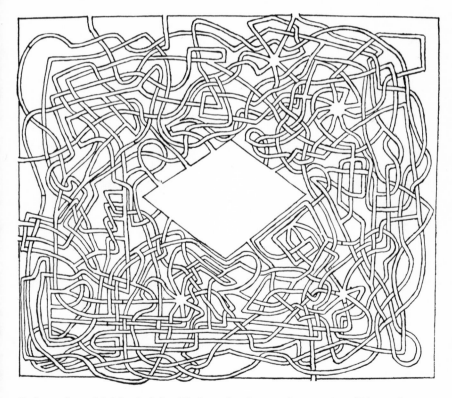

Dodgson drew this labyrinth for *Mischmasch*, a homemade magazine of his youth

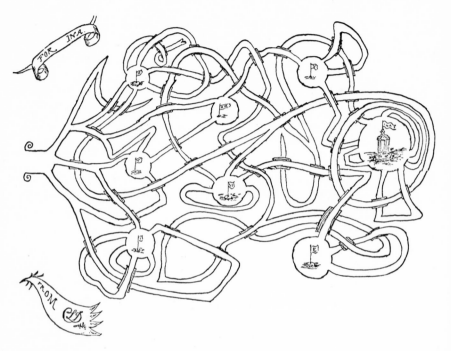

A labyrinth drawn by Lewis Carroll for his child friends

Later in life he would frequently draw mazes for his child-friends, often adding a personal touch. And so Georgina Watson, known familiarly as Ina, would have gathered letter clues spelling the names of her two sisters, 'Hartie' (Carroll's pet name for Harriett) and 'Mary', prior to reaching the destination signified by her own name.

Presumably the signposts had to be encountered in the order consistent with the spelling; otherwise the problem would appear to be naively simple. One certain way, incidentally, of solving a maze on paper, trickier on snow, is to adopt the reverse procedure of shading in all the blind alleys and false openings until only clear routes remain.

Facts

Were I to take an iron gun,
And fire it off towards the sun;
I grant 'twould reach its mark at last,
But not till many years had passed.

But should that bullet change its force,
And to the planets take its course;
'Twould *never* reach the *nearest* star,
Because it is so *very* far.

Useful and Instructive Poetry

The above poem from Carroll's earliest work, composed in 1845 when he was thirteen, although not published until 1932 in the collected edition of his verse, is the first literary indication of a puzzlist's mind at play. The fascination with astronomy persisted into his later years, as proved by a stray question discovered by Warren Weaver, the mathematician and pioneer of cybernetics, in Carroll's mathematical papers: 'What is the highest point on the moon visible to an observer on the earth?' The problem is obviously poorly defined and one wonders whether he meant it as anything more than a catch question, requiring an answer no more elaborate than 'the nearest point to earth'.

In books on astronomy available to Carroll it is stated that the highest lunar peaks are the Leibnitz Mountains which go up to around 30,000 ft., though astronomer Patrick Moore has pointed out that these have recently been discredited as a true range, the name itself having been deleted. If there is one aspect of this topic, however, which rings true in a typical Carrollian manner, it is that while the highest lunar mountains appear to be in excess of 25,000 ft., there is no sea level on the moon to act as a standard, a fact sufficiently telling for Carroll in his most tantalising mood to discredit the concept of height altogether!

Where does the day begin?

'If everybody minded their own business,' the Duchess said, in a hoarse growl, 'the world would go round a deal faster than it does.'

'Which would *not* be an advantage,' said Alice, who felt very glad to get an opportunity of showing off a little of her knowledge. 'Just think what work it would make with the day and night! You see the earth takes twenty-four hours to turn round on its axis –'

'Talking of axes,' said the Duchess, 'chop off her head!'

Alice's Adventures in Wonderland

Carroll was as young as seventeen when he posed the question of the above heading in *The Rectory Umbrella*, another pot-pourri magazine which he edited for his brothers and sisters:

Half of the world, or nearly so, is always in the light of the sun: as the world turns round, this hemisphere of light shifts round too, and passes over each part of it in succession.

Supposing on Tuesday, it is morning at London; in another hour it would be Tuesday morning at the west of England; if the whole world were land we might go on tracing[1] Tuesday morning, Tuesday morning all the way round, till, in twenty-four hours we got to London again. But we *know* that at London twenty-four hours after Tuesday morning it is Wednesday morning. Where, then, in its passage round the earth, does the day change its name? Where does it lose its identity?

Practically there is no difficulty in it, because a great part of the journey is over water, and what it does out at sea no one can tell: and besides there are so many different languages that it would be hopeless to attempt to trace the name of any one day all the year round. But is the case inconceivable that the same land and the same language should continue all round the world? I cannot see that it is: in that case either[2] there would be no distinction at all between each successive day, and so week, month, etc., so that we should have to say, 'The Battle of Waterloo happened to-day, about two million hours ago', or some line would have to be fixed where the change should take place, so that the inhabitants of one house would wake and say, 'Heigh-ho,[3] Tuesday morning!' and the inhabitants of the next (over the line), a few miles to the west would wake a few minutes afterwards and say, 'Heigh-ho! Wednesday morning!' What hopeless confusion the people who happened to live *on* the line would be in, is not for me to say. There would be a quarrel every morning as to what the name of the day should be. I can imagine no third case, unless everybody was allowed to choose for

---

[1]The best way is to imagine yourself walking round with the sun and asking the inhabitants as you go, 'What morning is this?' If you suppose them living all the way around, and all speaking one language, the difficulty is obvious.

[2]This is clearly an impossible case, and is only put as an hypothesis.

[3]The usual exclamation at waking, generally said with a yawn.

[4]'If all the world were apple pie, And all the sea were ink, And all the trees were bread and cheese, What *should* we have to drink?'

themselves, which state of things would be rather worse than either of the other two.

I am aware that this idea has been started before – namely, by the un-known author of that beautiful poem beginning, 'If all the world were apple pie', etc.[4] The particular result here discussed, however, does not appear to have occurred to him as he confines himself to the difficulties in obtaining drink which would certainly ensue.

Here was a problem that would trouble him for the next thirty years. On February 23, 1857, he wrote a letter on the matter to *The Illustrated London News*, where it appeared on April 18:

> Observing that this question is now under discussion in your columns (a question which occurred to myself years ago, and for which I have never been able to meet with a satisfactory solution), I am anxious that your correspondents should be aware what the real difficulty is. According to the statement of 'T. J. Buckton, Lichfield', the day is always commencing at some point or other on the globe; so that if one could travel round it in twenty-four hours, arriving everywhere exactly at midnight by the time of the place, we should find each place in a transition of name. But if for midnight we substitute midday we are at once involved in a difficulty: the case may be briefly stated thus:– Suppose yourself to start from London at midday on Tuesday, and to travel with the sun, thus reaching London again at midday on Wednesday. If at the end of every hour you ask the English residents in the place you have reached the name of the day, you must at last reach some place where the answer changes to Wednesday. But at that moment it is still Tuesday (1 p.m.) at the place you left an hour before. Thus you find two places within an hour in time of each other using different names for the same day, and that not at midnight when it would be natural to do so, but when one place is at midday and the other at 1 p.m. Whether two such places exist, and whether, if they do exist, any com-munication can take place between them without utter confusion being the result, I shall not pretend to say: but I shall be glad to see any rational solution suggested for the difficulty as I have put it.

Later, in 1860, he also made it the subject of a lecture to the Ashmolean Society. Collingwood recalls how the problem 'cast a gloom over many a pleasant party', and throughout his life Carroll troubled government offices and telegraph companies with the dilemma. He would, for example, write to the cable office in some city in Australia and say, 'If I despatched a cable to you at 11.00 p.m. on Monday evening, at what time and on what day of the week would you receive it?' The reply was usually curt: 'Consult our time-tables.'

A practical answer to the basic problem did not exist until 1878 when Sandford Fleming suggested the 'time zones' we know today. Even then it was six years before the International Date Line was established as a reality. It is unlikely, however, if the problem itself was ever fully resolved in Carroll's mind. Here was one among many fascinating instances of the topsy-turvy, illogical way in which time could behave. It's hard to believe that both the Red Queen, running as fast as she can to stay in the same place, and the White Queen, with her reference to 'one of the last set of Tuesdays', were not themselves caught up in the confused unravelling of the mystery in Carroll's mind.

Florence Becker Lennon in the revised edition of *Victoria through the Looking-Glass*, her painstaking life of Carroll, has brought up to date the whole area of speculation occasioned by the problem and the nature of time in general: 'When an astronaut has seen three sunsets and three dawns in five hours, is he three days older?' Certainly to Carroll the conventional divisions of time which we take for granted were meaningless, if not without use; and yet take them away and the world would be timeless, each fraction of a second its own paradox in the mind of this inveterate diarist.

The young Carroll's frontispiece to *The Rectory Umbrella*

24

The two clocks paradox

'Well, I'd hardly finished the first verse,' said the Hatter, 'when the Queen bawled out "He's murdering the time! Off with his head!" '

'How dreadfully savage!' exclaimed Alice.

'And ever since that,' the Hatter went on in a mournful tone, 'he won't do a thing I ask! It's always six o'clock now.'

A bright idea came into Alice's head. 'Is that the reason so many tea-things are put out here?' she asked.

'Yes, that's it,' said the Hatter with a sigh: 'it's always tea-time, and we've no time to wash the things between whiles.'

Alice's Adventures in Wonderland

There is not too wide a chasm between the Mad Hatter's dispute with time and the 'difficulty' of the two clocks also included by Carroll in *The Rectory Umbrella* and which he had already set his sister Elizabeth in letter form the year before in 1849.

Which is the best, a clock that is right only once a year, or a clock that is right twice every day? 'The latter,' you reply, 'unquestionably.' Very good, reader, now attend.

I have two clocks: one doesn't go *at all*, and the other loses a minute a day: which would you prefer? 'The losing one,' you answer, 'without a doubt.' Now observe: the one which loses a minute a day has to lose twelve hours, or seven hundred and twenty minutes before it is right again, consequently it is only right once in two years, whereas the other is evidently right as often as the time it points to comes round, which happens twice a day. So you've contradicted yourself *once*: 'Ah, but,' you say, 'What's the use of it being right twice a day, if I can't tell when the time comes?' Why, suppose the clock points to eight o'clock, don't you see that the clock is right *at* eight o'clock? Consequently when eight o'clock comes your clock is right. 'Yes, I see *that*,' you reply. Very good, then you've contradicted yourself *twice*: now get out of the difficulty as you can, and don't contradict yourself if you can help it.

and then by way of a footnote:

You *might* go on to ask, 'How am I to know when eight o'clock *does* come? My clock will not tell me.' Be patient, reader: you know that when eight o'clock comes your clock is right: very good; then your rule is this, keep your eye fixed on your clock, and *the very moment it is right* it will be eight o'clock. 'But—' you say. There, that'll do, reader: the more you argue, the farther you get from the point, so it will be as well to stop.

Carroll's preoccupation with capricious time schemes which on closer examination revealed ideas of greater moment continued throughout his life. In *The Annotated Alice*, Martin Gardner recalls that Arthur Stanley Eddington, in his book *Space, Time and Gravitation*, as well as lesser writers on relativity theory, have compared the Mad Hatter's Tea Party where time stands still with the portion of De Sitter's model of the cosmos where this is the case for ever. In a similar way the Red Queen's remark that 'it takes all the running *you* can do, to keep in the same place', is its own lesson in relativity.

In *Sylvie and Bruno* the German Professor's 'Outlandish Watch' is a logical progression from Alice's earlier contact with backwards time whereby, according to the White Queen, one's memory works both ways and the sentence precedes the trial which precedes the crime. It is not only possible to set the 'six or eight' hands on the German's watch back, so that events with alterations as prescribed immediately happen all over again from a specified moment, but also by pressing a 'reversal peg' one can set events moving backwards with a greater, if not total, consistency than in the earlier work. And so in the description of a time-reversed dinner the procedure of eating and then serving is carried out in meticulous, some would say tedious, others nauseous, detail – with the exception of the conversation. Individual remarks are placed in the desired sequence, but the actual words are uttered in a forwards time direction.

No one has visualised the difficulties inherent in the time-reversal of one's entire bodily and mental processes and one's environment more clearly than Martin Gardner in a brilliant article, separate from his regular column, in *Scientific American* for January, 1967. Gardner sees the events pertaining to the 'Outlandish Watch' as a kind of 'looking-glass reversal of time's linear dimension'. But whereas one can see a reversed world, merely by looking into a mirror, it is impossible for an observer in one world ever to see another world that is time-reversed. Each would be totally invisible to the other since light, while radiating from one, would seem to be going back towards its point of origin in the other. In his book *Cybernetics*, the study of which he founded, Norbert Wiener concluded that communication between individuals living in opposite time directions would be impossible. If you did manage to convey some piece of information to a time-reversed counterpart, he would forget it as soon as you had spoken, the remark passing into the hinterland of his 'future' rather than the prospect of his 'past'.

Court Circular

'Who cares for *you*?' said Alice (she had grown to her full size by this time). 'You're nothing but a pack of cards!'

At this the whole pack rose up into the air, and came flying down upon her . . .

Alice's Adventures in Wonderland

Carroll completed the rules for the following card game on January 25, 1858 and published them in pamphlet form in January, 1860. This was his first published game, its invention anticipating by four and a half years the breathtaking shuffle of his own memory and imagination which led to the court of the King and Queen of Hearts and the above quotation.

RULES FOR COURT CIRCULAR
(A New Game of Cards for Two or More Players)
SECTION I. *(For Two Players)*

I

Cut for precedence. Highest is 'first hand'; lowest 'dealer'. Dealer gives 6 cards to each, one by one, beginning with first-hand, and turns up the 13th, which is called the 'Lead'. It is convenient that the same player should be dealer for the whole of each game.

II

First-hand then plays a card; then the other player, and so on, until 6 cards have been played, when the trick is complete, and he who can make (out of the 3 cards he has played, with or without the Lead), the best 'Line', wins it.

First-hand

N.B. The cards in the figure are numbered in the order of playing.

III

A 'Line' consists of 2, or all 3, of the cards put down by either player, with or without the Lead. In making a Line, it does not matter in what order the 3 cards have been put down. Lines rank as follows:

(1) 3, or 4, CARDS, (LEAD *included*)
Trio—i.e. 3 of a sort, (e.g. 3 Kings, or 3 Nines.)
Sequence—i.e. 3, or 4, in Sequence, (e.g. Eight, Nine, Ten, Knave.)

Sympathy—i.e. 3, or 4, Hearts.

Court— i.e. 3, or 4, Court-cards, (if 4, it is called Court Circular.)

N.B. In this Class a Line of 4 cards beats a *similar* Line of 3. The Lead must not be reckoned in the middle of a Sequence.

(2) 3 CARDS, (LEAD *excluded*)

Names as above.

N.B. In making a Sequence, the Ace may be reckoned either with King, Queen, or with Two, Three.

(3) 2 CARDS, (LEAD *excluded*)

Pair—i.e. 2 of a sort.

Valentine—i.e. 2 Hearts.

Etiquette—i.e. 2 Court-cards.

IV

If both have made Lines of the same kind, he whose Line contains the best card wins the trick; and if neither has made a Line, he who has played the best card wins it. Cards rank as follows:

(1) Hearts.

(2) The rest of the pack, in order Aces, Kings, &c.

N.B. If no Hearts have been played, and the highest cards on each side are equal, (e.g. if each have played an Ace,) they rank in the order Diamonds, Clubs, Spades.

V

The winner of a trick chooses, as Lead for the next trick, any one of the cards on the table, except the old Lead; he then takes the rest, turning them face upwards, if he be first-hand, but if not, face downwards; and he becomes first hand for the next trick.

VI

The dealer then gives cards to each, one by one, beginning with first-hand, until each hand is made up again to 6 cards.

VII

At any time during a trick, after the first card of it has been played, and before either has played 3 cards, he whose turn it is to play may 'resign' instead; in which case no more cards are played in that trick, and the other player wins it and proceeds as in Rule V. But when either has played 3 cards, the other must not resign.

VIII

When the pack is exhausted neither player may resign. The winner of the last trick clears the board. Each then reckons up the cards he has won, which count as follows:

> Cards face upwards .... 2 each.
>   downwards 1
> Hearts 1
> Court-cards 1

(so that a Court-Heart, if face upwards, counts 4 altogether.) The winner scores the difference between his own and the loser's marks, the loser scoring nothing. Game is 20 or 50.

SECTION II. *(For Three or More Players)*

The same rules apply with the following necessary changes. The Lead is placed in the middle; first-hand then plays a card; then the player on his left-hand, and so on all round, each putting down his 3 cards in a row from the Lead towards himself. He who makes the best Line wins the trick, and is first-hand for the next trick. At any time during a trick, after the first card of it has been played, and before any one has played 3 cards, he whose turn it is to play may 'resign' instead; in which case he loses his chance of winning that trick, and the other players go on without him. But when any one has played 3 cards, no other player may resign. In the case where all players but one 'resign', he who is left to the last wins the trick. At the end of each game all the players but the lowest score the difference between their own marks and those of the lowest, the lowest scoring nothing. Game is 50.

Disintegrating fan

After a time she heard a little pattering of feet in the distance, and she hastily dried her eyes to see what was coming. It was the White Rabbit returning splendidly dressed, with a pair of white kid gloves in one hand and a large fan in the other: he came trotting along in a great hurry, muttering to himself, as he came, 'Oh! the Duchess, the Duchess! Oh! *won't* she be savage if I've kept her waiting!' Alice felt so desperate that she was ready to ask help of any one: so, when the Rabbit came near her, she began, in a low, timid voice, 'If you please, sir—' The Rabbit started violently, dropped the white kid gloves and the fan, and scurried away into the darkness as hard as he could go.

Alice's Adventures in Wonderland

As we have seen, Carroll made no secret of the fact that the White Rabbit was a magician's rabbit. The fan, the white gloves, the watch are all conventional attributes of the popular conception of a drawing-room wizard of that time. In dropping the fan for the White Rabbit, Carroll may even have had a specific trick fan in mind: this, when handed to the audience to open, would fall apart in their hands. The conjuror would then take it back, breathe upon it, and it would become whole again.

The secret hinged upon the basic construction of the fan, strung together in such a way that when opened from left to right in the ordinary manner, it appeared as one would expect. But when it was opened in the opposite direction, from right to left, it disintegrated. In actual fact the second illustration shows the more accurate state of affairs. The fan was not strung together properly; merely gave the appearance of being normal, due to the cunning construction of flanges that engaged to keep the slats together when opened in one direction.

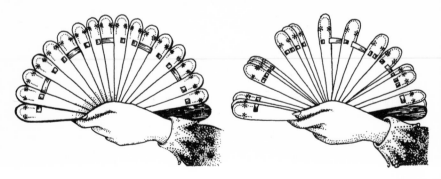

Watch wizardry

.... but when the Rabbit actually *took a watch out of its waistcoat-pocket*, and looked at it, and then hurried on, Alice started to her feet, for it flashed across her mind that she had never before seen a rabbit with either a waistcoat-pocket, or a watch to take out of it, and, burning with curiosity, she ran across the field after it, and was just in time to see it pop down a large rabbit-hole under the hedge.

Alice's Adventures in Wonderland

The watch trick was a favourite pièce de resistance of the drawing-room entertainer. After its ritual and hilarious destruction the timepiece would be reproduced from places as varied as a loaf of bread, a glass of milk or a nest of locked boxes. A favourite means of sabotage involved a specially constructed pestle and mortar. Having requested a watch from a member of the audience, the performer, under the pretext that it required regulating, would place it in the mortar and then with little subtlety bring the pestle crashing down. The sound of fragmented glass would be heard and after the appropriate pounding the pieces poured for all to see from mortar to hand and back. The mortar used embodied a special hemi-spherical cavity in the base where the actual fragments of an old watch had been placed beforehand. These were concealed by a loose section, 'b', which fitted into the lower portion of the pestle. The pestle, 'a', when engaged with 'b', itself contained a considerable cavity, large enough to carry off the watch when required.

During the performance the mortar was introduced with 'b' in the base concealing the fragments; the watch was placed on top of 'b'; the pestle, its head for the moment kept away from the audience, brought down on 'b'. A slight pounding motion caused 'a' to connect with 'b',

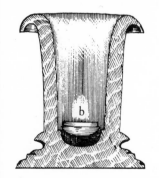

taking the watch with it. There was no reason now why the performer couldn't 'finish the job' by applying the additional force of poker or hammer. After revealing the fragments he would cause them to vanish in some probably equally cumbersome device, eventually recovering the spectator's watch from the pestle and depositing it as required in the eventual place of discovery.

A hole through the centre of the earth

Down, down, down. Would the fall *never* come to an end? 'I wonder how many miles I've fallen by this time?' she said aloud. 'I must be getting somewhere near the centre of the earth. Let me see: that would be four thousand miles down, I think—' (for, you see, Alice had learnt several things of this sort in her lessons in the schoolroom, and though this was not a *very* good opportunity for showing off her knowledge, as there was no one to listen to her, still it was good practice to say it over) '—yes, that's about the right distance – but then I wonder what Latitude or Longitude I've got to?' (Alice had not the slightest idea what Latitude was, or Longitude either, but she thought they were nice grand words to say.)

Presently she began again. 'I wonder if I shall fall right *through* the earth! How funny it'll seem to come out among the people that walk with their heads downwards! The Antipathies, I think—' (she was rather glad there *was* no one listening, this time, as it didn't sound at all the right word) '—but I shall have to ask them what the name of the country is, you know. Please, Ma'am, is this New Zealand or Australia?' (and she tried to curtsey as she spoke – fancy, *curtseying* as you're falling through the air! Do you think you could manage it?) 'And what an ignorant little girl she'll think me for asking! No, it'll never do to ask: perhaps I shall see it written up somewhere.'

Down, down, down.

Alice's Adventures in Wonderland

Speculation continued to be rife in Carroll's day regarding the outcome of a projected fall, assuming such to be possible, through a hole in the centre of the earth. The problem, which also courted the attention of Plutarch, Bacon, and Voltaire, had been correctly assessed by Galileo. Alice would fall with increasing speed and decreasing acceleration until she came to the exact centre of the earth, where her acceleration would be zero. Subsequently her speed would decrease, with increasing deceleration, until she reached, as she half suspected, the opening on the other side, where she would fall back again, and again, and again, oscillating back and forth forever, air resistance eventually bringing her to rest at the centre of the earth. As Gardner has pointed out, the solution does not take into account the effects of Coriolis force as a result of the earth's rotation, although if one imagines the fall as from pole to pole this is unnecessary.

That Carroll's own interest in the problem persisted is shown by the following intriguing excerpt from *Sylvie and Bruno Concluded*, where, as Gardner shows, the duration of time needed for the train to travel from one end of the tunnel to the other would take exactly the same time as Alice's fall to 'The Antipathies' – just over forty-two minutes, regardless of the length of the tunnel!

'They run their railway-trains without any engines – nothing is needed but machinery to *stop* them with. Is *that* wonderful enough, Miladi?'

'But where does the *force* come from?' I ventured to ask.

Mein Herr turned quickly round, to look at the new speaker. Then he took off his spectacles, and polished them, and looked at me again, in evident bewilderment. I could see he was thinking – as indeed *I* was also – that we *must* have met before.

'They use the force of *gravity*,' he said. 'It is a force known also in *your* country, I believe?'

'But that would need a railway going *down-hill*,' the Earl remarked. 'You can't have *all* your railways going down-hill?'

'They *all* do,' said Mein Herr.

'Not from *both* ends?'

'From *both* ends.'

'Then I give it up!' said the Earl.

'Can you explain the process?' said Lady Muriel. 'Without using that language, that I ca'n't speak fluently?'

'Easily,' said Mein Herr. 'Each railway is in a long tunnel, perfectly straight: so of course the *middle* of it is nearer the centre of the globe than the two ends: so every train runs half-way *down*-hill, and that gives it force enough to run the *other* half *up*-hill.'

'Thank you. I understand that perfectly,' said Lady Muriel. 'But the velocity, in the *middle* of the tunnel, must be something *fearful*!'

Four times five is twelve

'I'm sure I'm not Ada,' she said, 'for her hair goes in such long ringlets, and mine doesn't go in ringlets at all; and I'm sure I can't be Mabel, for I know all sorts of things, and she, oh, she knows such a very little! Besides, *she's* she, and *I'm* I, and – oh dear, how puzzling it all is! I'll try if I know all the things I used to know. Let me see: four times five is twelve, and four times six is thirteen, and four time seven is – oh dear! I shall never get to twenty at that rate!

Alice's Adventures in Wonderland

Alexander L. Taylor, in his book *The White Knight*, advances the theory that in a number system based on the scale 18, 4 times 5 actually is 12. On the scale 18, the numbers progress 1, 2, 3, 4, 5, 6, 7, 8, 9, (10) (11) (12) (13) (14) (15) (16) (17) 10, 11, 12 and so on. Similarly 4 times 6 equals 13 on the scale 21, where the numbers progress 1, 2, 3, 4, 5, 6, 7, 8, 9 (10) (11) (12) (13) (14) (15) (16) (17) (18) (19) (20) 10, 11, 12, 13. Increasing the scale by three each time, one arrives at:

4 times 7 equals 14 on the scale 24;

4 times 8 equals 15 on the scale 27;

4 times 9 equals 16 on the scale 30;

4 times 10 equals 17 on the scale 33;

4 times 11 equals 18 on the scale 36;

4 times 12 equals 19 on the scale 39.

But, and here Taylor finds the answer why Alice will never get to 20, 4 times 13 does not equal 20 on the scale 42, where the numbers go 1, 2, 3, 4, 5, 6, 7, 8, 9, (10, 11, 12. . . . 39, 40, 41) 10, 11, 12, 13, 14, 15, 16, 17, 18, 19, 1(10), etc., the last notation being 1, in the 42s column, followed by whatever symbol is adopted for ten.

Gardner does give a simpler explanation of the problem, based on the traditional practice of teaching multiplication tables to 12 and no further. And so 4 times 5 is 12, 4 times 6 is 13, 4 times 7 is 14, 4 times 8 is 15, and so on until 4 times 12 is 19, where normal teaching stops, just one this side of 20. It is, however, hard not to accept Taylor's theory that Carroll was anxious to make the most of two worlds; the problem as interpreted by Taylor interested him, and although it wouldn't interest Alice there was no reason why he shouldn't use it to entertain her on the level of nonsense. It is even more difficult to suppose that he, a mathematical don, inserted the puzzle in the book without realising it. As Taylor said in the Winter, 1971 edition of *Jabberwocky*, the official quarterly of the Lewis Carroll Society, 'If you find a watch in the Sahara Desert you don't think it grew there. In this case we know who put it there, so if he didn't record it that tells us something about his recording habits. It doesn't tell us that the mathematical puzzle isn't a mathematical puzzle.'

Thimble thaumaturgy

'But she must have a prize herself, you know,' said the Mouse.
'Of course,' the Dodo replied very gravely. 'What else have you got in your pocket?' it went on, turning to Alice.
'Only a thimble,' said Alice sadly.
'Hand it over here,' said the Dodo.
Then they all crowded round her once more, while the Dodo solemnly presented the thimble, saying, 'We beg your acceptance of this elegant thimble'; and, when it had finished this short speech, they all cheered.

Alice's Adventures in Wonderland

In October, 1950, during structural alterations to Croft Rectory, the house where Carroll spent the latter part of his boyhood, a small horde of childhood ephemera was found beneath a loose board in the floor of what had been the Dodgson nursery. Although Carroll had almost certainly outgrown the nursery by the time he moved to Croft in 1843, there is evidence, principally in the form of handwriting by both Mrs. Dodgson and her son, Charles, as described in full by Derek Hudson in his life of Carroll, that points to his being responsible for the buried treasure. Among such insignificant articles as a hair-slide, a lid from a doll's tea-set, a piece of clay pipe and a miniature penknife, were three objects of extraordinary relevance: a small white glove, a small left-hand shoe, and a thimble. The White Rabbit and Alice's discovery when diminished that she could put on one of his gloves; the White Knight and his reference to a right-hand foot squeezed into a left-hand shoe; the Dodo and the thimble all come rushing to mind. But the thimble is especially relevant to the theme of this book. Carroll's fascination with thimbles would have extended far beyond Alice, far beyond *The Hunting of the Snark* where 'They sought it with thimbles, they sought it with care'. No object was more readily adaptable to manipulative purposes for the adept young prestidigitateur.

The standard thimble routine in its simplest form involves the passage of a thimble from the forefinger of one hand to that of the other. To duplicate the effect one must first learn how to thumb-palm a thimble. This entails bending the appropriate forefinger into the crotch of the thumb, which closes upon it. The finger is then immediately extended again, leaving the thimble behind palmed. To recover the thimble at the tip of the forefinger reverse the movement. If the move is performed while the arm is making a larger movement, the smaller movement of the finger will remain undetected. Obviously the back of the hand must be kept towards the audience.

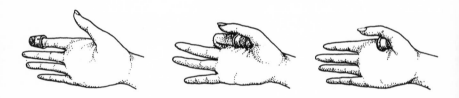

With this sleight one can make the motion of placing the thimble against the open left palm which immediately closes around the right forefinger as if gripping it. In actual fact the thimble is thumb-palmed towards the end of the movement of bringing the right hand across to the left. Only the bare forefinger eventually comes into contact with the left hand. For effect, one can now pat oneself on the head with the left hand and in an instant recover the thimble as if from the mouth. Or one can apparently place the thimble in the mouth (thumb-palming again), swallow as if for real, and then reproduce it from behind one's neck. Another variation involves putting the thimble in the mouth, then blowing out a lighted candle (as if blowing the thimble at the candle); the right hand then reproduces the thimble from beneath the candlestick or plucks it out of the wick.

36

To pass the thimble from forefinger to forefinger, a duplicate second thimble is needed. This is obtained secretly by the left hand and held in the thumb-palm position. It is now possible to place the thimble in the mouth as already described, and reproduce it from the back of the neck with the other hand. The most effective transposition, however, involves standing with one's hands at knee level. The hands, forefingers extended, one thimble visible, now tap the knees three times in unison. On the split-second count of 'three' one thimble is palmed, the other retrieved from the palm position. With practice the illusion is perfect.

Smoke rings and caterpillars

She stretched herself up on tiptoe, and peeped over the edge of the mushroom, and her eyes immediately met those of a large blue caterpillar, that was sitting on the top, with its arms folded, quietly smoking a long hookah, and taking not the smallest notice of her or of anything else . . . . at last the Caterpillar took the hookah out of its mouth, and addressed her in a languid, sleepy voice.

'Who are *You*?' said the Caterpillar.

Alice's Adventures in Wonderland

One of the ingenious embellishments of the Alice story in Walt Disney's animated film version was the way in which the Caterpillar illustrated his words by Technicoloured smoke rings which assumed the frail shape of letters and objects, in a way that would surely have appealed to the author of the puzzle letter reproduced on p. 57. This association between smoke and sound recalls the actual link between smoke rings and sound rings. The principle of adapting a cardboard box, preferably cylindrical, to produce perfect smoke rings is well known. If the box has no lid cover the end with stiff paper, fastened with an elastic band. In the centre of the lid now make a hole half an inch in diameter. Fill the box with smoke and, holding it horizontally, tap sharply against the base with the knuckle. A perfect smoke ring will spring out of the hole.

The difference between plain sound rings and smoke rings is that the former are invisible. One can, however, prove their existence in a most magical fashion. Empty the box of smoke. Then light a candle and, aiming the hole of the lid, tap the box on the bottom as before. If you aim correctly the sound ring produced from one small tap will magically extinguish the candle from a distance of more than three feet away.

Wine that isn't there

'Have some wine,' the March Hare said in an encouraging tone.

Alice looked all round the table, but there was nothing on it but tea. 'I don't see any wine,' she remarked.

'There isn't any,' said the March Hare.

'Then it wasn't very civil of you to offer it,' said Alice angrily.

Alice's Adventures in Wonderland

To the Victorian conjuror non-existent wine could be materialised out of thin air with greater ease than either Alice or the March Hare could have imagined. Required was a specially constructed bottle, made of tin, painted murky green to resemble glass. This was divided inside into four or five separate compartments arranged around a central space, each tapering to a narrow-mouthed tube which terminated about an inch from the top. A minute hole was drilled through the outer surface of the bottle into each compartment, the holes arranged along the side so that when the bottle is held in the hand, each hole may be covered by a finger or the thumb. The outer compartments were each filled with a different wine or spirit by means of a funnel and the conjuror was then ready to perform.

He would begin by openly pouring water into the bottle from a jug and back again, indirectly proving the bottle empty. The water passed into the central space only and when it was poured out again care had to be taken to hold the fingers and thumb tightly pressed against the holes on the side, excluding air from entering the compartments and thus causing the premature release of the wine already in the bottle. He would now ask members of his audience which drink they would prefer from those for which he had secretly made provision. On the appropriate request he would pour from the bottle, releasing the relevant finger to cause the required flow of liquid, and then, with the glass full, again block the air hole. In this way non-existent drinks could be conjured up for the entire front row!

Flower painting

> A large rose-tree stood near the entrance of the garden: the roses growing on it were white, but there were three gardeners at it, busily painting them red. Alice thought this a very curious thing, and she went nearer to watch them, and, just as she came up to them, she heard one of them say, 'Look out now, Five! Don't go splashing paint over me like that!'
>
> *Alice's Adventures in Wonderland*

Carroll would have known of an intriguing experiment used to demonstrate the capillary action that carries water up from the soil to the very tips of the leaves and petals of a plant producing a striking visual effect that could have saved the Queen's gardeners the anxiety of impending decapitation. Fill two glasses with water, one of which is coloured red with dye or food colouring. Take a plain white rose and carefully split the stem, placing half in one glass, half in the other, as in the illustration. Then sit back and watch. After a few hours one side of the bloom will have turned the red the gardeners desired. The two-coloured rose that results is in itself a fascinating curiosity, although it is, of course, possible to change the colour of the whole flower without the need to split the stem.

Biting out of a teacup

'Give your evidence,' said the King; 'and don't be nervous, or I'll have you executed on the spot.'

This did not seem to encourage the witness at all: he kept shifting from one foot to the other, looking uneasily at the Queen, and in his confusion he bit a large piece out of his teacup instead of the bread-and-butter.

Alice's Adventures in Wonderland

All you need to recreate some of the confusion caused by the Mad Hatter at the tea table is a ten-penny piece concealed in the fingers of the left hand. Pick up a cup in your right hand and raise the left to steady it as you make for your lips. One edge of the coin should be clipped secretly between your first and second finger, the other held against the china. Press firmly with your second finger and as you proceed to drink withdraw the first, causing the coin to snap sharply against the cup. For a moment there will be panic as everyone imagines you have bitten a piece straight out of the china. At once remove the cup and place it back on the table with your right hand, while the left casually drops to the lap where it leaves the coin, all other eyes directed towards the cup itself.

Castle Croquet

Alice thought she had never seen such a curious croquet-ground in her life:
it was all ridges and furrows: the croquet balls were live hedgehogs, and
the mallets live flamingoes, and the soldiers had to double themselves up
and stand on their hands and feet, to make the arches.

    The chief difficulty Alice found at first was in managing her flamingo:
she succeeded in getting its body tucked away, comfortably enough, under
her arm, with its legs hanging down, but generally, just as she had got its
neck nicely straightened out, and was going to give the hedgehog a blow
with its head, it *would* twist itself round and look up in her face, with such
a puzzled expression that she could not help bursting out laughing; and,
when she had got its head down, and was going to begin again, it was very
provoking to find that the hedgehog had unrolled itself, and was in the act
of crawling away: besides all this, there was generally a ridge or a furrow
in the way wherever she wanted to send the hedgehog to, and, as the
doubled-up soldiers were always getting up and walking off to other parts
of the ground, Alice soon came to the conclusion that it was a very difficult
game indeed.

Alice's Adventures in Wonderland

Long before Carroll conjured up the eccentric croquet ground of the
Queen of Hearts he was ringing elaborate variations on the standard
game for Alice Liddell and her sisters, prevented from playing anything
noisier within the precincts of Christ Church, Oxford, where their
father was Dean. Originally entitled 'Croquet Castles', this version was
published with considerable revision under the above name in 1866.

RULES FOR CASTLE CROQUET
(A game for four players)

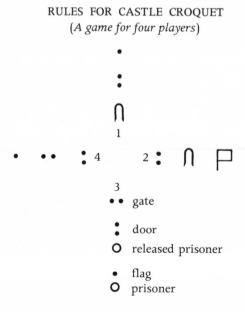

I.

This game requires 8 balls, 8 arches, and 4 flags; 4 of the balls are called 'soldiers', the others 'sentinels'. The arches and flags are set up as in the figure, making 4 'castles', and each player has a castle, a soldier, and a sentinel. To begin the game, the soldier is placed just within the gate, and the sentinel half-way between the gate and the door.

(N.B.—The distance from one gate to the next should be 6 or 8 yards, and the distance from the gate to the door, or from the door to the flag, 2 or 3 yards.)

II.

The soldiers are played first, in the order given in the figure, then the sentinels in the same order, and so on. Each player has to bring his soldier out of its castle, and with it 'invade' the other castles in order (*e.g.*, No. 3 has to invade castles 4, 1, 2), re-enter his own, and touch the flag, and then to touch it with his sentinel (which, if out of the castle, must re-enter for this purpose); and whoever does all this first, wins. To 'invade' a castle, the soldier must enter at the gate, go through the door (either way), touch the flag, and come out at the gate again.

(N.B.—No ball can enter or leave a castle except at the gate. A sentinel, that has not left his castle, is said to be 'on duty,' wherever he happen to be.)

III.

If a sentinel and soldier touch, while both are within the sentinel's castle, or if a soldier enter a castle while its sentinel and his own are both 'on duty,' the soldier becomes 'prisoner' and is placed behind the flag. He cannot move till released which is done either by his own sentinel (on duty) coming and touching the flag, or by the sentinel leaving the castle. In the former case, his own sentinel is put back where he was at the beginning of the game; and in either case the released soldier is placed behind the door, and cannot be again taken prisoner until after his next turn.

IV.

When a soldier goes through an arch, or touches a flag, in his proper course, or plays after being released, or when a sentinel enters or leaves his castle, or takes a prisoner, he may be played again; but a sentinel may not enter or leave his castle twice in one turn.

(N.B.—A sentinel can only enter or leave *his own* castle: no account is taken of his going through any arch other than his own gate.)

V.

If a ball touch another (except a sentinel on duty, a prisoner, or a released prisoner who has not played since his release), the player may use it to croquêt his own with; but may not move it in doing so, unless it be his own sentinel (not on duty). He may not croquêt himself twice in one turn with the same ball, unless he has done one of the things mentioned in Rule IV. meanwhile. In this game, croquêting does not give (as in the ordinary game) the right of playing again.

N.B.—The following arrangement of the 8 balls as soldiers and sentinels will be found convenient:

Soldiers	Sentinels
Blue	Green
Black	Brown
Orange	Yellow
Red	Pink

The flags should match the soldiers in colour.

This game may be adapted for five players, by the addition of a light-blue and a light-green ball, and the 10 balls may be arranged thus:

Soldiers	Sentinels
Blue	Light Blue
Black	Brown
Orange	Yellow
Green	Light Green
Red	Pink

Enigma

> They roused him with muffins – they roused him with ice –
>   They roused him with mustard and cress –
> They roused him with jam and judicious advice –
>   They set him conundrums to guess.

The Hunting of the Snark

In November, 1866, long before he ventured an answer to his own most famous riddle, Carroll had printed for private circulation an *Explication of the Enigma* [of Bishop Samuel Wilberforce]. The original riddle, reprinted separately by Carroll, went as follows:

> I have a large Box, with two lids, two caps, three established Measures, and a great number of articles a Carpenter cannot do without. – Then I have always by me a couple of good Fish, and a number of a smaller tribe, – besides two lofty Trees, fine Flowers, and the fruit of an indigenous Plant; a handsome Stag; two playful Animals; and a number of a smaller and less tame Herd: – Also two Halls, or Places of Worship; some Weapons of warfare; and many Weathercocks: – The Steps of an Hotel; The House of Commons on the eve of a Dissolution; Two Students or Scholars, and some Spanish Grandees, to wait upon me.
>
> All pronounce me a wonderful piece of Mechanism, but few have numbered up the strange medley of things which compose my whole.

There is no positive proof of Carroll's authorship of the Explication, but the fact that he kept it apart from the *Enigma* during printing would seem to suggest that what follows is by him:

> The WHOLE, –is MAN.
>
> The PARTS are as follows:
>
> A large box – The Chest.
> Two lids – The Eye lids.
> Two Caps – The Knee Caps.
> Three established Measures – The nails, hands, and feet.
> A great number of articles a Carpenter cannot do without – Nails.
> A couple of good Fish – The Soles of the Feet.
> A number of a smaller tribe – The Muscles. (Mussels).
> Two lofty Trees – The Palms (of the hands).
> Fine Flowers – Two lips, (Tulips), and Irises.
> The fruit of an indigenous Plant – Hips.
> A handsome Stag – The Heart. (Hart).
> Two playful Animals – The Calves.

A number of a smaller and less tame Herd – The Hairs. (Hares).
Two Halls, or Places of Worship – The Temples.
Some Weapons of Warfare – The Arms, and Shoulder blades.
Many Weathercocks – The Veins. (Vanes).
The Steps of an Hotel – The Insteps. (Inn-Steps).
The House of Commons on the eve of a Dissolution – Eyes and Nose.
(Ayes and Noes).
Two Students or Scholars – The Pupils of the Eye.
Some Spanish Grandees – The Tendons. (Ten Dons).

Double acrostics

'Next, when you are describing
A shape, or sound, or tint;
Don't state the matter plainly,
But put it in a hint;
And learn to look at all things
With a sort of mental squint.'

Rhyme? and Reason?

The Double Acrostic is commonly thought to be the forerunner of
the modern crossword puzzle, exploiting the intersection of mutual
letters with greater complexity than possibly any previous type of
word play. With far greater scope for stylistic literary effect than the
crossword itself, it set a fashion which lasted throughout the English
speaking world from the middle of the nineteenth century until the First
World War. Although it's not possible to credit Carroll with the distant
invention of the crossword puzzle, as Langford Reed would have in his
biography, he made many exceptional contributions to the earlier form.
In *The World's Best Word Puzzles*, published in 1925, no less than Henry
E. Dudeney, the great English puzzle inventor, does in fact attribute the
invention of the double acrostic to none other than Queen Victoria, citing
an earlier (1861) work: *Victorian Enigmas; or, Windsor Fireside Researches: Being a Series of Acrostics Enigmatically Propounded* by Char-

lotte Eliza Capel, in which the author traces her inspiration back to a double acrostic given her five years previously by a friend at Windsor Castle who had seen it written out by the Queen for her children. The horizontal words defined in the numbered stanzas, or lights, were Naples, Elbe, Washington, Cincinatti, Amsterdam, Stanboul, Tornea, Lepanto and ecliptic, giving an initial upright of NEWCASTLE and a final one, read in reverse, of COAL MINES.

Carroll's finest double acrostic was first published in his collection of poems entitled *Phantasmagoria* in 1869. Composed, according to his diary entry for June 25, 1867, while he listened to the music of the Christ Church Commemoration Ball at the insistence of the niece of one of his students, it was intended as 'a specimen of what might be done by making the Double Acrostic *a connected poem* instead of what it has hitherto been, a string of disjointed Stanzas . . . about as interesting to read straight through as a page of a cyclopedia.' The first two stanzas define the two uprights to be discovered by taking the initial and final letters of the answers to the subsequent lights.

There was an ancient City, stricken down
With a strange frenzy, and for many a day
They paced from morn to eve the crowded town,
And danced the night away.

I asked the cause: the aged man grew sad:
They pointed to a building gray and tall,
And hoarsely answered 'Step inside, my lad,
And then you'll see it all.'

Yet what are all such gaieties to me
Whose thoughts are full of indices and surds?
$$x^2 + 7x + 53$$
$$= \frac{11}{3}.$$

But something whispered 'It will soon be done:
Bands cannot always play, nor ladies smile:
Endure with patience the distasteful fun
For just a little while!'

A change came o'er my Vision – it was night:
We clove a pathway through a frantic throng:
The steeds, wild-plunging, filled us with affright:
The chariots whirled along.

Within a marble hall a river ran –
  A living tide, half muslin and half cloth:
And here one mourned a broken wreath or fan
    Yet swallowed down her wrath:

And here one offered to a thirsty fair
  (His words half-drowned amid those thunders tuneful)
Some frozen viand (there were many there),
    A tooth-ache in each spoonful.

There comes a happy pause, for human strength
  Will not endure to dance without cessation;
And every one must reach the point at length
    Of absolute prostration.

At such a moment ladies learn to give,
  To partners who would urge them overmuch,
A flat and yet decided negative –
    Photographers love such.

There comes a welcome summons – hope revives,
  And fading eyes grow bright, and pulses quicken:
Incessant pop the corks, and busy knives
    Dispense the tongue and chicken.

Flushed with new life, the crowd flows back again:
  And all is tangled talk and mazy motion –
Much like a waving field of golden grain,
    Or a tempestuous ocean.

And thus they give the time, that Nature meant
  For peaceful sleep and meditative snores,
To ceaseless din and mindless merriment
    And waste of shoes and floors.

And One (we name him not) that flies the flowers,
  That dreads the dances, and that shuns the salads,
They doom to pass in solitude the hours,
    Writing acrostic-ballads.

How late it grows! The hour is surely past
  That should have warned us with its double knock?
The twilight wanes, and morning comes at last –
    'Oh, Uncle, what's o'clock?'

The Uncle gravely nods, and wisely winks.
  It *may* mean much, but how is one to know?
He opes his mouth – yet out of it, methinks,
    No words of wisdom flow.

Carroll did not offer a solution in *Phantasmagoria*. The anonymous editor of *The Collected Verse of Lewis Carroll*, published in 1932, appended 'COMMEMORATION, MONSTROSITIES', but without giving the all-important lights. In *The Strand Magazine* for December, 1915, H. Cuthbert Scott suggested a far more feasible solution: 'QUASI-INSANITY, COMMEMORATION', with the lights to substantiate it:

1	Q uadrati	C
2	U nderg	O
3	A lar	M
4	S trea	M
5	I c	E
6	I nteri	M
7	N	O
8	S uppe	R
9	A ren	A (or A rist A)
10	N igh	T
11	I	I
12	T w	O
13	Y aw	N

Martin Gardner, in *Scientific American* for September, 1967, re-opened the controversy by suggesting AurorA for the unsatisfactory ninth light, although Dmitri A. Borgmann, the American specialist in word play, concentrating on 'tangled talk' rather than 'mazy motion', proposes the more attractive AbracadabrA. Borgmann also suggests ScriM, a coarse cotton cloth, as an alternative for StreaM. Other likely alternatives submitted to Gardner by readers included SwarM, StoicisM ('swallowed down her wrath') and SchisM; AmericA and AgorA.

The alphabet-cipher

'I quite agree with you,' said the Duchess; 'and the moral of that is – "Be what you would seem to be" – or, if you'd like it put more simply – "Never imagine yourself not to be otherwise than what it might appear to others that what you were or might have been was not otherwise than what you had been would have appeared to them to be otherwise." '

'I think I should understand that better,' Alice said very politely, 'if I had it written down: but I can't quite follow it as you say it.'

Alice's Adventures in Wonderland

The following is a development of 'The Telegraph-Cipher' invented by Carroll during the night of April 22, 1868. The exact date of composition is unknown, but it seems reasonable to place it soon after 'The Telegraph-Cipher'; not that Carroll hadn't been devising less worthy versions for more than ten years prior to finding the definitive one.

Each column of this table forms a dictionary of symbols representing the alphabet: thus, in the A column, the symbol is the same as the letter represented; in the B column, A is represented by B, B by C, and so on.

To use the table, some word or sentence should be agreed on by two correspondents. This may be called the 'key-word', or 'key-sentence', and should be carried in the memory only.

In sending a message, write the key word over it, letter for letter, repeating it as often as may be necessary: the letters of the key-word will indicate which column is to be used in translating each letter of the message, the symbols for which should be written underneath: then copy out the symbols only, and destroy the first paper. It will now be impossible for any one, ignorant of the key-word, to decipher the message, even with the help of the table.

For example, let the key-word be *vigilance*, and the message 'meet me on Tuesday evening at seven', the first paper will read as follows–

```
v i g i l a n c e v i g i l a n c e v i g i l a n c e v i
m e e t m e o n t u e s d a y e v e n i n g a t s e v e n
h m k b x e b p x p m y l l y r x i i q t o l t f g z z v
```

The second will contain only 'h m k b x e b p x p m y l l y r x i i q t o l t f g z z v.'

The receiver of the message can, by the same process, retranslate it into English.

```
  A B C D E  F G H I  J  K L M N O  P Q R S T  U V W X Y Z

A a b c d e  f g h i  j  k l m n o  p q r s t  u v w x y z  A
B b c d e f  g h i j  k  l m n o p  q r s t u  v w x y z a  B
C c d e f g  h i j k  l  m n o p q  r s t u v  w x y z a b  C
D d e f g h  i j k l  m  n o p q r  s t u v w  x y z a b c  D
E e f g h i  j k l m  n  o p q r s  t u v w x  y z a b c d  E
F f g h i j  k l m n  o  p q r s t  u v w x y  z a b c d e  F
G g h i j k  l m n o  p  q r s t u  v w x y z  a b c d e f  G
H h i j k l  m n o p  q  r s t u v  w x y z a  b c d e f g  H
I i j k l m  n o p q  r  s t U v w  x y z a b  c d e f g h  I
J j k l m n  o p q r  s  t u v w x  y z a b c  d e f g h i  J
K k l m n o  p q r s  t  u v w x y  z a b c d  e f g h i j  K
L l m n o p  q r s t  u  v w x y z  a b c d e  f g h i j k  L
M m n o p q  r s t u  v  w x y z a  b c d e f  g h i j k l  M
N n o p q r  s t u v  w  x y z a b  c d e f g  h i j k l m  N
O o p q r s  t u v w  x  y z a b c  d e f g h  i j k l m n  O
P p q r s t  u v w x  y  z a b c d  e f g h i  j k l m n o  P
Q q r s t u  v w x y  z  a b c d e  f g h i j  k l m n o p  Q
R r s t u v  w x y z  a  b c d e f  g h i j k  l m n o p q  R
S s t u v w  x y z a  b  c d e f g  h i j k l  m n o p q r  S
T t u v w x  y z a b  c  d e f g h  i j k l m  n o p q r s  T
U u v w x y  z a b c  d  e f g h i  j k l m n  o p q r s t  U
V v w x y z  a b c d  e  f g h i j  k l m n o  p q r s t u  V
W w x y z a  b c d e  f  g h i j k  l m n o p  q r s t u v  W
X x y z a b  c d e f  g  h i j k l  m n o p q  r s t u v w  X
Y y z a b c  d e f g  h  i j k l m  n o p q r  s t u v w x  Y
Z z a b c d  e f g h  i  j k l m n  o p q r s  t u v w x y  Z

  A B C D E  F G H I  J  K L M N O  P Q R S T  U V W X Y Z
```

N.B.—If this table be lost, it can easily be written out from memory, by observing that the first symbol in each column is the same as the letter naming the column, and that they are continued downwards in alphabetical order. Of course it would only be necessary to write out the particular columns required by the key-word: such a paper, however, should not be preserved, as it would afford means for discovering the key-word.

'The Telegraph-Cipher' itself had originally consisted of two separate pieces of card, each measuring 4 by $\frac{7}{8}$ inches, which fitted together to form a whole card 4 by $1\frac{3}{4}$ inches. The top half, designated 'Key Alphabet', contained the 26 letters from 'a' to 'z' along the lower edge; the bottom half, designated 'Message Alphabet', contained the same, with an additional 'a' following hard on the 'z', along the top edge. The procedure of writing the key word over the message is the same as in the more elaborate version. To deduce the cipher, find the first letter of the key-word on the Key card, and the first letter of the message on the Message card, and bring both letters into alignment, sliding the cards against each other as with a slide rule. Whatever letter on the Key card now falls over the letter 'a' on the Message card becomes the first letter of the cipher. In a letter dated April 29, 1868 Carroll sent a prototype to child-friend Edith Argles, together with the following example of the cipher at work:

Key-word:	t r i c k/t r i c k/t r
Message:	c o me t o mo r r o w
Cipher:	r d w y r f f u l t f v

which translates back:

Cipher:	r d w y r f f u l t f v
Key-word:	t r i c k/t r i c k/t r
Translation:	c o me t o mo r r o w

Anagrams

November 25, 1868:
Wrote a letter to the *Standard*, commenting on a wonderful sentence in *The Times* leader on Gladstone's defeat in Lancashire yesterday: 'The failure of the Liberal policy in one populous district only gives greater weight to the general decision of the country.' I also sent them an anagram which I thought out lying awake the other night: 'William Ewart Gladstone: Wilt tear down *all* images?' I heard of another afterwards, made on the same name: 'I, wise Mr. G, want to lead all' – which is well answered by 'Disraeli: I lead, Sir!'

The Diaries

Neither letter nor anagram was published, but this is not to dispute his mastery of the anagram itself. He later devised two even better ones for Gladstone:

A wild man will go at trees.
Wild agitator! Means well.

Florence Nightingale inspired him to 'Flit on, cheering angel'; and Edward Vaughan Kenealy, the defending counsel for the Tichborne Claimant, 'Ah! We dread an ugly knave!' Composing anagrams on the names of prominent people enjoyed some vogue in Carroll's day and still maintains an enthusiastic outlet among addicts. Borgmann has listed several brilliant examples on the names of American presidents:

Grover Cleveland: 'Govern, clever lad!'
Theodore Roosevelt: 'Hero told to oversee'
President Franklin Delano Roosevelt: 'Lo! Real keen person voted first in land!'
Dwight D. Eisenhower: 'Wow! He's right indeed!'

Since we began this section with Gladstone and Disraeli, it is worth mentioning the similarity between them and the Lion and the Unicorn respectively in Tenniel's illustration. Rather than read any overt political significance into this on Carroll's part (he was at heart a Conservative with a distrust in Gladstone), it should be remembered that Tenniel himself achieved his principal fame in his own day through his political cartoons in *Punch*. There is a similar visual parallel between Gladstone and the Mad Hatter, and also between Disraeli and the man in the white paper suit, a uniform ironically appropriate for a Prime Minister.

Now is also the time to mention the virtual word game Charles

Lutwidge Dodgson played in arriving at his own immortal nom de plume. While writing verse for a short-lived monthly publication, *The Train*, in 1856, he submitted five possibilities for a pseudonym: 'Dares', an abbreviation of Daresbury, his Cheshire birthplace; two anagrams of his Christian names, 'Edgar Cuthwellis' and 'Edgar U. C. Westhill'; and by a complicated process of Latinization, reversal and retranslation, from Carolus Ludovicus through Ludovicus Carolus, 'Louis Carroll' and 'Lewis Carroll'. The editor, Edmund Yates, chose the latter, first used to sign the poem *Solitude* in March, 1856.

Carroll himself, not surprisingly, even resorted to mathematics to give vent to his strong Tory resentment. In *The St. James's Gazette* for March 23, 1882, he followed to its logical conclusion Gladstone's 'Resolution' that 'Closure voted by a bare majority can be carried legitimately by the same bare majority':

> 'May I presume to anticipate *The Daily News* in making an announcement which will shake to its centre the whole scientific world? The ''Perpetuum Mobile'' is discovered. We may confidently expect that a clock will shortly be exhibited, which, as often as it runs down, is able to wind itself up again. The discoverer of this marvellous principle – the mere details of construction being trifles that any watchmaker can arrange – is no less a person than Mr. Gladstone, on whose great mind it has dawned, for the first time in the world's history, that a body of men *can confer on themselves* rights over another body of men which they do not already possess. That is to say, Mr. Pyke will first introduce Mr. Pluck, and then Mr. Pluck, being regularly introduced, will be qualified to introduce Mr. Pyke. . . .'

Flower riddle

Tell me truly, Maidens three,
Where can all these wonders be ?
Where tooth of lion, eye of ox,
And foot of cat and tail of fox,
With ear of mouse and tongue of hound
And beard of goat, together bound
With hair of Maiden, strew the ground.

The above was dedicated to Harriett, Mary and Georgina Watson, whom Carroll used to address collectively with the portmanteau word 'Harmarina'. It is impossible to date the riddle, but towards the end of 1869 Carroll was applauding himself in his diary for the excellent photographs he had taken of the three daughters of the Rev. George William Watson, sometime Postmaster of Merton College, Oxford, who had died in 1863.

The riddle is based on the most literal rendering of some of the more imaginative names for flowers and grasses, perhaps with reference to some garden or countryside haunt all four knew well. It was a surprising choice for Carroll, since Isa Bowman, the child actress and friend who played the name part in the stage production of *Alice in Wonderland* at the Royal Globe Theatre in December, 1888, tells us in her *Story of Lewis Carroll* that he did not like flowers. Describing the long walks they went on together, she recalls: 'Once, and once only, I remember him to have taken an interest in a flower, and that was because of the folklore that was attached to it, and not because of the beauty of the flower itself. . . . he took a foxglove from the heap that lay in my lap and told me the story of how they came by their name.'

Do you see that Fox-Glove growing close to the tree? And do you know why it's called a *Fox-Glove*? Perhaps you think it's got something to do with a Fox? No indeed! *Foxes* never wear gloves!

The right word is *Folk's*-Gloves. Did you ever hear that Fairies used to be called 'the good Folk'?

The Nursery Alice

The [chestnuts]

My [deer] Ina,

Though [eye] don't give birthday presents, still [eye]
April
... write a birthday [letter].
June
[ear] came 2 your [door] 2
wish U many happy returns
of the day, [barrel] the [cat] met
me, [hand] took me for a [mouse],
[hand] hunted me [hand] and [hand]
till [foot] could hardly [well].
However somehow [eye] got
into the [house], [hand] there
a [snake] met me, [hand] took me
for a [frog], and pelted me

Part of a letter from Carroll at 'The Chestnuts', his sisters' home in Guildford, to Georgina Watson, revealing the lengths to which he would go to tantalise his child-friends

The three squares

The poor King looked puzzled and unhappy, and struggled with the pencil for some time without saying anything; but Alice was too strong for him, and at last he panted out 'My dear! I really *must* get a thinner pencil. I can't manage this one a bit: it writes all manner of things that I don't intend—'

Through the Looking-Glass

In Collingwood's *Life and Letters* Isabel Standen recalls being shown by Carroll on August 21, 1869 a puzzle 'so thoroughly characteristic of him in its quaint humour', in which one had to draw three interlaced squares in one continuous line without going over any parts of the line twice, without intersecting the line, and without taking the pencil off the paper.

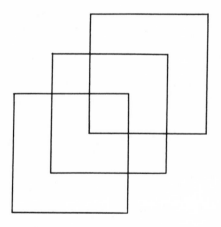

Thomas O'Beirne, the Scottish author of *Puzzles and Paradoxes*, has proposed a certain method for solving such puzzles. First colour the alternate areas as shown and then literally pull them apart at the appropriate points in such a way that the coloured areas form one continuous mass, free of any enclosed non-coloured areas. The edge of this shape approximates topologically to the more precise line required by the solution.

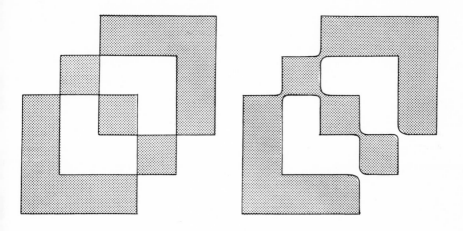

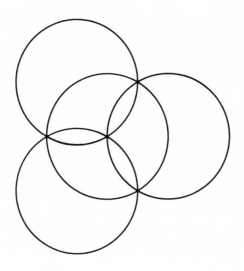

O'Beirne himself has proposed a four-circle variation of Carroll's problem, the solution of which will be found on page 271.

Double acrostic

I sing a place wherein agree
All things on land that fairest be,
All that is sweetest of the sea.

Nor can I break the silken knot
That binds my memory to the spot
And friends too dear to be forgot.
.   .   .   .   .

On rocky brow we loved to stand
And watch in silence, hand in hand,
The shadows veiling sea and land.

Then dropped the breeze; no vessel passed:
So silent stood each taper mast,
You would have deemed it chained and fast.

Above the blue and fleecy sky:
Below, the waves that quivering lie,
Like crispèd curls of greenery.

'A sail!' resounds from every lip.
Mizen, no, square-sail – ah, you trip!
Edith, it cannot be a ship!

So home again from sea and beach,
One nameless feeling thrilling each.
A sense of beauty, passing speech.

Let lens and tripod be unslung!
'Dolly!' 's the word on every tongue;
Dolly must sit, for she is young!

Photography shall change her face,
Distort it with uncouth grimace –
Make her bloodthirsty, fierce, and base.

I end my song while scarce begun;
For I should want, ere all was done,
Four weeks to tell the tale of one:

And I should need as large a hand,
To paint a scene so wild and grand,
As he who traversed Egypt's land.

What say you, Edith? Will it suit ye?
Reject it, if it fails in beauty:
You know your literary duty!

Composed on a train journey between Torquay and Guildford on September 28, 1869, this double acrostic was dedicated by Carroll to Miss

E. M. Argles, and was first printed together with the following solution in the Catalogue for the exhibition in London to commemorate the centenary of his birth:

1	B luf	F
2	A ncho	R
3	B roccol	I
4	B arqu	E
5	A ppreciatio	N
6	C hil	D
7	O diou	S
8	M ont	H
9	B elzon	I
10	E ditorshi	P

Puzzles from Wonderland

'You should learn not to make personal remarks,' Alice said with some severity: 'It's very rude.'

The Hatter opened his eyes very wide on hearing this; but all he *said* was, 'Why is a raven like a writing-desk?'

'Come, we shall have some fun now!' thought Alice. 'I'm glad they've begun asking riddles – I believe I can guess that,' she added aloud.

'Do you mean that you think you can find out the answer to it?' said the March Hare.

'Exactly so,' said Alice.

'Then you should say what you mean,' the March Hare went on.

'I do,' Alice hastily replied; 'at least – at least I mean what I say – that's the same thing, you know.'

'Not the same thing a bit!' said the Hatter. 'Why, you might just as well say that "I see what I eat" is the same thing as "I eat what I see"!'

Alice's Adventures in Wonderland

The Mad Hatter's famous unanswered riddle caused much conjecture at the time and eventually Carroll was forced to supply an answer in a preface to the edition of the eighty-sixth thousand, dated 1896, in much the same way that in the introduction to *The Hunting of the Snark* he

explained the 'portmanteau' words in *Jabberwocky* with fifteen years between the two publications: 'Enquiries have been so often addressed to me, as to whether any answer to the Hatter's Riddle can be imagined, that I may as well put on record here what seems to me to be a fairly appropriate answer, viz: "Because it can produce a few notes, tho they are *very* flat; and it is never put with the wrong end in front!" This, however, is merely an afterthought; the Riddle, as originally invented, had no answer at all.'

Sam Loyd, the American puzzle king, ventured posthumously in his *Cyclopedia of Puzzles*, 1914, the solution that 'The notes for which they are noted are not noted for being musical notes.' Loyd also reminded the world that 'Poe wrote on both' and that 'bills and tales are among their characteristics.'

Five years after the publication of *Alice's Adventures in Wonderland*, in December, 1870, Carroll continuing his penchant for riddles, published seven 'Puzzles from Wonderland' in *Aunt Judy's Magazine*. Answers appeared the following month, signed 'Eadgyth', but there is doubt as to whether they are by Carroll himself, since there are many other contributions that are certainly not his signed similarly between 1869 and 1878. *The Lewis Carroll Handbook* suggests that the solutions were penned by

Horatia K. F. Gatty, who later succeeded her mother as editor of the magazine.

Carroll mentions in his diary for November 30, 1870 that the puzzles 'were originally written for the Cecil children'. In June of that year he had met Lord Salisbury on his installation as Chancellor at Oxford and made friends with them then. Presumably at a later date he wrote out the first puzzle for another friend, Mary Watson, a letter notable for the fact that this was one of the few occasions when Lewis Carroll signed himself as such and not 'C. L. Dodgson'.

Mary dear,
    Here is a riddle for you. Put your three heads together, & see if you can guess it.

Dreaming of apples on a wall,
    And dreaming often, dear,
I dreamed that, if I counted all,
    How many would appear?

Your loving friend,
    Lewis Carroll.

PUZZLES FROM WONDERLAND

1.

Dreaming of apples on a wall,
And dreaming often, dear,
I dreamed that, if I counted all,
—How many would appear?

2.

A stick I found that weighed two pound:
I sawed it up one day
In pieces eight of equal weight!
How much did each piece weigh?
(Everybody says 'a quarter of a pound,' which is wrong.)

3.

John gave his brother James a box:
About it there were many locks.

James woke and said it gave him pain;
So gave it back to John again.

The box was not with lid supplied,
Yet caused two lids to open wide:

And all these locks had never a key—
What kind of box, then, could it be?

4.

What is most like a bee in May?
'Well, let me think: perhaps—' you say.
Bravo! You're guessing well to-day!

5.

Three sisters at breakfast were feeding the cat,
The first gave it sole – Puss was grateful for that:
The next gave it salmon – which Puss thought a treat:
The third gave it herring – which Puss wouldn't eat.
(Explain the conduct of the cat.)

6.

Said the Moon to the Sun,
'Is the daylight begun?'
Said the Sun to the Moon,
'Not a minute too soon.'

'You're a Full Moon,' said he.
She replied with a frown,
'Well! I never *did* see
So uncivil a clown!'
(Query. Why was the moon so angry?)

7.

When the King found that his money was nearly all gone, and that he really *must* live more economically, he decided on sending away most of his Wise Men. There were some hundreds of them – very fine old men, and magnificently dressed in green velvet gowns with gold buttons: if they *had* a fault, it was that they always contradicted one another when he asked for their advice – and they certainly ate and drank *enormously*. So, on the whole, he was rather glad to get rid of them. But there was an old law, which he did not dare to disobey, which said that there must always be

'Seven blind of both eyes:
Ten blind of one eye:
Five that see with both eyes:
Nine that see with one eye.'
(Query. How many did he keep?)

SOLUTIONS TO PUZZLES FROM WONDERLAND

1.

If ten the number dreamed of, why 'tis clear
That in the dream ten apples would appear.

2.

In Shylock's bargain for the flesh was found
No mention of the blood that flowed around:
So when the stick was sawed in pieces eight,
The sawdust lost diminished from the weight.

3.

As curly-wigg'd Jemmy was sleeping in bed,
His brother John gave him a blow on the head;
James opened his eyelids, and spying his brother,
Doubled his fist, and gave him another.
This kind of a box then is not so rare;
The lids are the eyelids, the locks are the hair,
And as every schoolboy can tell to his cost,
The key to the tangles is constantly lost.

4.

'Twixt 'Perhaps' and 'May be'
Little difference we see:
Let the question go round,
The answer is found.

5.

That salmon and sole Puss should think very grand
    Is no such remarkable thing.
For more of these dainties Puss took up her stand;
But when the third sister stretched out her fair hand
    Pray why should Puss swallow her ring?

6.

'In these degenerate days,' we oft hear said,
    'Manners are lost and chivalry is dead!'
No wonder, since in high exalted spheres
    The same degeneracy, in fact, appears.
The Moon, in social matters interfering,
    Scolded the Sun, when early in appearing;
And the rude Sun, her gentle sex ignoring,
    Called her a fool, thus her pretensions flooring.

7.

Five seeing, and seven blind
    Give us twelve, in all, we find;
But all of these, 'tis very plain,
    Come into account again.
For take notice, it may be true,
    That those blind of one eye are blind of two;
And consider contrariwise,
    That to see with your eye you may have your eyes;
So setting one against the other—
    For a mathematician no great bother—
And working the sum, you will understand
    That sixteen wise men still trouble the land.

It is worth mentioning here Carroll's earliest recorded riddle, included by him without solution in *Mischmasch* and used by Collingwood as the climax to his article, 'Before "Alice": The Boyhood of Lewis Carroll' in *The Strand Magazine*, December, 1898:

A monument – men all agree—
Am I in all sincerity,
    Half cat, half hindrance made.
If head and tail removed should be,
Then most of all you strengthen me;
Replace my head, the stand you see
    On which my tail is laid.

Collingwood hoped that the rediscovered teaser would set the world racking its brain as feverishly as the Mad Hatter's riddle. Certainly it was thirty-one years before an attempt at an answer, almost certainly the correct one ('tablet'), appeared in print in the first edition of the *Handbook*.

The coin and the ball of wool

. . . . while Alice was sitting curled up in a corner of the great armchair, half talking to herself and half asleep, the kitten had been having a grand game of romps with the ball of worsted Alice had been trying to wind up, and had been rolling it up and down till it had all come undone again; and there it was, spread over the hearth-rug, all knots and tangles, with the kitten running after its own tail in the middle.

Through the Looking-Glass

A ball of wool with its very own labyrinthine intricacy made a favourite prop for the drawing-room magician of a hundred years ago. Here was the most effective climax to the marked coin trick Carroll would have known, the reappearance of the coin delayed to the last possible suspense-laden moment while the wool was unwound.

Apart from a ball of wool about four to five inches in diameter, one needs a flat metal tube about four inches long, thick enough for a coin to slide from end to end, the edges of one end opened slightly as shown.

Wind the wool around the opposite end of the tube, so that when the wool is finally wound into a ball the opened end will protrude for about an inch and a half. This is placed out of sight behind some other prop on the magician's table.

During the performance a member of the audience marks a coin for later identification and then lends it to the magician, who wraps it in a piece of paper about four inches by six inches, folded lengthwise in such a way that one long edge overlaps the other by about an inch. The coin is placed in the fold and the fold closed against the coin as in the first illustration. Holding the paper in the left hand with the shorter half towards you, fold the two edges of the paper forward as shown (2 and 3). Then fold forward the top of the packet (4). This gives the impression of the coin being securely trapped, but in actual fact the top is still open because initially one side of the packet was made shorter than the other. Take the packet in the right hand, reversing it in the process, and tap it against a glass; the coin will sound, proof that it is still there. Then in passing it back to the left hand, allow the coin to slip secretly into the right fingers (5). Place the packet in a prominent position. The right hand now reaches for the ball of wool, dropping the coin into the tube and quickly withdrawing and then releasing the latter before showing it. Hand the ball to the owner of the coin, your fingers smoothing over any traces of a hole in the wool, and then proceed to vanish the coin, either by tearing the paper into shreds or, if flash paper has been used, allowing it to burst into flame instantly. The spectator now unwinds the wool, the most convenient way to do this being to keep the ball in a glass so that he merely has to pull on the loose end. The coin will soon make its presence felt, clinking dramatically against the side of the glass.

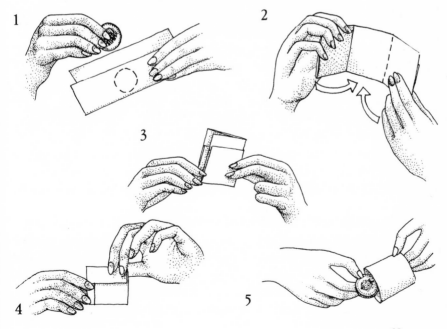

Through a looking-glass

There was a book lying near Alice on the table, and while she sat watching the White King (for she was still a little anxious about him, and had the ink all ready to throw over him, in case he fainted again), she turned over the leaves, to find some part that she could read, '—for it's all in some language I don't know,' she said to herself.

It was like this.

JABBERWOCKY

'Twas brillig, and the slithy toves
  Did gyre and gimble in the wabe:
All mimsy were the borogoves,
  And the mome raths outgrabe.

She puzzled over this for some time, but at last a bright thought struck her. 'Why, it's a Looking-glass book, of course! And, if I hold it up to a glass, the words will all go the right way again.'

Through the Looking-Glass

Throughout his life Carroll lived in a world of his own where topsy-turvy held sway, his own fascination with the idea of mirror-reversal being merely one manifestation of a cherished norm. He would relax by playing his music boxes backwards. He frequently wrote letters back to front, not only in mirror-writing but with the last word first and vice-versa so that one had to start reading from the end. The following example to Nellie Bowman was included by her sister Isa in her *Story of Lewis Carroll*. The facsimile of the 'Looking-Glass letter' to another child friend, Edith Hall, was included by Collingwood in his *Life and Letters*.

Other apparently more straightforward letters provided him with a platform for acting out his fantasy for backwards-living. In one he explained how writing letters tired him so much that 'generally I go to bed again the next minute after I get up; and sometimes I go to bed again a minute *before* I get up! Did you ever hear of anyone being so tired as that?' His obsession with inversion extended not surprisingly to mathematics where he devised a new multiplication process whereby the multiplier is written backwards and above the number to be multiplied. He actually claims to have written *The Hunting of the Snark* in reverse order after the sudden initial inspiration of the last line, 'For the Snark

Nov. 1. 1891.

CD, Uncle loving
your! Instead grand
-son his to it give to
had you that so, years
80 or 70 for it forgot
you that was it pity,
a what and : him of fond
So were you wonder don't
I and, gentleman old
nice very a was he. For
it made you that him
been have *must* it see
you so: grandfather ony
was, *then* alive was that,
"Dodgson Uncle" only,
the. Born was I before

Part of a back-to-front letter from Lewis Carroll to Nellie Bowman

was a Boojum, you see.' Only later did he fit a stanza to the line, and then over the next two years the rest of the poem to fit the final stanza. In a comprehensive note in *The Annotated Alice*, Martin Gardner explores this theme of inversion as the basic mainstay of Carrollian humour.

[Mirror-writing letter:]

Nov. 6, 1893.

My dear Edith,

I know you won't
be pleased to get your own
little letter: once I hope
you will write me a letter
Norwich that you have
wish, now that you have
some. get the real one.
I will send you the
other book, about "Through the Looking-Glass"
that you had better not here
It just say, for now.

That he should then have a more than passing interest in the peculiarities of mirror reflection is not surprising. In *The Times* for January 22, 1932, Alice Raikes, a distant cousin, tells how she played her own vivid part in the evolution of his second most famous work:

'As children we lived in Onslow Square and used to play in the garden behind the houses. Charles Dodgson used to stay with an old uncle there,

An example of a looking-glass letter, from Carroll to Miss Edith Hall

and walk up and down, his hands behind him, on the strip of lawn. One day, hearing my name, he called me to him saying, ''So you are another Alice. I'm very fond of Alices. Would you like to come and see something which is rather puzzling?' We followed him into his house which opened, as ours did, upon the garden, into a room full of furniture with a tall mirror standing across one corner.'

' ''Now,'', he said, giving me an orange, ''first tell me which hand you have got that in.'' ''The right,'' I said. ''Now,'' he said, ''go and stand before

that glass, and tell me which hand the little girl you see there has got it in." After some perplexed contemplation, I said, "The left hand." "Exactly," he said, "and how do you explain that?" I couldn't explain it, but seeing that some solution was expected, I ventured, "If I was on the *other* side of the glass, wouldn't the orange still be in my right hand?" I can remember his laugh. "Well done, little Alice," he said. "The best answer I've had yet." '

The amateur magician in him found mirrors stimulating, a reliable means of baffling his young friends. With Carroll, however, magic was not 'all done by mirrors', the secret means to a miracle, but openly with them, although he was grateful for their mysterious innate qualities.

By taking two small pocket mirrors held at right angles to each other, he could with adjustment show how they formed a perfect reflection of one's face, a reflection of a reflection, so that now if Alice Raikes had,

say, winked her right eye, her image would also wink its right eye, in direct contradiction of what she would have seen, and with the orange did see, in a single mirror.

Another stunt involved painting on the face of a convex mirror a simple shape in a weak solution of gum arabic. In normal daylight this would be invisible, but as soon as the mirror was made to reflect the sun or a strong light, the pattern would immediately become apparent, its shadow projected on an opposite wall, due to the interception of the rays by the coated parts.

A more sophisticated version of another reflection trick involves attaching a thin strip of gummed paper to a small rectangular mirror from half way along one long edge to the same point on the opposite edge. Place the long edge of the mirror at right angles to the page along the line AB, aligning the paper strip with the black column. You will not be able to read the words reversed as they are in the mirror. Now turn the page upside down and place the long edge at right angles to the page along the line CD. Amazingly the right hand side will still appear back to front as well as upside-down, while the words on the left will be as readable as they are on the page!

A   B

QUALITY	CHOICE
GLOVES	KID
PAGES	COOKBOOK
GAMBLE	DICE
NUTS	BEECH

D   C

The reason for this curious phenomenon is that the letters comprising CHOICE, KID, COOKBOOK, DICE, BEECH all have a horizontal axis of symmetry, with the result that they appear unchanged when viewed horizontally in mirror-image. The other letters, like corkscrews and scissors, Alice and her orange and Tenniel's cunning monogram, are assymetrical with the result that they are not superposable on their mirror-images. A similar effect, incidentally, can be obtained along a vertical axis with words like:

T	T	A	M	H
O	I	U	O	O
M	M	T	T	I
A	O	O	I	T
T	T	M	V	Y
O	H	A	I	T
	Y	T	T	O
		A	Y	I
				T
				Y

The fact that Alice, in order to read *Jabberwocky*, had to reverse its image in a mirror suggests that she herself was not reversed by her journey through the Looking-Glass, a condition held suspect by modern scientific theory because of its portended consequences. The reader is recommended to consult Martin Gardner's absorbing work *The Ambidextrous Universe* for an explanation of why Alice was unlikely to have existed for more than a fraction of a second in such a world; why, to answer her own question, Looking-Glass milk would almost certainly have been of no nutritional value whatsoever!

It is though worth recording the aftermath of a lecture given on this very topic by Edward Teller, the 'father of the Hydrogen Bomb', in 1956. In reply to Teller, Harold P. Furth, a Californian physicist, gave a vivid description of what would happen when matter did come into contact with anti-matter in a poem published in *The New Yorker* for November 10, 1956, under the title 'Perils of Modern Living'. By courtesy of the Atomic Energy Commission an anonymous Teller is transported to the extra-terrestrial home of his counterpart, Dr. Anti-Teller. Overjoyed to see how they complement each other 'lentil' fashion – "their right hands clasped, and the rest was gamma rays."

Levitation

She just kept the tips of her fingers on the hand-rail, and floated gently down without even touching the stairs with her feet: then she floated on through the hall, and would have gone straight out at the door in the same way, if she hadn't caught hold of the door-post. She was getting a little giddy with so much floating in the air, and was rather glad to find herself walking again in the natural way.

Through the Looking-Glass

W. H. Cremer's 'Saloon of Magic' at 210, Regent Street, was a frequent haunt of Carroll on his visits to London. Cremer's edition of *The Magician's Own Book*, published in 1871, contains instructions for a domestic levitation effect in which the subject of the experiment relaxes on a table or bench his own length, with legs extended and heels touching. Four persons, two on each side, stand around the table and place their extended forefingers under his knees and shoulders. At a given signal from the magician those eight fingers alone lift the body soaring into the air – but only after the two persons at his shoulders have bent over and exhaled deeply upon his chest, and those at his knees similarly upon his legs, preferably in unison, for about fifteen times without stopping! As a postscript Cremer suggests that the subject should expel the air from his own lungs immediately prior to the signal for levitation to proceed.

Shopping dilemma

'I should like to buy an egg, please,' she said timidly. 'How do you sell them?'
  'Fivepence farthing for one – twopence for two,' the Sheep replied.
  'Then two are cheaper than one?' Alice said in a surprised tone, taking out her purse.
  'Only you *must* eat them both, if you buy two,' said the Sheep.
  'Then I'll have *one*, please,' said Alice, as she put the money down on the counter. For she thought to herself, 'They mightn't be at all nice, you know.'

Through the Looking-Glass

The following problem in purchasing was described as a favourite of Carroll by Collingwood in *The Lewis Carroll Picture Book*. A customer bought goods in a shop to the pre-decimal amount of 7s. 3d. The only money he had with him was a half-sovereign (10s.), a florin (2s.), and a sixpence. So he needed change; but the shopkeeper himself only had a crown (5s.), a shilling and a penny. Then a friend entered the shop with a double-florin (4s.), a half-crown (2s. 6d.), a fourpenny-bit, and a threepenny-bit. Could they manage it?

The way to resolve the dilemma is for all three individuals to place what currency they do possess on the counter. Since the cost of the purchase was 7s. 3d., obviously the shopkeeper has to receive that sum plus his original 6s. 1d., a total of 13s. 4d. Therefore the half-sovereign must go to the shopkeeper, who in addition takes the sixpence, the half-crown, and the fourpenny-bit. The customer, needing 5s. 3d. change, takes the double-florin, the shilling, and threepenny-bit. Finally the friend takes back his 7s. 1d., now comprising florin, crown and penny. There are other combinations, but this is the most logistically pleasing, as it will be seen that not one of the three persons retains any one of his own coins.

Doubtless the seeming paradox of the following problem would also have appealed to Carroll, a version of which was discovered among the notebooks of fellow author and recreational mathematician, Samuel Taylor Coleridge. A farmer's wife took her basket of eggs to market. To the first customer she sold half her eggs and half an egg; to the second half of what remained and half an egg; to the third half of what she then had left and half an egg. And yet at no time did she break any eggs! Three eggs remained. How many did she start out with? The paradox disappears as soon as one realises that the most unlikely of conditions can be fulfilled if she starts with an odd number of eggs. The specific answer is thirty-one.

The upright egg

The Sheep took the money, and put it away in a box: then she said 'I never put things into people's hands – that would never do – you must get it for yourself.' And so saying, she went off to the other end of the shop, and set the egg **upright** on a shelf.

Through the Looking-Glass

There have been many solutions proposed for duplicating Columbus' reputed feat of balancing an egg on end. Legend has it that his own method entailed cracking the wide end slightly, thus flattening the shell into an actual base. Another variation involves shaking the egg violently so that the contents merge, enabling the centre of gravity to lie in the direct line of balance. In what is probably the best version with an ungimmicked egg one pours a small mound of salt on to the table. It is easy to set the egg upright in this. Then very, very carefully, with a fine camel hair brush, remove the grains until only a few remain. The egg will stay standing with no apparent means of support.

Sam Loyd developed the theme of the Columbus egg, conjecturing the true origin of the story which caused the navigator to remark, 'It's the easiest thing in the world when you are shown how.' He proposed an old gambling game to be played between two people who have to

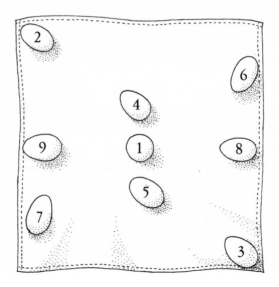

place eggs of equal size alternatively upon a square napkin. After one egg is placed it must not be moved or touched by another. This continues until the napkin is so crowded there is no room for another egg, the winner the person to place an egg last. Loyd explained that if the first player begins by placing an egg exactly in the centre of the napkin, on end as shown, all he has to do to ensure eventual victory is to duplicate the play of his opponent at each successive placing as depicted in the illustration, where the numbers indicate the order of play for the beginning of a specimen game.

The secret of Haigha's bag

'Come, fetch out the plum-cake, old man!' the Unicorn went on, turning from her to the King. 'None of your brown bread for me!'

'Certainly – certainly!' the King muttered, and beckoned to Haigha. 'Open the bag!' he whispered. 'Quick! Not that one – that's full of hay!'

Haigha took a large cake out of the bag, and gave it to Alice to hold, while he got out a dish and carving-knife. How they all came out of it Alice couldn't guess. It was just like a conjuring-trick, she thought.

Through the Looking-Glass

The pose adopted by Haigha in Tenniel's illustration as he produces the White King's ham sandwich from his intriguing bag of plenty is nothing if not a magician's pose. Moreover, the proximity of the Humpty Dumpty episode to the above does nothing to weaken the idea that, as Carroll wrote this sequence, prominent in his mind was a standard item of every conjuror's repertoire, the Egg Bag.

In its simplest form, as detailed in *The Secret's Out*, edited by Cremer, c. 1871, the bag, preferably made of thin and necessarily opaque material, was really two bags sewn together, the equivalent of one with a division across. In one side was sewn a series of pockets, each containing an egg. The bag could be turned inside out and shown empty, revealing the empty partition, and then folded back and an egg produced for as many times as the size of the bag and number of pockets dictated.

In later years a more subtle version was developed involving a bag about eight inches by six, again double, but the partition being folded down from the mouth of the bag for about two thirds of its depth and left open at its lower edge. Stitched at the sides, this produced a kind of pocket, mouth downward, within the bag. Drop an egg in and turn the bag upside down and the egg will fall into the pocket rather than crash to the floor. As long as you keep the pocket side towards yourself you may turn the bag inside out and upside down without the audience suspecting that the bag is anything but empty.

With this version it is possible to approximate the earlier effect using only one egg. Begin with the egg in the bag. Turn the bag upside down and inside out, proving the bag empty. For a moment hold the bag in the teeth to show both hands absolutely empty. Take the bag in the left hand, dip the right hand inside and produce an (the) egg. This is placed in the mouth where it is apparently swallowed (in actual fact,

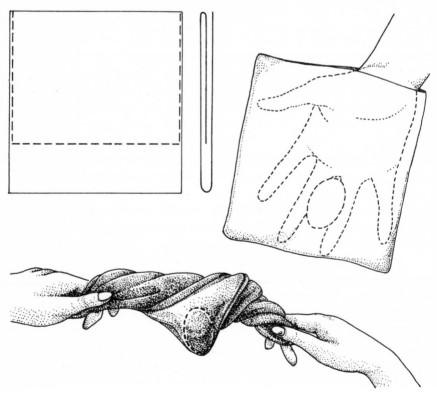

although it *is* placed in the mouth, after a brief pause the egg is instantly pushed out with the tongue under cover of the right hand where it is palmed). The hand now returns to the bag, which it shows empty (working the egg back into the pocket), and then reproduces a second egg, which is disposed of in the same way. And so on, ad infinitum, until the magician has produced and swallowed up to a dozen eggs conjured out of the empty bag.

Throughout the routine it is possible to ring the changes in demonstrating the emptiness of the bag. By placing the bag perfectly flat on the hand and spreading the fingers apart, the egg will sink down below the level of the hand as shown. You can now pat your hands together, making the bag seem so flat that it would appear to be more impossible than ever for it to contain anything so large and fragile as an egg.

Again, by letting the egg settle in one corner it is possible to take the bag by the opposite corners and twist it as tight as possible. It is natural for the unheld corners to stick up when this is done, so even though the egg is in one of them, there is no reason to suppose that the bag is anything other than empty.

Also, by holding the egg through the cloth at the top of the bag you can go up to a member of the audience and ask him to feel in the bag with his right hand. He will find nothing. Then ask him to feel with his left. By this time you have released the egg and he produces it for you! The permutation of the basic moves are, of course, limitless and each performer develops his own. The trend in recent years, however, has been towards a comedy mock-exposure sequence whereby the performer pretends to demonstrate how an egg can be secreted out of the bag and into his pocket or under his arm and back again. The second time he demonstrates this the egg is left in the bag and a half-closed hand makes as if to leave the egg in its secret hideaway. With spectators holding his wrists, the performer then challenges them to stop him reaching for his pocket or wherever. Needless to say, the egg, having never left the 'empty' bag, reappears regardless.

A looking-glass apple

Alice had seated herself on the bank of a little brook, with the great dish on her knees, and was sawing away diligently with the knife. 'It's very provoking!' she said, in reply to the Lion (she was getting quite used to being called "the Monster"). 'I've cut several slices already, but they always join on again!'

'You don't know how to manage Looking-glass cakes,' the Unicorn remarked. 'Hand it round first, and cut it afterwards.'

This sounded nonsense, but Alice very obediently got up, and carried the dish round, and the cake divided itself into three pieces as she did so. '*Now* cut it up,' said the Lion, as she returned to her place with the empty dish.

Through the Looking-Glass

Alice's experiences with the Looking-Glass cake will almost certainly have jogged Carroll's memory of an old parlour trick featuring an apple, inspected as genuine by a spectator, and then magically divided into quarters with its skin left intact. To prove what has happened the magician now allows the spectator to peel the apple, which neatly falls apart in his hands, an instance of 'slice it first, and peel it afterwards'.

The only preparation necessary is to take a needle and thread and sew round the apple just beneath the skin, inserting the needle 'each time at the exit of the previous stitch. You start and finish as indicated at the stem, where you then cross the two ends and pull smartly until the polygon loop comes right out. This slices the apple into two halves; repeat at right angles to slice into quarters. The blemishes left by the needle are hardly distinguishable and merge discreetly into the natural texture of the peel.

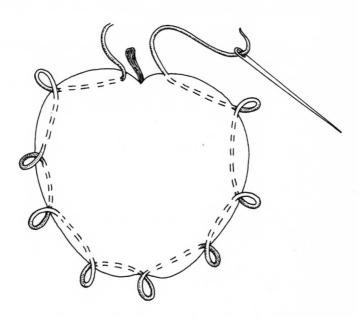

Looking-glass Chess

'I wouldn't mind being a Pawn, if only I might join – though of course I should *like* to be a Queen, best.'

She glanced rather shyly at the real Queen as she said this, but her companion only smiled pleasantly, and said 'That's easily managed. You can be the White Queen's Pawn, if you like, as Lily's too young to play; and you're in the Second Square to begin with: when you get to the Eighth Square you'll be a Queen—'

Through the Looking-Glass

Few of Carroll's puzzles have caused more head-scratching among experts than the difficulties posed innocently by him in the game on which which *Through the Looking-Glass* is based. The chess motif is far more prominent in the later book than the playing card and croquet motifs in *Alice's Adventures in Wonderland*; not only is a chess diagram included at the beginning, but a problem is posed, namely 'White Pawn (Alice) to play, and win in eleven moves':

RED

WHITE

1. Alice meets R. Q.	1. R. Q. to K. R's 4th
2. Alice through Q's 3d *(by railway)* to Q's 4th *(Tweedledum and Tweedledee)*	2. W. Q. to Q. B's 4th *(after shawl)*
3. Alice meets W. Q. *(with shawl)*	3. W. Q. to Q. B's 5th *(becomes sheep)*
4. Alice to Q's 5th *(shop, river, shop)*	4. W. Q. to K. B's 8th *(leaves egg on shelf)*
5. Alice to Q's 6th *(Humpty Dumpty)*	5. W. Q. to Q. B's 8th *(flying from R. Kt.)*
6. Alice to Q's 7th *(forest)*	6. R. Kt. to K's 2nd (ch.)
7. W. Kt. takes R. Kt.	7. W. Kt. to K. B's 5th
8. Alice to Q's 8th *(coronation)*	8. R. Q. to K's sq. *(examination)*
9. Alice becomes Queen	9. Queens castle
10. Alice castles *(feast)*	10. W. Q. to Q. R's 6th *(soup)*
11. Alice takes R. Q. & wins	

As if to anticipate the strictures of Falconer Madan in the early edition of the *Handbook* that 'the chess framework is full of absurdities and impossibilities', and that 'hardly a move has a sane purpose', Carroll added a preface dated 'Christmas, 1896' to the revised edition of 1897:

As the chess-problem, given on the next page, has puzzled some of my readers, it may be well to explain that it is correctly worked out, so far as the *moves* are concerned. The *alternation* of Red and White is perhaps not so strictly observed as it might be, and the 'castling' of the three Queens is merely a way of saying that they entered the palace: but the 'check' of The White King at move 6, the capture of the Red Knight at move 7, and the final 'checkmate' of the Red King, will be found, by any one who will take the trouble to set the pieces and play the moves as directed, to be strictly in accordance with the laws of the game.

This does not, however, resolve the two most glaring inconsistencies with regard to the game as it is played today. There is no explanation of why White makes thirteen moves to Red's three, eight of them in succession; nor why the White Queen, in its final move, ignores the check by the Red Queen on the White King!

The best solution of both problems so far offered is to be found in an article by the Rev. Ivor Ll. Davies in *The Anglo-Welsh Review* for August, 1970. Drawing inspiration from the fact that Carroll was an afficianado of complicated games and the last person to break rules for the sake of breaking them, he attempts to rationalise the circumstances under which the erratic procedure of moves could have been founded upon an actual game, perhaps one of those Carroll played with the young Alice Liddell when teaching her this most addictive, most dynamic of mental recreations.

The Catalogue for the Sale of Carroll's effects held after his death includes three chess books: *The Art of Chess-Play: A New Treatise on the Game of Chess* (1846), by George Walker; *The Chess-Player's Companion: Comprising a New Treatise on Odds, and a Collection of Games* (1849) and *The Chess Tournament, A Collection of the Games Played at this Celebrated Assemblage* (namely at the St. George's Club to mark the Great Exhibition) (1852), both by Howard Staunton. Scrupulous research by Davies among the contents of these volumes has revealed variations of play prominent in Carroll's day yet alien to the game as it is known today, variations that iron out the two major inconsistencies in the game detailed above and annul the need for the tired, facile explanation that the topsy-turvy logic of a Looking-Glass world would have demanded a zany upheaval of the rules of the game. Walker's Law XX states: 'When you give check, you must apprize your adversary, by saying aloud "check"; or he need not notice it, but may move as though check were not given.' Why had White ignored the check by the Red Queen on his King? Davies reminds us that on the arrival of the Queen at King one, the Queen had explained to Alice, now her equal on the final rank, 'Speak when you're spoken to!' Since on her arrival no one had spoken to her, the Red Queen could not break her own stipulation by volunteering 'check' herself.

With regard to the unfair advantage of White over Red by ten moves, Davies resorts most convincingly to Book V of Staunton's *Companion*, entitled *On Odds*: 'At the remote period of its birth in India it belonged to the widespread family of human games based on chance and "the moves were governed by the casts of dice".' In a world of pure chance where

success is determined by the fall of a die, the ratio of thirteen wins to three in favour of one player is not so improbable. White has more moves simply because he is more successful with the bones. Certainly no one can dispute that Carroll well prepared his readers for the extra hazards which this added uncertainty would impart to Alice's adventures: ' "They don't keep this room so tidy as the other," Alice thought to herself, as she noticed several of the chessmen down in the hearth among the cinders; but in another moment, with a little "Oh!" of surprise, she was down on her hands and knees watching them.'

The knight's tour

'Kitty, can you play chess? Now, don't smile, my dear, I'm asking it seriously. Because, when we were playing just now, you watched just as if you understood it: and when I said "Check!" you purred! Well, it *was* a nice check, Kitty, and really I might have won, if it hadn't been for that nasty Knight, that came wriggling down among my pieces. Kitty, dear, let's pretend—'

Through the Looking-Glass

No single word could more effectively describe the movement of the knight across the chessboard than 'wriggling'. This is the most complicated move in the game. If one imagines a rectangle comprising six squares, two by three, the knight's move always represents a diagonal journey from one corner of such a rectangle to the opposite one. He can move in any direction provided he goes two squares vertically or horizontally, and then one square to the right or left at right angles to the first part of the move.

The intricacy of the move was put to puzzling effect by conjurors in Carroll's day in a feat known as 'The Knight's Tour', in which, with only legitimate moves, the knight is made to visit every single square on the board, landing on no square more than once before returning to the starting position. The demonstration represents an impressive and baffling display of mental agility, which does not demand a knowledge of the game in order to be appreciated by an audience, although master chess players themselves will find it little short of dumbfounding. A chess grid is depicted on a black-board, the squares of which are numbered from 1 to 64, starting at the top left-hand corner and going from left to right. A member of the audience calls a number from 1 to 64, this representing the starting point. Another spectator takes the chalk, rings round that square and proceeds to chart the tour as detailed by the performer from square to square. The performer himself has his back turned to the board, heightening the effect of the presentation yet at the same time enabling him to read off a small chart concealed in his hand or attached to his watch face! This reads as follows:

1	51	55	62	64	14	10	3
11	36	40	45	54	29	25	20
17	21	30	60	48	44	35	5
2	6	13	50	63	59	52	15
12	16	7	33	53	49	58	32
27	31	24	43	38	34	41	22
42	46	39	37	23	19	26	28
57	61	56	47	8	4	9	18

First find the starting number and then read off down the columns, from left to right, returning to the top left-hand corner after 18. So if told to start at 50, one calls out 33, 43, 37, 47, 64, etc. All one has to remember is the starting number, so that you will know when all sixty-four squares have been visited. The final path will look like this:

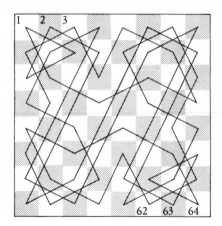

It's easy to compile separate charts for repeat performances to cover the following equally elegant designs:

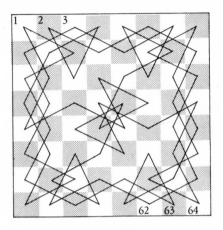

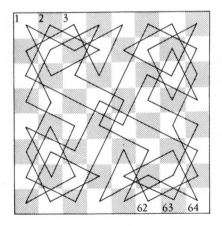

A geometrical paradox

Alice laughed. 'There's no use trying,' she said: 'one *can't* believe impossible things.'

'I daresay you haven't had much practice,' said the Queen. 'When I was your age, I always did it for half-an-hour a day. Why, sometimes I've believed as many as six impossible things before breakfast. There goes the shawl again!'

Through the Looking-Glass

Of all Carroll's conundrums and paradoxes what follows is probably the most impossible to believe. Given an uncoloured chessboard of 64 squares, divided as shown along the heavy lines, one reassembles the four pieces to form a rectangle.

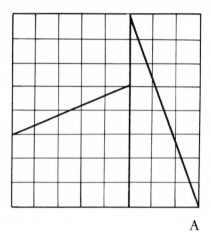

A

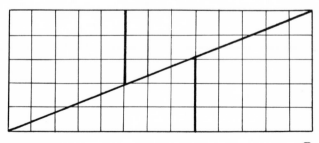

B

A quick count of the small squares along either side of the rectangle will result in 5 and 13. Therefore the area must be 65 square units, a fact which may be verified by counting the small squares individually. Where has the extra square appeared from?

If the chessboard is constructed accurately, the rectangle will eventually *not* have an accurate diagonal. The area of the space along the diagonal, long enough for it to be unnoticeable, is equivalent to the mysterious square unit. Carroll himself generalised the paradox in an equation that produces the dimensions of all the possible squares that can be dissected in the same fashion (squares, for example, with sides 21 and 55) and was described fully by Warren Weaver in *The American Mathematical Monthly* for April, 1938. The equation, pieced together from incomplete notes with skilled detective work by Weaver, dates to the period between 1890 and 1893.

The paradox was included by Collingwood as a 'favourite puzzle' of Carroll in *The Lewis Carroll Picture Book*. It is doubtful, however,

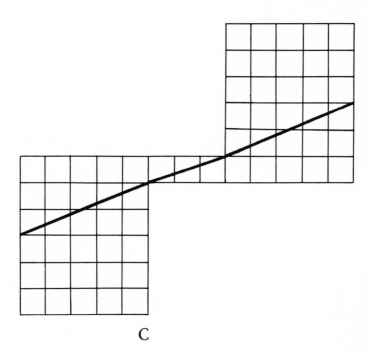

C

whether he originated the problem. Sam Loyd claims in his *Cyclopedia of Puzzles* to have presented it to the American Chess Congress in 1858 and once referred to it as the ancestor of his 'Get off the Earth' puzzle, telling the readers of his column in the *Brooklyn Daily Eagle* that when they understood the paradox they would 'know something about the Chinese methods of getting off the earth'. Sam Loyd's son, incidentally, was the first to discover that the four pieces could also be reassembled to form an area reduced to 63 squares, as in Fig. C.

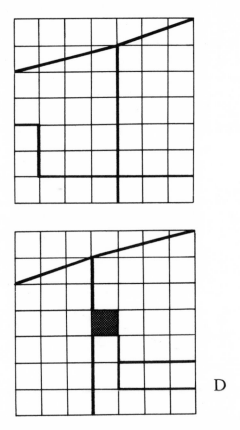

D

An interesting development of the chessboard paradox was conceived by prolific New York mathemagician Paul Curry, who had the ingenious idea of dissecting a square and reassembling its parts to form an identical square with a hole inside! For this see D and E.

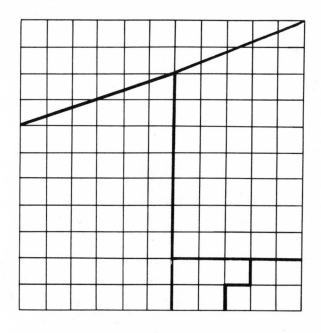

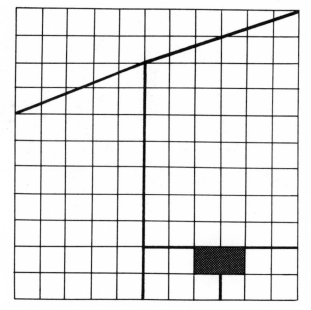

E

When the reader has puzzled enough over these, he may like to give his attention to the Loyd Chinamen already mentioned. The first illustration shows a cardboard circle, riveted at the centre to a cardboard background. The figures overlap both disc and background. Count the

warriors and they total thirteen; turn the wheel slightly until the parts fit differently and one warrior will be found to have disappeared! It is exciting to think that the inventor of the Cheshire Cat may have had a small part in this quite different vanishing trick.

Tangrams

'She can't do Subtraction,' said the White Queen. 'Can you do Division? Divide a loaf by a knife – what's the answer to *that*?'

'I suppose—' Alice was beginning, but the Red Queen answered for her. 'Bread-and-butter, of course. . . .'

Through the Looking-Glass

Dissection problems abound in recreational mathematics. In a field where Greek crosses and horseshoes have long mingled with no sense of incongruity, where doughnuts have consistently had to be divided into thirteen pieces with only three plane cuts, no puzzle professes a greater claim to antiquity than the Tangram. Of Chinese origin and at least 4,000 years old, it has amazingly maintained its original form from the time when the legendary Tan first dissected a small black square exactly as shown in the illustration:

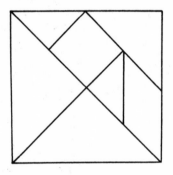

That simple operation opened up an infinite range of enchanting designs and pictorial representations. No less fascinated than Tan was Lewis Carroll whose library included a small book entitled *The Fashionable Chinese Puzzle* and containing 323 Tangram shapes to be constructed from the seven pieces. On Carroll's death this book passed into the hands of Henry E. Dudeney who was inspired to produce designs for the March Hare and Mad Hatter.

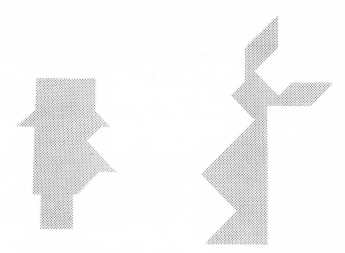

Of equal interest to Carroll would have been Dudeney's Tangram paradox. The following illustration presents two figures who appear to be identical in all respects except that one has a foot missing. And yet they both comprise all seven Tangram pieces. Where, then, does the second gentleman get his foot from? You will find the answers later in the book.

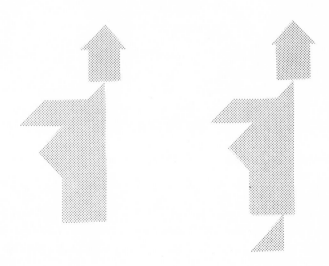

The four-colour map problem

For some minutes Alice stood without speaking, looking out in all directions over the country – and a most curious country it was. There were a number of tiny little brooks running straight across it from side to side, and the ground between was divided up into squares by a number of little green hedges, that reached from brook to brook.

'I declare it's marked out just like a large chess-board!' Alice said at last.

Through the Looking-Glass

Another favourite puzzle of Carroll, undated by Collingwood, involved the famous topological problem of designating regions on a map by colours. Carroll saw it as a game for two players:

> A is to draw a fictitious map divided into counties.
>
> B is to colour it (or rather mark the counties with *names* of colours) using as few colours as possible.
>
> Two adjacent counties must have *different* colours.
>
> A's object is to force B to use as *many* colours as possible. How many can he force B to use?

By 'adjacent' it is understood that Carroll meant touching along a line, as distinct from touching at a single point. With this accepted, A can easily force B to use as many as four colours:

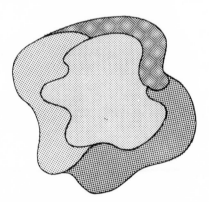

No one has, in fact, ever found either a plane or spherical map for which four colours are not sufficient, but it would be wrong to mistake this for a general proof that four are sufficient. Perhaps one day a map requiring five colours will be discovered. H. S. M. Coxeter, writing in *Mathematics Teacher* for April, 1959, allows himself 'to make a conjecture that a map requiring five colours may be possible, but that the simplest such map has so many faces (maybe hundreds or thousands) that nobody, confronted with it, would have the patience to make all the necessary tests that would be required to exclude the possibility of colouring it with four colours.' Moebius himself made the assertion in 1840 that it is impossible to draw a map of five countries on a plane so that each pair shares a common border (a problem equivalent to joining each of five dots placed on a plane to the others by non-intersecting straight lines), but this is a long way from proving the need for five colours on a map of 'n' countries. As the problem stands, one can assume that five colours are sufficient, four necessary. The world awaits the breakthrough in mathematics leading to the proof that four are both necessary and sufficient.

Of interest to Carroll would have been a development of his own game by science fiction writer, Stephen Barr, described by Martin Gardner, in which A first draws a country; B then colours it and adds a new country; A colours the new one and adds a third, and so on, each player colouring the area just drawn by his opponent until one is forced to lose the game . . . by using a fifth colour.

In both *The Hunting of the Snark* and *Sylvie and Bruno Concluded* Carroll continued to play cartographical games. In the former the Bellman brought a map of the sea which the crew could all understand:

'Other maps are such shapes, with their islands and capes!
  But we've got our brave Captain to thank'
(So the crew would protest) 'that he's bought *us* the best –
  A perfect and absolute blank!'

By way of contrast to the blank map Carroll supplied, the map of the German Professor in the later work is not lacking in one single detail:

Mein Herr looked so thoroughly bewildered that I thought it best to change the subject. 'What a useful thing a pocket-map is!' I remarked.

'That's another thing we've learned from *your* Nation,' said Mein Herr, 'map-making. But we've carried it much further than *you*. What do you consider the *largest* map that would be really useful?'

'About six inches to the mile.'

'Only *six inches*!' exclaimed Mein Herr. 'We very soon got to six *yards* to the mile. Then we tried a *hundred* yards to the mile. And then came the grandest idea of all! We actually made a map of the country, on the scale of *a mile to the mile*!'

'Have you used it much?' I enquired.

'It has never been spread out, yet,' said Mein Herr: 'the farmers objected: they said it would cover the whole country, and shut out the sunlight! So we now use the country itself, as its own map, and I assure you it does nearly as well.'

Jorge Luis Borges, in his essay 'Partial Magic in the Quixote', included in his *Labyrinths*, quotes Josiah Royce in the first volume of his work *The World and the Individual* (1899): 'Let us imagine that a portion of the soil of England has been levelled off perfectly and that on it a cartographer traces a map of England. The job is perfect; there is no detail of the soil of England, no matter how minute, that is not registered on the map; everything has there its correspondence. This map, in such a case, should contain a map of the map, which should contain a map of the map of the map, and so on to infinity.'

The artist, Mark Boyle, has more recently taken Carroll's initially wild assumption one step nearer to reality in a project entitled 'Journey to the Surface of the Earth'. Boyle's self-imposed task, described at length by Philip Oakes in *The Sunday Times* for September 27, 1970, involves the exact reconstruction of specific sites on the earth's surface, ranging from six to eight feet square, chosen at random by blindfolded people aiming darts at a map of the world. The query of British logician R. B. Braithwaite, in *The Mathematical Gazette* for July, 1932 – 'Can a symbol symbolise itself?' – was nearer to an answer than he knew.

Arithmetical Croquet

'Can you play croquet?'

The soldiers were silent, and looked at Alice, as the question was evidently meant for her.

'Yes!' shouted Alice.

'Come on, then!' roared the Queen, and Alice joined the procession, wondering very much what would happen next.

Alice's Adventures in Wonderland

Carroll's long held ambition to devise a version of croquet which could actually be played in the head while walking along with his child-friends became a reality a short time before October 24, 1872. On that date he recorded in his diary that he had sent the rules of the game, then entitled 'Numerical Croquet', to Gwendolyn Cecil. Later intended for his projected *Original Games and Puzzles*, a revised version as follows was found among his papers dated April 22, 1889:

Arithmetical Croquet, for two Players. 1. The first player names a number not greater than 8: the second does the same: the first then names a higher number, not advancing more than 8 beyond his last; and so on alternately – whoever names 100, which is 'winning peg', wins the game.

2. The numbers 10, 20, etc. are the 'hoops'. To 'take' a hoop, it is necessary to go, from a number below it, to one the same distance above it: e.g. to go from 17 to 23 would 'take' the hoop 20: but to go to any other number above 20 would 'miss it', in which case the player would have, in his next turn, to go back to a number below 20, in order to 'take' it properly. To miss a hoop twice loses the game.

3. It is also lawful to 'take' a hoop by playing *into* it, in one turn, and out of it, to the same distance above it in the next turn: e.g. to play from 17 to 20, and then from 20 to 23 in the next turn, would 'take' the hoop 20. A player 'in' a hoop may not play out of it with any other than the number so ordered.

4. Whatever step one player takes, bars the other from taking an equal step, or the difference between it and 9: e.g. if one player advances 2, the other may not advance 2 or 7. But a player has no 'barring' power when playing *into* a hoop, or when playing from any number between 90 and 100, unless the other player is also at such a number.

5. The 'winning-peg', like the 'hoops', may be 'missed' once, but to miss it twice loses the game.

6. When one player is 'in' a hoop, the other can keep him in, by playing the number he needs for coming out, so as to bar him from using it. He can also do it by playing the difference between this and 9. And he may thus go on playing the 2 barring numbers alternately: but he may not play either twice running: e.g. if one player has gone from 17 to 20, the other can keep him in by playing 3, 6, 3, 6, etc.

Carroll's original version of the Queen's croquet party from
Alice's Adventures Under Ground

Miss Ella Monier Williams, the daughter of electrical pioneer, Sir Monier Monier Williams, reminiscing in *The Lewis Carroll Picture Book*, recalls how she was once 'rewarded by an hour of (his) happy companionship, mainly occupied as we walked along by playing a game of croquet in our heads. How it was done I cannot recollect, but his clever original brain planned it out by some system of mathematical calculation.'

The game itself is not far removed from one frequently used by conjurors in recent years. In this the first player names a number not greater than 10. His opponent similarly mentions a number not greater than 10 and (unlike in Carroll's game where two totals are computed simultaneously) this is added to the first number. And so on in turns until someone reaches 100 and is proclaimed winner. Its appeal to conjurors is perhaps explained by the existence of a system which ensures you can't lose – when you know the secret! This is based upon the key numbers 12, 23, 34, 45, 56, 67, 78 and 89. Each key is 11 more than the one before. After your opponent has named a number not greater than 10 you add, apparently at random, whatever will bring the total to the first key. After your opponent had added his second number, you subsequently bring the total to the second key. And so on until you reach 89, when it is now impossible for your opponent to reach 100. The maximum he can add is 10, and whatever he names you quickly bring the total to 100. Whether the comparative simplicity of the above would have appealed to a man whose thoughts were literally 'full of indices and surds? $x^2 + 7x + 53 = \frac{11}{3}$', as much as it would probably have been preferred by his child friends, is impossible to determine.

The square window

Christ Church,
Oxford.
March 15, 1873.

My Dear Helen,
    I don't know if you are fond of puzzles, or not. If you are, try this. If not, never mind. A gentleman (a nobleman let us say, to make it more interesting) had a sitting-room with only one window in it – a square window, 3 feet high and 3 feet wide. Now he had weak eyes, and the window gave too much light, *so* (don't you like '*so*' in a story?) he sent for the builder, and told him to alter it, so as only to give half the light. Only, he was to keep it square – he was to keep it 3 feet high – and he was to keep it 3 feet wide. How did he do it? Remember, he wasn't allowed to use curtains, or shutters, or coloured glass, or anything of that sort.
    I must tell you an awful story of my trying to set a puzzle to a little girl the other day. It was at a dinner-party, at dessert. I had never seen her before, but, as she was sitting next me, I rashly proposed to her to try the puzzle (I daresay you know it) of 'the fox, and goose, and bag of corn.' And I got some biscuits to represent the fox and the other things. Her mother was sitting on the other side, and said, 'Now mind you take pains, my dear, and do it right!' The consequences were awful! She *shrieked* out 'I can't do it! I can't do it! Oh, Mamma! Mamma!', threw herself into her mother's lap, and went off into a fit of sobbing which lasted several minutes! That was a lesson to me about trying children with puzzles. I do hope the square window won't produce any awful effects on *you*!
    I am,
        Your very affectionate friend,
            C. L. DODGSON.

Whether Helen Feilden, the girl to whom Carroll addressed the above, ever discovered the solution to the window problem, Collingwood, in

The Lewis Carroll Picture Book, from which the above is taken, does not say. The secret is little more than a visual quibble and will be found towards the end of the book.

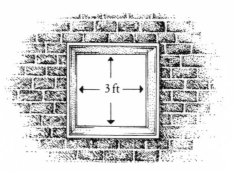

Dudeney, in *The Canterbury Puzzles*, his thought-provoking sequel to Chaucer's *Tales*, later proposed a variation under the title 'The Donjon Keep Window'. This was a square aperture one foot wide and one foot high, divided by narrow bars into four sections or 'lights', each half a foot on every side:

The challenge was to build another window, the sides of which also measured a foot, to be divided by bars into eight lights, the sides of which must all be equal, again measuring six inches.

Hoax riddle

My dear Gaynor, – So you would like to know the answer to that riddle? Don't be in a hurry to tell it to Amy and Frances: triumph over them for a while!

My first lends its aid when you plunge into trade.

Gain. Who would go into trade if there were no gain in it?

My second in jollifications—

Or [The French for 'gold'—] Your jollifications would be *very* limited if you had no money.

My whole, laid on thinnish, imparts a neat finish
  To pictorial representations.

Gaynor. Because she will be an ornament to the Shakespeare Charades – only she must be 'laid on thinnish,' that is, *there musn't be too much of her.*

Yours affectionately,
C. L. D<small>ODGSON</small>

My dear Gaynor,—Forgive me for having sent you a sham answer to begin with.

My first – *Sea.*   It carries the ships of the merchants.

My second – *Weed.*   That is, a cigar, an article much used in jollifications.

My whole – *Seaweed.*   Take a newly painted oil-picture: lay it on its back on the floor, and spread over it, 'thinnish,' some wet seaweed. You will find you have 'finished' that picture.

Yours affectionately,
C. L. D<small>ODGSON</small>

The above two letters to Gaynor Simpson, one of Carroll's young Guildford friends, date back to the beginning of 1874. The *actual* answer according to Collingwood in *The Life and Letters* is 'Co-pal'.

Acrostics to child-friends

Inscribed to a dear Child:
in memory of golden summer hours
and whispers of a summer sea

Girt with a boyish garb for boyish task,
  Eager she wields her spade: yet loves as well
Rest on a friendly knee, intent to ask
  The tale he loves to tell.

Rude spirits of the seething outer strife,
  Unmeet to read her pure and simple spright,
Deem, if you list, such hours a waste of life
  Empty of all delight!

Chat on, sweet Maid, and rescue from annoy
  Hearts that by wiser talk are unbeguiled.
Ah, happy he who owns that tenderest joy,
  The heart-love of a child!

Away, fond thoughts, and vex my soul no more!
  Work claims my wakeful nights, my busy days –
Albeit bright memories of that sunlit shore
  Yet haunt my dreaming gaze!

Carroll wrote scores of acrostics concealing the names of his child friends, of which the above, used to preface by way of dedication *The Hunting of the Snark*, is one of the most ingenious. Not only do the initial letters spell the name Gertrude Chataway, but the first words of each stanza themselves provide a phonetic equivalent. Carroll composed the verses on October 25, 1875 and the same day mailed them to Gertrude's mother, asking for her permission to print them. Their cryptic nature must have escaped her since after receiving her reply and prior to actual publication early the following year, Carroll wrote yet again, this time underlining the acrostic and asking wi·ether this made any difference to her permission: 'If I print them, I shan't tell anyone it is an acrostic – but someone will be sure to find out before long.'

In the same way the dedicatory poem of *Sylvie and Bruno* is an acrostic to Isa Bowman and *Through the Looking-Glass* to the original Alice herself. The latter is certainly the most famous of all his puzzle poems, its own mellow account of the 'golden afternoon' when Carroll first conjured up Alice's curious adventures:

A boat, beneath a sunny sky
Lingering onward dreamily
In an evening of July –

Children three that nestle near,
Eager eye and willing ear,
Pleased a simple tale to hear –

Long has paled that sunny sky:
Echoes fade and memories die:
Autumn frosts have slain July.

Still she haunts me, phantomwise,
Alice moving under skies
Never seen by waking eyes.

Children yet, the tale to hear,
Eager eye and willing ear,
Lovingly shall nestle near.

In a Wonderland they lie,
Dreaming as the days go by,
Dreaming as the summers die:

Ever drifting down the stream –
Lingering in the golden gleam –
Life, what is it but a dream?

Anagrammatic sonnet

In a letter to Maud Standen dated December 18, 1877 Carroll contrived the very last word in anagrams. About the sonnet he writes:

> Each line has 4 feet, and each foot is an anagram, i.e. the letters of it can be rearranged so as to make one word. Thus there are 24 anagrams, which will occupy your leisure moments for some time, I hope. Remember I don't limit myself to substantives, as some do. I should consider 'we dish = wished' a fair anagram.

> As to the war, try elm. I tried.
> The wig cast in, I went to ride
> 'Ring? Yes'. We rang. 'Let's rap'. We don't.
> 'O shew her wit!' As yet she won't.
> Saw eel in Rome. Dry one: he's wet.
> I am dry. O forge Th'rogue Why a net?

To these you may add 'abcdefgi', which makes a good compound word – as good a word as 'summer-house'.

The Lewis Carroll Handbook gives the following as a possible solution:

> OATS – WREATH – MYRTLE – TIDIED
> WEIGHT – SCIANT – TWINE – RIOTED
> SYRINGE – GNAWER – PLASTER – WONTED
> WHOSE – WITHER – YEAST – NEW-SHOT
> WEASEL – MOIREN(?) – YONDER – THEWES
> MYRIAD – FOREGO – ROUGETH – HAY WENT.

But Roger Lancelyn Green points out that it is possible to make another actual poem from the original with almost as much sense:

> So at the raw myrtle it died.
> Weight I scant – twine, or tied
> In Grey's new rag. Plaster! End tow,
> Whose whither at – yes, the snow!
> We seal no mire, or deny the wet:
> My raid forego? Th'rouge – nay whet!

Even more impressively, in a subsequent reprint of the *Handbook* Green was able to append a better final couplet:

> We seal no mire, or deny hew set:
> My raid forego? Hot urge – nay whet!

This not only improves the sense by the merest fraction, but also corrects one letter in the penultimate line which was wrong in his earlier version.

The extra word to be arranged from the letters ABCDEFGI, by the way, is 'big-faced'.

Charade one

They both make a roaring, a roaring all night:
They both are a fisherman – father's delight:
They are both, when in fury, a terrible sight!

The first nurses tenderly three little hulls,
To the lullaby-music of shrill-screaming gulls,
And laughs when they dimple his face with their skulls.

The Second's a tidyish sort of a lad,
Who behaves pretty well to a man he calls 'Dad',
And earns the remark, 'Well, he isn't so bad!'

Of the two put together, oh, what shall I say?
Tis a time when 'to live' means the same as 'to play':
When the busiest person does nothing all day.

When the grave College Don, full of love inexpressi-
Ble, puts it all by, and is forced to confess he
Can think but of Agnes and Evie and Jessie.

The above was devised by Carroll for three child friends, Agnes, Eveline
and Jessie Hull, and sent to Maud Standen in the letter which also included the Anagrammatic Sonnet. The answer is 'a Sea-Son'.

The fox, goose and bag of corn

Christ Church,
Oxford,
January 22, 1878

My dear Jessie,
. . . . Tell Sally it's all very well to say she can do the two thieves and the
five apples, but can she do the fox and the goose and the bag of corn? That
the man was bringing from market, and he had to get them over a river, and
the boat was so tiny he could only take *one* across at a time; and he couldn't
ever leave the fox and the goose together, for then the fox would eat the
goose; and if he left the goose and the corn together, the goose would eat
the corn. So the only things he *could* leave safely together were the fox and
the corn, for you never see a fox eating corn, and you hardly ever see corn
eating a fox. Ask her if she can do *that* puzzle . . .
Your affectionate friend,
LEWIS CARROLL

This is almost certainly the oldest of all crossing-river problems. The man takes the goose over first, returns for the fox, which he leaves on the other side, while he takes back the goose. He crosses with the corn, and returns alone for the goose. In this way the fox has never been left alone with the goose, nor the goose with the corn!

The jealous husbands

> He was thoughtful and grave – but the orders he gave
> Were enough to bewilder a crew.
> When he cried, 'Steer to starboard, but keep her head larboard!'
> What on earth was the helmsman to do?
>
> *The Hunting of the Snark*

A logical, if more complex, development of the fox and goose problem, again mentioned by Collingwood as among Carroll's regular arcana, is the problem of the four men with their wives who wanted to cross a river in a boat only large enough to hold two of them at one time. The conditions here are that no man must leave his wife on either bank unless by herself or in the company of women alone. Needless to say, someone must always bring the boat back. How did they do it?

There is no way of telling from *The Lewis Carroll Picture Book* whether Collingwood was actually quoting Carroll or posing the problem in his own words. As both Sam Loyd and Dudeney found, however, it is impossible to arrive at a solution under the given conditions for *four* couples, without setting down an island in mid-stream for people to use as a half-way stage.

Loyd gives the additional condition that no man is to get into the boat by himself when there happens to be a woman alone on the island or river bank other than his own wife. Obviously one assumes that at no time is a man to be in the boat together with another man's wife. The point is to get the four couples safely across from bank to bank in the least possible number of moves. When only three couples are involved, the island is unnecessary, and it would appear that this was the form in which Carroll knew the problem, assuming he had a solution. The following chart in which ABC represent the three husbands and abc the three wives should explain itself:

	BANK	OTHER SIDE
1.	ABCabc	
2.	ABC c	ab
3.	ABC bc	a
4.	ABC	abc
5.	ABC b	a c
6.	B b	A ca c
7.	AB ab	C c
8.	ab	ABC c
9.	abc	ABC
10.	b	ABCa c
11.	bc	ABCa
12.		ABCabc

The quickest solution to the four couple variation is likewise as detailed:

	BANK	ISLAND	OTHER SIDE
1.	ABCDabcd		
2.	ABCD cd		ab
3.	ABCD bcd		a
4.	ABCD d	bc	a
5.	ABCD cd	b	a
6.	CD cd	b	AB a
7.	BCD cd	b	A a
8.	BCD	bcd	A a
9.	BCD d	bc	A a
10.	D d	bc	ABC a
11.	D d	abc	ABC
12.	D d	b	ABC a c
13.	B D d	b	A C a c
14.	d	b	ABCDa c
15.	d	bc	ABCDa
16.	d		ABCDabc
17.	cd		ABCDab
18.			ABCDabcd

Charade two

The following charade of six stanzas was published privately by Carroll for distribution among his friends:

B. H.
from C. L. D

A CHARADE.

[NB FIVE POUNDS will be given to any one who succeeds in writing an original poetical Cha- -rade, introducing the line " My First is followed by a bird," but making no use of the answer to this Charade   Ap 8 1878
(signed)
Lewis Carroll]

My First is singular at best
   More plural is my Second
. My Third is far the pluralest —
So plural-plural, I protest,
   It scarcely can be reckoned !

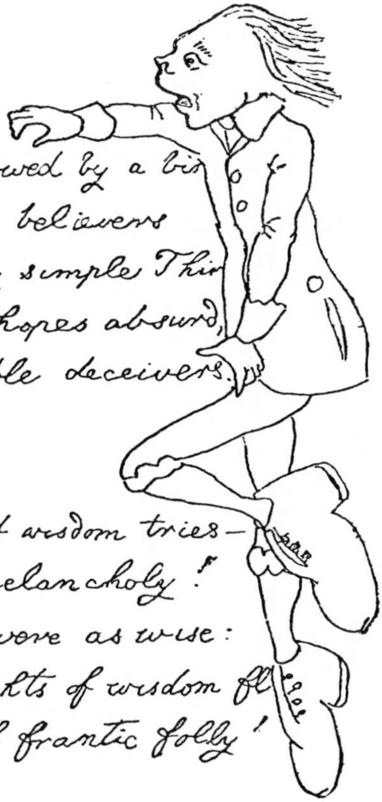

My First is followed by a bir
  My Second by believers
In magic art · my simple Thir
Follows, too often, hopes absurd,
  And plausible deceivers.

My First to get at wisdom tries —
  A failure melancholy!
My Second men revere as wise:
My Third from heights of wisdom fl
  To depths of frantic folly!

My First is ageing day by day,
  My Second's age is ended
My Third enjoys an age, they say,
That never seems to fade away,
  Through centuries extended!

My Whole? I need a Poet's pen
    To paint her myriad phases
The monarch, and the slave, of men —
A mountain-summit, and a den
    Of dark and deadly mazes!

A flashing light — a fleeting shade —
    Beginning, end, and middle
Of all that human art hath made,
Or wit devised! Go, seek her aid,
    If you would guess my riddle!

Falconer Madan, looking for some deeper relevance in the sketches of the man and goose, suggested in the *Handbook* that a possible answer could be 'anserine'. The correct solution is in fact 'I-Magi-nation'.

The Queen's basket escape

'But I *must* go back, *now*. You see I left off at a comma, and it's so awkward not knowing how the sentence finishes! Besides, you've got to go through Dogland first, and I'm always a little nervous about dogs. But it'll be quite easy to come, as soon as I've completed my new invention – for carrying one's-*self*, you know. It wants just a *little* more working out.'

'Won't that be very tiring, to carry *yourself*?' Sylvie enquired.

'Well, no, my child. You see, whatever fatigue one incurs by *carrying*, one saves by *being carried*! Good-bye, dears! Good-bye, Sir!' he added to my intense surprise, giving my hand an affectionate squeeze.

'Good-bye, Professor!'

Sylvie and Bruno

Carroll embodied a more realistic, though still bizarre approach to the problem of physical weight in the following problem quoted from Collingwood:

A captive Queen and her son and daughter were shut up in the top room of a very high tower. Outside their window was a pulley with a rope round it, and a basket fastened at each end of the rope of equal weight. They managed to escape with the help of this and a weight they found in the room, quite safely. It would have been dangerous for any of them to come down if they weighed more than 15 lbs. more than the contents of the lower basket, for they would do so too quick, and they also managed not to weigh less either.

The one basket coming down would naturally of course draw the other up. How did they do it?

The Queen weighed 195 lbs., daughter 105, son 90, and the weight 75.

In principle we are not far away from the river-crossing problems encountered earlier. The solution is as follows:

1. The weight is sent down; the empty basket comes up.
2. The son goes down; the weight comes up.
3. The weight is taken out; the daughter goes down; the son comes up.
4. The son gets out; the weight goes down; empty basket comes up.
5. The Queen does down; the daughter and weight come up together; the daughter gets out.
6. The weight goes down; empty basket comes up.
7. The son goes down; the weight comes up.
8. The daughter removes the weight and goes down; the son comes up.
9. The son sends down the weight; empty basket comes up.
10. The son goes down; the weight comes up.
11. The son gets out; the weight falls to the ground.

As if not content with the logistical triumph of the above, Carroll devised a postscript in which besides her son and daughter and the weight, the Queen had with her in the room a pig weighing 60 pounds, a dog 45, and a cat 30. The object is to bring these down safely as well under the same conditions. But even Carroll, master of anthropomorphism, couldn't see himself clear of stipulating an additional person at each end to lift the animals into and out of the baskets!

Memoria Technica

> The loss of his clothes hardly mattered, because
> He had seven coats on when he came,
> With three pair of boots – but the worst of it was,
> He had wholly forgotten his name.

The Hunting of the Snark

Collingwood recalls the two blind spots in Carroll's otherwise 'wonderfully good' memory, namely with regard to faces and dates. On a visit to London to dine with a friend whom he had not known for long he found himself being greeted the following morning by a stranger in the street. 'I beg your pardon,' said Carroll, 'but you have the advantage of me. I have no remembrance of having seen you before this moment.' 'That's very strange,' the other replied, 'for I was your host last night!' To save himself the embarrassment of such incidents he devised the following mnemonic system which he circulated among his friends. He mentions it in his diary as early as October, 1875 and although he dated the circular June, 1888, as there is no mention of the system around that time in his diary there is reason to believe he may have misdated it.

> My *Memoria Technica* is a modification of Gray's; but, whereas he used both consonants and vowels to represent digits, and had to content himself with a syllable of gibberish to represent the date or whatever other number was required, I use only consonants, and fill in with vowels *ad libitum*, and thus can always manage to make a real word of whatever has to be represented.

The principles on which the necessary 20 consonants have been chosen are as follows:

1. 'b' and 'c', the first two consonants in the alphabet.
2. 'd' from 'duo', 'w' from two'.
3. 't' from 'tres', the other may wait awhile.
4. 'f' from 'four', 'q' from 'quattuor'.
5. 'l' and 'v', because 'l' and 'v' are the Roman symbols for 'fifty' and 'five'.
6. 's' and 'x' from 'six'.
7. 'p' and 'm' from 'septem'.
8. 'h' from 'huit', and 'k' from the Greek 'okto'.
9. 'n' from 'nine'; and 'g' because it is so like a '9'.
0. 'z' and 'r' from 'zero'.

There is now one consonant still waiting for its digit, viz., 'j', and one digit waiting for its consonant, viz., '3', the conclusion is obvious.

The result may be tabulated thus:

1	2	3	4	5	6	7	8	9	0
b	d	t	f	l	s	p	h	n	z
c	w	j	q	v	x	m	k	g	r

When a word has been found, whose last consonants represent the number required, the best plan is to put it as the last word of a rhymed couplet, so that, whatever other words in it are forgotten, the rhyme will secure the only really important word.

Now suppose you wish to remember the date of the discovery of America, which is 1492; the '1' may be left out as obvious; all we need is '492'.

Write it thus:

4	9	2
f	n	d
q	g	w

and try to find a word that contains 'f' or 'q', 'n' or 'g', 'd' or 'w'. A word soon suggests itself – 'found'.

The poetic faculty must now be brought into play, and the following couplet will soon be evolved:

> 'Columbus sailed the world around,
> Until America was FOUND'.

> If possible, invent the couplets for yourself; you will remember them
> better than any others.
>
> *June*, 1888

His application of the system ranged from the serious to the frivolous.
He took great delight in showing his friends around the sights of Oxford
and was able to impress them by committing to memory the dates of the
colleges. In this way Carroll had only to see the beautiful lawns of St.
John's College to recall the year of its foundation, 1555, (l,v,l), through
his couplet:

> They must have a bevel
> To keep them so LEVEL.

Likewise the famous 'Brazen Nose' over the door of Brasenose College:

> With a nose that is brazen
> Our gate we EMBLAZON.

helped to pinpoint in his memory the date of that particular foundation
as 1509, (l,z,n), while this reference to the great bell 'Tom,' which hung
in Christ Church's 'Tom Tower', near Carroll's rooms:

> Ring Tom when you please:
> We ask but SMALL FEES.

indicated the correct date of his own college, 1546, (l,f,s).

The system also had its uses for 'giving pi to 71 decimal places' and
'logarithms of all primes under 100'. At one point he even planned to
issue a booklet based on the system entitled *Logarithms by Lightning: a
Mathematical Curiosity*. It would be interesting to know if he ever
used it while performing his arduous mental calculations and 'Pillow-
Problems', converting sub-totals to a word which could be summoned
instantly when required rather than over-burdening the mind with
unnecessary figures.

Fish riddle

'First, the fish must be caught.'
That is easy: a baby, I think, could have
    caught it.
  'Next, the fish must be bought.'
That is easy: a penny, I think, would have
    bought it.

  'Now cook me the fish!'
That is easy, and will not take more than a
    minute.
  'Let it lie in a dish!'
That is easy, because it already is in it.

  'Bring it here! Let me sup!'
It is easy to set such a dish on the table.
  'Take the dish-cover up!'
Ah, *that* is so hard that I fear I'm unable!

  For it holds it like glue –
Holds the lid to the dish, while it lies in the
    middle:
  What is easiest to do,
Un-dish-cover the fish, or dishcover the
    riddle?'

Through the Looking-Glass

In Part 4 of a parody entitled 'Alice in Numberland', featured in the series 'Specimens of Celebrated Authors' by the magazine *Fun* for October 30, 1878, the White Queen's riddle is quoted in its entirety together with an answer of similar length submitted anonymously, but polished by Carroll prior to publication. The four stanzas of the solution run as follows:

> First pull up the fish.
> It can't swim away: for a fish this is funny!
>   Next 'tis bought; and I wish
> That a penny was always its adequate money.
>
>   Make it ready to eat –
> Fetching pepper and vinegar won't take a minute.
>   Dish with cover complete,
> Of lovely shell china, already 'tis in it.
>
>   Now 'tis time we should sup.
> What's one only, you dolt? Set a score on the table!
>   Take the dish-cover up –
> With mere finger and thumb you will never be able.
>
>   Get an oyster-knife strong,
> Insert it 'twixt cover and dish, in the middle;
>   Then you shall before long
> Un-dish-cover the OYSTERS – dishcover the riddle!

Lanrick

December 31, 1878:
Called on the Housemans; also on Mr. Sant. Back to the Drurys to luncheon, and, after a few games of my new invention *Natural Selection*, afterwards called *Lanrick*, I left for Brighton.

The Diaries

This is the first recorded mention of the game which took its final title from a passage in Scott's *Lady of the Lake*: 'The muster-place be Lanrick-mead.' Various versions of the rules appeared in *The Monthly Packet* through 1880-1881, before they were published in pamphlet form alongside *Syzygies* in 1893. A game for two players, it requires a chess or

draughts board, eight men of one colour and eight of another, and nine pieces of card the size of a chess square to act as markers. The men have the move power of a Queen in chess; the players require sufficient memory power to keep the following 'Rules' and 'Definitions' in mind during play.

DEFINITIONS:

Def. 1.

A 'Rendezvous' is a set of squares, into which each Player tries to get his men. The position of its central square is determined by that of the Mark, and the number of its squares is always one less than that of the men which are on the Board when the Mark is set. There are two kinds of Rendezvous, 'close' and 'open'.

Def. 2.

A Rendezvous must be 'close,' when the number of its squares is odd. It consists of the marked square and certain adjacent squares, as shown in the following diagrams, in which the Players are supposed to be at the upper and lower edges. The numerals indicate the number of Rendezvous-squares, the letter 'm' the Mark, and the asterisks the Rendezvous-squares.

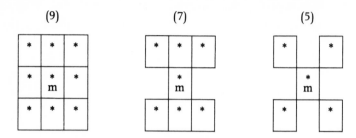

A 3-square Rendezvous consists of a line of 3 squares having the marked square in the middle, in any position, straight or slanting, chosen by the Player who sets the Mark.

Def. 3.

A Rendezvous must be 'open,' when the number of its squares is even. It consists of certain border-squares, which would be in 'check' if the Mark were a chess-queen, as shown in the following diagrams, which are to be interpreted as in Def. 2.

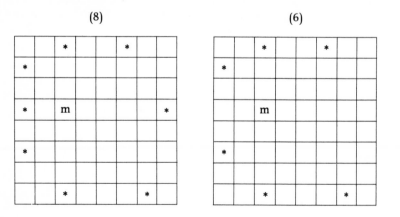

(4)

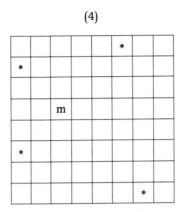

For any but a 9-square Rendezvous, it will be found convenient to mark the Rendezvous-squares with pieces of card.

RULES.

Rule 1.

Each man may be moved along any line of unoccupied squares, straight or slanting, but may not (except in the case named in Rule 6) change its direction.

Rule 2.

To begin the game, ten men are set as in this diagram, in which the five B's indicate black men, and the five W's white men. Then one Player sets the Mark. Both then try to play their men into the Rendezvous thus determined, he, who did not set the Mark, having the first turn.

BLACK

	B			W			B
W							
							W
B							
							B
W			B			W	

WHITE

Rule 3.

In playing the first turn for a Rendezvous, a Player may move 2 squares only. In any other turn he may move 5, 4, or 3 squares, according as he has on the Board more than 4, 4, or less than 4 men. He may divide these squares among his men as he likes, but may not move more than 3 of them with any one man, unless it be his only man outside the Rendezvous. He need not move more than one square in one turn. While playing, he should count aloud the squares through or into which he moves a man. After once playing a man and letting go of it, he may not move it again in that turn.

Rule 4.

The Mark, for any Rendezvous, may be set on any but a border-square; for a 3-square Rendezvous it may be set on any but a corner-square, provided that he, who sets it, has no man in the Rendezvous thus determined.

Rule 5.

When the Mark has been set, he, who did not set it, may, before playing, demand an 'interchange'; in which case he, who set the Mark, must interchange all his own men with whichever he chooses of the others.

Rule 6.

In playing for an open Rendezvous, a Player may move any man, that is on the border, along it, without regarding the corners, as if it were one continuous line of squares; and any such man, if not moved beyond the first Rendezvous-square, reckons as having been moved *one* square only; but, if it be moved beyond, each square so moved must be counted as in Rule 3.

Rule 7.

When a Player has got all his men into the Rendezvous, it being not yet full, he removes one of the outlying men from the Board, replacing it with a fresh man of his own colour; and this ends his turn.

Rule 8.

When a Player has got all his men into the Rendezvous, it being now full, he removes the outlying man from the Board. Then he who has fewest men on the Board, or in case of equality he who has just lost a man, sets the Mark for the next Rendezvous, as in Rule 4.

Rule 9.

When a Player has only one man left, he has lost the Game.

What Carroll fails to make clear from a cursory reading of the rules, something the original title intimated more successfully, is the specific idea followed through in the game of contraction and expansion down the numerical scale. Thus after Rule 8, when the close '9' rendezvous has just been occupied and the men reduced by one, play then expands into an open '8' rendezvous, then again contracts to a close '7', and so on backwards and forwards until the survival of the fittest as inferred from Rule 9.

As if to compensate for what he left contestants to read in between Rules 8 and 9, he appended several 'Hints to Players', emphasising that in playing for a close rendezvous you have *two* aims in view – not merely to get your own men in, but also to keep the enemy out, so that a mere race for the rendezvous is not always the wisest course. Carroll also stressed the advantage of getting hold of the central square of a close rendezvous for ushering other men in. This presupposes the additional hold of a square at the corner or side of the rendezvous where you wish to bring in the new man. As soon as the latter has reached a square adjoining the corner-man, he can be played in by first moving the centre-man into a vacant rendevous square, then the corner-man into the centre-square, and then the outsider into the corner-square.

And then towards the end Carroll belatedly allows just a glimmer of the old mischievousness to filter through the instructions, so far so involved as to deny all hope of humour. It is almost as if he were proffering a prize to all his admirers, not for winning at Lanrick but for persevering with the rules, at once his own private game and idea of 'Natural Selection'.

You should also arrange your men, that are already *in* the Rendezvous, so as to make things comfortable for those of the enemy's men who are on their way towards it. For instance, if it be a 9-square Rendezvous, and if there are four such men approaching from the East: by placing three of your men in the squares marked with askerisks, you may form an inpenetrable wall across the Rendezvous, and thus provide a set of *three* vacant squares to accommodate the *four* weary travellers – a polite attention which they will not soon forget. Similarly, if there are *two* of the enemy's men approaching from the North-East: by placing three of your men, as here indicated, you will provide *one* vacant square for the two guests, who will probably indulge in the pathetic strain, 'Now one of us must stop outside, But that one won't be *me*! So, Tommy, make room for your Uncle!'

Should you find that the enemy is likely to get all his men into the Rendezvous, while you still have two or three men outside, remember that, as soon as all his men are in, he will replace one of your outlying men with a fresh man of his own colour; and that he will most certainly choose for this purpose whichever of the outlying men is nearest to the Rendezvous. Consequently, *your* best course is to have no one of them nearer than the others. Keep them all together, at the same distance from the Rendezvous, so that, whichever of them he transforms into an enemy, you can at once bar its progress with your other outlying men.

The advice I have given, as to barring the progress of the enemy's men rather than merely hurrying on with your own, is also worth remembering when playing for an 'open' Rendezvous.

In carrying out the operation described in Rule 5 – the interchanging of the two sets of men – difficulties may arise, when men have been taken off their squares, in settling *which* squares they came from. These difficulties may lead to angry disputes; thence to mutual accusations of unveracity; thence to estrangement of friends; and thence to family feuds, lasting through several generations. These deplorable results may all be avoided by observing the following simple Rule:

Move every one of the men, which are to be interchanged, into a corner of its square. Place a card-marker on a square occupied by a white man (I am supposing the two colours to be 'white' and 'black'), and take the white man off its square. Place this white man in the centre of a square occupied by a *black* man, and take the *black* man off its square. Place this *black* man in the centre of a square occupied by another *white* man. Proceed thus till all the men on the Board are in the centres of squares, and you have one black man in hand, which of course you place on the square indicated by the card-marker.

Rule 5 serves to prevent the Mark from being so set that he who sets it is quite certain to get his men in first – which certainly would rob the Game of much of its interest. In playing for a final 3-square Rendezvous, the mere setting of the Mark would, but for this Rule, decide the Game.

Charade three

The following was written after seeing Marion Terry perform in Gilbert's *Pygmalion and Galatea*, the three stanzas respectively describing 'my first', 'my second' and 'my whole'.

A Charade.

Dedicated,
without permission,
to
Miss Marion Terry.

I. My First.

The air is bright with hues of light,
    And rich with laughter & with singing:
Young hearts beat high in ecstasy,
    And banners wave, and bells are ringing:
But silence falls with falling day,
And there's an end to mirth and play.
    Ah, well-a-day!

II. My Second.

Rest your old bones, ye ancient crones!
    The kettle sings, the firelight dances:
Deep be its quaffed, the magic draught
    That fills the soul with golden fancies:
For youth & pleasance will not stay,
And ye are withered, worn, and gray.
    Ah, well-a-day!

III. My Whole.

O fair cold face! O form of grace,
    For human passion madly yearning!
O weary air of dumb despair,
    From marble won, to marble turning!
"Leave us not thus!" we fondly pray.
"We cannot let thee pass away!"
    Ah, well-a-day!

23. 1879.   Lewis Carroll.

129

The solution refers back to his initial inspiration to put pen to paper, namely 'GALA-TEA'.

Carroll was familiar with all members of the Terry family. Later that same year he recorded a strange dream he experienced about Marion:

> May 15, 1879:
> Last night I had a dream which I recorded as a curiosity, so far as I know, in the literature of dreams. I was staying, with my sisters, in some suburb of London, and had heard that the Terrys were staying near us, so went to call, and found Mrs. Terry at home, who told us that Marion [Polly] and Florence were at the theatre, the 'Walter House,' where they had a good engagement. 'In that case,' I said, 'I'll go on there at once and see the performance – and may I take Polly with me?' 'Certainly,' said Mrs. Terry. And there was Polly, the child, seated in the room, and looking about nine or ten years old: and I was distinctly conscious of the fact, yet without any feeling of surprise at its incongruity, that I was going to take the *child Polly* with me to the theatre, to see the *grown-up* Polly act!

Lewis Carroll would weave this puzzling idea of multiple existence into the several layers of his ill-conceived fantasy *Sylvie and Bruno*, in which the fairy-child Sylvie and the adult Lady Muriel are one and the same person.

Doublets

Christ Church,
Oxford,
June 5, 1879

My Dear Edith,
. . . You will find this puzzle very soothing: what doctors call 'an alterative', i.e. if you happen to have a headache, it will charm it away: but if you haven't one, it will probably give you one. . . .

Yours affectionately,

C. L. DODGSON

It is almost certain that the puzzle Carroll is referring to in the above letter to Edith Jebb is the one he had introduced as follows in the pages of *Vanity Fair* around March of the same year.

Dear Vanity, – Just a year ago last Christmas, two young ladies – smarting under that sorest scourge of feminine humanity, the having 'nothing to do' – besought me to send them 'some riddles'. But riddles I had none at hand, and therefore set myself to devise some other form of verbal torture which should serve the same purpose. The result of my meditations was a new kind of Puzzle – new at least to me – which, now that it has been fairly tested by a year's experience, and commended by many friends, I offer to you, as a newly-gathered nut, to be cracked by the omnivorous teeth which have already masticated so many of your Double Acrostics.

The rules of the Puzzle are simple enough. Two words are proposed, of the same length; and the Puzzle consists in linking these together by interposing other words, each of which shall differ from the next word *in one letter only*. That is to say, one letter may be changed in one of the given words, then one letter in the word so obtained, and so on, till we arrive at the other given word. The letters must not be interchanged among themselves, but each must keep to its own place. As an example, the word 'head' may be changed into 'tail' by interposing the words 'heal, teal, tell, tall.' I call the two given words 'a Doublet', the interposed words 'Links', and the entire series 'a Chain', of which I here append an example:

HEAD

heal

teal

tell

tall

TAIL

It is, perhaps, needless to state that it is *de rigueur* that the links should be English words, such as might be used in good society.

The easiest 'Doublets' are those in which the consonants in one word answer to consonants in the other, and the vowels to vowels; 'head' and 'tail' constitute a Doublet of this kind. Where this is not the case, as in 'head' and 'hare,' the first thing to be done is to transform one member of the Doublet into a word whose consonants and vowels shall answer to those in the other member (*e.g.*, 'head, herd, here,') after which there is seldom much difficulty in completing the 'Chain'.

I am told that there is an American game involving a similar principle. I have never seen it, and can only say of its inventors, *'pereant qui ante nos nostra dixerunt!'*

LEWIS CARROLL

The above letter to the editor of *Vanity Fair* around March 1879 eventually revitalised the competitive appeal of the magazine. Its weekly 'Acrostics and Hard cases' had become tired and passé, and after trial runs of 'Doublets' for three weeks from March 29 the first full-scale competition was mounted on April 19, ushering in its own prize-gathering craze.

The simplicity of having to complete the chain of words in the least possible number of links was outweighed by Carroll's own strictures on which words were permissible in them. Lest his game be taken in vain, he included in the published edition a glossary of about 1,400 words of from three to six letters. The preface to this incorporates a passage first published in *Vanity Fair*, May 17, 1879, using to amusing effect many taboo words already submitted by competitors:

> Choker humbly presents his compliments to the four thousand three hundred and seventeen (or thereabouts) indignant Doubleteers who have so strongly shent him, and pre to being soaked in the spate of their wrath, asks for a fiver of minutes for reflection. Choker is in a state of complete pye. He feels that there must be a stent to the admission of spick words. He is quite unable to sweal the chaffy spelt, to sile the pory cole, or to swill a spate from a piny ait to the song of the spink. Frils and the mystic Gole are strangers in his sheal: the chanceful Gord hath never brought him gold, nor ever did a cate become his ain. The Doubleteers will no doubt spank him sore, with slick quotations and wild words of yore, will pour upon his head whole steres of steens and poods of spiles points downwards. But he trusts that those alone who habitually use such words as these in good society, and whose discourse is universally there understood, will be the first to cast a stean at him.

For practical purposes it is enough to say that proper names should not be used for linking purposes and all words should be accessible in a standard current dictionary. Specific Carrollian vagaries outlawed nouns formed from verbs (as 'reader' from 'read'), hence the strained pseudonym 'Choker', and all abbreviations with the exception of 'e'en' and 'e'er'!

To complete the chain in the least possible number of links is to reach the maximum possible score for any one Doublet, the number of points equal to the total number of letters in the two words given. For every extra link used beyond the number specified one point is deducted from this score. The following is a record of the Doublets set in *Vanity Fair* for four months from the beginning of the competition, as appended by Carroll to the second published edition of the rules:

PRELIMINARY DOUBLETS

		Links Needed
March 29.	Drive PIG into STY	4
	Raise FOUR to FIVE	6
	Make WHEAT into BREAD	6
April 5.	Dip PEN into INK	5
	Touch CHIN with NOSE	5
	Change TEARS into SMILE	5
April 12	Change WET to DRY	3
	Make HARE into SOUP	6
	PITCH TENTS	5

FIRST COMPETITION.

April 19.	Cover EYE with LID	3
	Prove PITY to be GOOD	6
	STEAL COINS	7
26.	Make EEL into PIE	3
	Turn POOR into RICH	5
	Prove RAVEN to be MISER	3
May 3.	Change OAT to RYE	3
	Get WOOD from TREE	7
	Prove GRASS to be GREEN	7
10.	Evolve MAN from APE	5
	Change CAIN into ABEL	8
	Make FLOUR into BREAD	5
17.	Make TEA HOT	3
	Run COMB into HAIR	6
	Prove a ROGUE to be a BEAST	10
24.	Change ELM into OAK	7
	Combine ARMY and NAVY	7
	Place BEANS on SHELF	7
31.	HOOK FISH	6
	QUELL a BRAVO	10
	Stow FURIES in BARREL	5
June 7.	BUY an ASS	7
	Get COAL from MINE	5
	Pay COSTS in PENCE	9
14.	Raise ONE to TWO	7
	Change BLUE to PINK	8
	Change BLACK to WHITE	6

21.	Change FISH to BIRD	4
	Sell SHOES for CRUST	6
	Make KETTLE HOLDER	9
28.	REST on SOFA	4
	Trace RIVER to SHORE	10
	CARESS PARENT	2
July 5.	Change GRUB to MOTH	9
	Turn WITCH into FAIRY	12
	Make WINTER SUMMER	13
12.	Save LAMB from LION	2
	Crown TIGER with ROSES	5
	Lay QUILT on SHEET	13
19.	Put LOAF into OVEN	9
	Make BREAD into TOAST	6
	Put ROUGE on CHEEK	16
26.	WHY NOT?	3
	MANY will FAIL	7
	to get	
	PRIZES from CHOKER	9

SOLUTIONS TO DOUBLETS

PRELIMINARY DOUBLETS

March 29.

```
P I G      W H E A T      N O S E       W E T      P I T C H
w i g      c h e a t      n o t e       b e t      p i n c h
w a g      c h e a p      c o t e       b e y      w i n c h
w a y      c h e e p      c o r e       d e y      w e n c h
s a y      c r e e p      c o r n      D R Y       t e n c h
S T Y      c r e e d      c o i n                  t e n t h
           b r e e d     C H I N                   T E N T S
           B R E A D
```

April 12.

April 5.

```
F O U R    P E N        T E A R S     H A R E
f o u l    e'e n        s e a r s     h a r k
f o o l    e e l        s t a r s     h a c k
f o o t    e l l        s t a r e     s a c k
f o r t    i l l        s t a l e     s o c k
f o r e    i l k        s t i l e     s o a k
f i r e   I N K         S M I L E     s o a p
F I V E                               S O U P
```

FIRST COMPETITION

April 19.

EYE
dye
die
did
LID

PITY
pits
pins
fins
find
fond
food
GOOD

STEAL
steel
steer
sheer
shier
shies
shins
chins
COINS

April 26.

EEL
e'en
pen
pin
PIE

POOR
boor
book
rook
rock
rick
RICH

RAVEN
riven
risen
riser
MISER

May 3.

OAT
rat
rot
roe
RYE

TREE
free
flee
fled
feed
weed
weld
wold
WOOD

GRASS
crass
cress
tress
trees
frees
freed
greed
GREEN

May 10.

APE
are
ere
err
ear
mar
MAN

CAIN
chin
shin
spin
spun
spud
sped
aped
abed
ABEL

FLOUR
floor
flood
blood
brood
broad
BREAD

May 17.

TEA
sea
set
sot
HOT

COMB
come
home
hole
hale
hall
hail
HAIR

ROGUE
vogue
vague
value
valve
halve
helve
heave
leave
lease
least
BEAST

May 24.

ELM
ell
all
ail
air
fir
far
oar
OAK

ARMY
arms
aims
dims
dams
dame
name
nave
NAVY

BEANS
beams
seams
shams
shame
shale
shall
shell
SHELF

May 31.

HOOK
hoot
host
hist
fist
FISH

QUELL
quill
quilt
guilt
guile
guide
glide
glade
grade
grave
brave
BRAVO

FURIES
buries
buried
burked
barked
barred
BARREL

June 7.

BUY
bud
bid
aid
aim
arm
ark
ask
ASS

FIRST COMPETITION *(continued)*

June 28.

M I N E	B L A C K	R E S T	W I T C H
m i n t	b l a n k	l e s t	w i n c h
m i s t	b l i n k	l o s t	w e n c h
m o s t	c l i n k	l o f t	t e n c h
m o a t	c h i n k	s o f t	t e n t h
c o a t	c h i n e	S O F A	t e n t s
C O A L	w h i n e		t i n t s
	W H I T E		t i l t s
C O S T S		R I V E R	t i l l s
p o s t s		r o v e r	f i l l s
p e s t s	*June 21.*	c o v e r	f a l l s
t e s t s	F I S H	c o v e s	f a i l s
t e n t s	f i s t	c o r e s	f a i r s
t e n t h	g i s t	c o r n s	F A I R Y
t e n c h	g i r t	c o i n s	
t e a c h	g i r d	c h i n s	W I N T E R
p e a c h	B I R D	s h i n s	w i n n e r
p e a c e		s h i n e	w a n n e r
P E N C E		s h o n e	w a n d e r
	S H O E S	S H O R E	w a r d e r
	s h o p s		h a r d e r
	c h o p s		h a r p e r
June 14.	c r o p s	C A R E S S	h a m p e r
O N E	c r o s s	c a r e s t	d a m p e r
o w e	c r e s s	p a r e s t	d a m p e d
e w e	c r e s t	P A R E N T	d a m m e d
e y e	C R U S T		d i m m e d
d y e			d i m m e r
d o e		*July 5.*	s i m m e r
t o e	K E T T L E	G R U B	S U M M E R
t o o	s e t t l e	g r a b	
T W O	s e t t e e	g r a y	*July 12.*
	s e t t e r	b r a y	L I O N
	b e t t e r	b r a t	l i m n
B L U E	b e t t e d	b o a t	l i m b
g l u e	b e l t e d	b o l t	L A M B
g l u t	b o l t e d	b o l e	
g o u t	b o l t e r	m o l e	T I G E R
p o u t	b o l d e r	m o t e	t i l e r
p o r t	H O L D E R	M O T H	t i l e s
p a r t			t i d e s
p a n t			r i d e s
p i n t			r i s e s
P I N K			R O S E S

FIRST COMPETITION *(continued)*

	July 19.		*July* 26.	
Q U I L T	L O A F	R O U G E	W H Y	C H O K E R
g u i l t	l e a f	r o u g h	w h o	c h o k e d
g u i l e	d e a f	s o u g h	w o o	c o o k e d
g u i d e	d e a r	s o u t h	w o t	l o o k e d
g l i d e	d e e r	s o o t h	N O T	l o o s e d
s l i d e	d y e r	b o o t h		n o o s e d
s l i c e	d y e s	b o o t s		n o i s e d
s p i c e	e y e s	b o a t s	M A N Y	p o i s e d
s p i n e	e v e s	b r a t s	m a n e	p r i s e d
s p i n s	e v e n	b r a s s	w a n e	p r i z e d
s h i n s	O V E N	c r a s s	w a l e	P R I Z E S
s h i e s		c r e s s	w i l e	
s h i e r	B R E A D	c r e s t	w i l l	
s h e e r	b r e a k	c h e s t	w a l l	
S H E E T	b l e a k	c h e a t	w a i l	
	b l e a t	c h e a p	F A I L	
	b l e s t	c h e e p		
	b l a s t	C H E E K		
	b o a s t			
	T O A S T			

In recent years the puzzle has attracted attention from learned quarters which Carroll himself could never have foreseen. The deranged narrator of Nabokov's *Pale Fire*, in his annotation to line 819 of the poem upon which the 'novel' hinges, mentions playing 'word golf' and remembers changing HATE to LOVE in two links, LASS to MALE in three, and LIVE to DEAD in four with LEND in the middle. The following are possible solutions:

HATE	LASS	LIVE
have	mass	line
hove	mast	lind
LOVE	malt	lend
	MALE	lead
		DEAD

In the same work Nabokov points out a related verbal curiosity, an 'absolutely extraordinary, unbelievably elegant case'. He instances the following series of English words arrived at by a process of deletion:

CROWN;   CROW;   COW

These words when translated into Russian and then transliterated into the Latin alphabet become

KORONA;   VORONA;   KOROVA

where a Doublet-style relationship is discernible between the first and second and the first and third words. Carroll, who visited the native country of his fellow verbal pyrotechnist in 1867, would no doubt have appreciated the rarity of such a parallel in word play between two languages, if denouncing the suggestion that Nabokov himself, author of the finest Russian translation of *Alice in Wonderland* (*Anya v strane chudes*) based his character Humbert Humbert in *Lolita* on Carroll's own penchant for young girls.

John Maynard Smith, exploring the process by which one species evolves from another in an essay entitled 'The Limitations of Molecular Evolution', from *The Scientist Speculates: an anthology of partly-baked ideas,* uses it to extend the analogy between the messages in words and the genetic instructions in chromosomes. He instances the change of WORD to GENE in three links:

W O R D
w o r e
g o r e
g o n e
G E N E

One has only to think of the helical DNA molecule as a word, with each successive change in that structure, the basis of evolution, as a change in letter, to realise that when Carroll evolved 'MAN from APE' he was closer to reality than he could have dreamed.

Borgmann in his *Language on Vacation* points out that the ideal Doublet involves the transformation of a word of 'n' letters in 'n' moves, given that initially the two words have no identical letters at the same positions (as with WORD to GENE). Borgmann himself provides the puzzle with the even apter title 'Word Ladders'. Gardner, in the pages of *Scientific American*, has revealed several solutions shorter than those reached by Carroll which he himself would have envied. Most appealing, since it does not rely on obscure words, is APE to MAN in four links:

A P E
a p t
o p t
o a t
m a t
M A N

It's interesting to note that the two girls with 'nothing to do', for whom Carroll invented the puzzle, were Julia and Ethel Arnold, the former later to marry Leonard Huxley and become mother of Sir Julian and Aldous Huxley. In a letter to *Jabberwocky* during the summer of 1970 Sir Julian himself recollects playing Doublets as a child. One wonders how significant a part, if any, the game played in his researches into Darwinian Theory and his book *Evolution: the Modern Synthesis*.

Cats and rats

We lived beneath the mat
Warm and snug and fat
But one woe, and that
Was the cat!

To our joys a clog,
In our eyes a fog,
On our hearts a log
Was the dog!

When the cat's away,
Then the mice will play,
But, alas! one day,
(So they say)

Came the dog and cat,
Hunting for a rat,
Crushed the mice all flat,
Each one as he sat
Underneath the mat,
Warm, and snug, and fat.
Think of that!

Alice's Adventures Under Ground

The final version of 'The Mouse's Tail', as it appears in *Alice's Adventures in Wonderland*, lacks the mouse's promised explanation of why he dislikes cats in addition to dogs. The following problem contributed by Carroll to *The Monthly Packet* in February, 1880, more than compensates with its feline emphasis:

If 6 cats kill 6 rats in 6 minutes, how many will be needed to kill 100 rats in 50 minutes?
This is a good example of a phenomenon that often occurs in working problems in double proportion; the answer looks all right at first, but, when we come to test it, we find that, owing to peculiar circumstances in the case, the solution is either impossible or else indefinite, and needing further data. The 'peculiar circumstance' here is that fractional cats or rats are excluded from consideration, and in consequence of this the solution is, as we shall see, indefinite.
The solution, by the ordinary rules of Double Proportion, is as follows:

$$\left.\begin{array}{l} 6 \text{ rats} \ : \ 100 \text{ rats} \\ 50 \text{ min.} \ : \ 6 \text{ min.} \end{array}\right\} \ : : 6 \text{ cats} : \text{ans.}$$

$$\therefore \text{ans.} = \frac{100 \cdot 6 \cdot 6}{6 \cdot 50} = 12$$

But when we come to trace the history of this sanguinary scene through all its horrid details, we find that at the end of 48 minutes 96 rats are dead, and that there remain 4 live rats and 2 minutes to kill them in: the question is, can this be done?

Now there are at least *four* different ways in which the original feat, of 6 cats killing 6 rats in 6 minutes, may be achieved. For the sake of clearness let us tabulate them:

A. All 6 cats are needed to kill a rat; and this they do in one minute, the other rats standing meekly by, waiting for their turn.

B. 3 cats are needed to kill a rat, and they do it in 2 minutes.

C. 2 cats are needed, and do it in 3 minutes.

D. Each cat kills a rat all by itself, and take 6 minutes to do it.

In cases A and B it is clear that the 12 cats (who are assumed to come quite fresh from their 48 minutes of slaughter) can finish the affair in the required time; but, in case C, it can only be done by supposing that 2 cats could kill two-thirds of a rat in 2 minutes; and in case D, by supposing that a cat could kill one-third of a rat in 2 minutes. Neither supposition is warranted by the data; nor could the fractional rats (even if endowed with equal vitality) be fairly assigned to the different cats. For my part, if I were a cat in case D, and did not find my claws in good working order, I should certainly prefer to have my one-third-rat cut off from the tail end.

In cases C and D, then, it is clear that we must provide extra cat-power. In case C *less* than 2 extra cats would be of no use. If 2 were supplied, and if they began killing their 4 rats at the beginning of the time, they would finish them in 12 minutes, and have 36 minutes to spare, during which they might weep, like Alexander, because there were not 12 more rats to kill. In case D, one extra cat would suffice; it would kill its 4 rats in 24 minutes, and have 24 minutes to spare, during which it could have killed another 4. But in neither case could any use be made of the last 2 minutes, except to half-kill rats – a barbarity we need not take into consideration.

To sum up our results. If the 6 cats kill the 6 rats by method A or B, the answer is '12'; if by method C, '14'; if by method D, '13'.

This, then, is an instance of a solution made 'indefinite' by the circumstances of the case. If an instance of the 'impossible' be desired, take the following: 'If a cat can kill a rat in a minute, how many would be needed to kill it in the thousandth part of a second?' The *mathematical* answer, of course, is '60,000,' and no doubt less than this would *not* suffice; but would 60,000 suffice? I doubt it very much. I fancy that at least 50,000 of the cats would never even see the rat, or have any idea of what was going on.

Or take this: 'If a cat can kill a rat in a minute, how long would it be killing 60,000 rats?' Ah, how long, indeed! My private opinion is that the rats would kill the cat.

For all its fantasy overtones, the problem, used by Carroll in an introduction to *A Tangled Tale*, soon assumed a ghostly reality. Lennon cites the 1912 travelogue *15,000 Miles in a Ketch*, by Captain Raymond Rallier Du Baty, which mentions Carroll's brother Edwin Dodgson being Vicar of the mid-Atlantic island of Tristan da Cunha from 1881 until 1889: 'In the time of the last chaplain, Mr. Dodgson, there was a plague of rats which threatened to destroy the whole population by eating up all their sustenance. . . . The islanders ignored the clergyman's plea that these ship rats should be at once exterminated, believing that they would not give trouble, as they were so far away. . . . On one occasion, when Mr. Dodgson was going to bed, he saw what he imagined to be his black kitten on the bed, a comfortable resting-place. Cats were imported into the island to exterminate this plague, but the rats exterminated the cats!'

Mischmasch

The name is German, and means in English 'midge-madge', which we need not inform the intelligent reader is equivalent to 'hodge-podge': our intention is to admit articles of every kind, prose, verse, and pictures, provided they reach a sufficiently high standard of merit.

Preface to Mischmasch

Carroll first contributed the following game, named after another of the whimsical magazines he used to write and edit for the amusement of himself and his brothers and sisters before going up to Oxford, to *The Monthly Packet* in June, 1881. Here is a slightly revised form of the game, for two players or two sets of players, with the same number of rules, as it appeared in the same magazine, November, 1882:

The essence of this game consists of one Player proposing a 'nucleus' (i.e. a set of two or more letters, such as 'gp', 'emo', 'imse'), and in the other trying to find a 'lawful word' (i.e. a word known in ordinary society, and not a proper name), containing it. Thus, 'magpie', 'lemon', 'himself', are lawful words containing the nuclei 'gp', 'emo', 'imse'.

A nucleus must not contain a hyphen (e.g. for the nucleus 'erga', 'flower-garden' is not a lawful word).

Any word, that is always printed with a capital initial (e.g. 'English'), counts as a proper name.

RULES

1. Each thinks of a nucleus, and says 'ready' when he has done so. When both have spoken, the nuclei are named. A Player may set a nucleus without knowing of any word containing it.

2. When a Player has guessed a word containing the nucleus set to him (which need not be the word thought of by the Player who set it), or has made up his mind that there is no such word, he says 'ready', or 'no word', as the case may be: when he has decided to give up trying, he says 'I resign'. The other must then, within a stated time (e.g. 2 minutes), say 'ready', or 'no word', or 'I resign', or 'not ready'. If he says nothing, he is assumed to be 'not ready'.

3. When both have spoken, if the first speaker said 'ready', he now names the word he has guessed: if he said 'no word', he, who set the nucleus, names, if he can, a word containing it. The other Player then proceeds in the same way.

4. The Players then score as follows – (N.B. When a Player is said to 'lose' marks, it means that the other scores them.)

Guessing a word, rightly,	scores 1.
„ „ wrongly,	loses 1.
Guessing 'no word', rightly,	scores 2.
„ „ wrongly,	loses 2.
Resigning	loses 1.

This ends the first move.

5. For every other move, the Players proceed as for the first move, except that when a Player is 'not ready', or has guessed a word wrongly, he has not a new nucleus set to him, but goes on guessing the one in hand, having first, if necessary, set a new nucleus for the other Player.

6. A 'resigned' nucleus cannot be set again during the same game. If, however, one or more letters be added or subtracted, it counts as a new one.

7. The move, in which either scores 10, is the final one; when it is completed, the game is over, and the highest score wins, or, if the scores be equal, the game is drawn.

A Tangled Tale

'A knot!' said Alice, already to make herself useful, and looking anxiously about her. 'Oh, do let me help to undo it!'

Alice's Adventures in Wonderland

This remark by Alice to the Mouse was used as a quotation by Carroll to preface the answer section to the series of puzzles, paradoxes and quibbles which he published under the above title in 1885. The tale itself was divided into 'knots', approximating to chapters, ten in all, which had already appeared in *The Monthly Packet* between April, 1880 and March, 1885. The tale itself sees Carroll at his playful best in combining tantalising whimsy with straightforward mathematics, its own affront to theorists who try to split his character into a dual identity where the Rev. C. L. Dodgson never met the successful author of nonsense books.

The problems themselves are interwoven into a story served by several narrative themes, all resolving at the end. A great deal of its appeal, however, must rest in an appendix, amounting to more than half the volume, in which, apart from the solutions, are featured the columns addressed by Carroll to his regular readers. Here he struck up a chatty relationship with contestants, classifying their answers in an amusing parody of the Oxford degree system and using them as the basis for a witty analysis of the wrong as well as the right ways in which a problem can be attacked. In the extracts which follow an attempt has been made to convey an element of this humour as well as give what is of most relevance to this volume, namely the germ of each problem and solution as detailed by Carroll at the head of each answer section.

Knot one: 'Excelsior'

' 'Twas three hours past high noon when we left our hostelry,' the young man said, musingly. 'We shall scarce be back by supper-time. Perchance mine host will roundly deny us all food!'

'He will chide our tardy return,' was the grave reply, 'and such a rebuke will be meet.'

'A brave conceit!' cried the other, with a merry laugh. 'And should we bid him bring us yet another course, I trow his answer will be tart!'

'We shall but get our deserts,' sighed the elder knight, who had never seen a joke in his life, and was somewhat displeased at his companion's untimely levity. ' 'Twill be nine of the clock,' he added in an undertone, 'by the time we regain our hostelry. Full many a mile shall we have plodded this day!'

'At a pace of six miles in the hour': frontispiece to
A Tangled Tale

Problem. 'Two travellers spend from 3 o'clock till 9 in walking along a level road, up a hill, and home again: their pace on the level being 4 miles an hour, up hill 3, and down hill 6. Find distance walked: also (within half an hour) time of reaching top of hill.'

Answer. '24 miles: half-past 6.'

Solution. A level mile takes $\frac{1}{4}$ of an hour, up hill $\frac{1}{3}$, down hill $\frac{1}{6}$. Hence to go and return over the same mile, whether on the level or on the hill-side, takes $\frac{1}{2}$ an hour. Hence in 6 hours they went 12 miles out and 12 back. If the 12 miles out had been nearly all level, they would have taken a little over 3 hours; if nearly all up hill, a little under 4. Hence $3\frac{1}{2}$ hours must be within $\frac{1}{2}$ an hour of the time taken in reaching the peak; thus, as they started at 3, they got there within $\frac{1}{2}$ an hour of $\frac{1}{2}$ past 6.

BLITHE has made so ingenious an addition to the problem, and SIMPLE SUSAN and CO. have solved it in such tuneful verse, that I record both their answers in full. I have altered a word or two in BLITHE'S – which I trust she will excuse; it did not seem quite clear as it stood.

'Yet stay,' said the youth, as a gleam of inspiration lighted up the relaxing muscles of his quiescent features. 'Stay. Methinks it matters little *when* we reached that summit, the crown of our toil. For in the space of time wherein we clambered up one mile and bounded down the same on our return, we could have trudged the *twain* on the level. We have plodded, then, four-

and-twenty miles in these six mortal hours; for never a moment did we
stop for catching of fleeting breath or for gazing on the scene around!'

'Very good,' said the old man. 'Twelve miles out and twelve miles in.
And we reached the top some time between six and seven of the clock.
Now mark me! For every five minutes that had fled since six of the clock when
we stood on yonder peak, so many miles had we toiled upwards on the
dreary mountainside!'

The youth moaned and rushed into the hostel.

BLITHE

> The elder and the younger knight,
>   They sallied forth at three;
> How far they went on level ground
>   It matters not to me;
> What time they reached the foot of hill,
>   When they began to mount,
> Are problems which I hold to be
>   Of very small account.
>
> The moment that each waved his hat
>   Upon the topmost peak—
> To trivial query such as this
>   No answer will I seek.
> Yet can I tell the distance well
>   They must have travelled o'er:
> On hill and plain, 'twixt three and nine,
>   The miles were twenty-four.
>
> Four miles an hour their steady pace
>   Along the level track,
> Three when they climbed – but six when they
>   Came swiftly striding back
> Adown the hill; and little skill
>   It needs, methinks, to show,
> Up hill and down together told,
>   Four miles an hour they go.
>
> For whether long or short the time
>   Upon the hill they spent,
> Two thirds were passed in going up,
>   One third in the descent.
> Two thirds at three, one third at six,
>   If rightly reckoned o'er,
> Will make one whole at four – the tale
>   Is tangled now no more.

SIMPLE SUSAN
MONEY SPINNER

Knot two: 'Eligible apartments'

That most fashionable of watering-places, Little Mendip, was 'chockfull' (as the boys expressed it) from end to end. But in one Square they had seen no less than four cards, in different houses, all announcing in flaming capitals 'ELIGIBLE APARTMENTS.' 'So there's plenty of choice, after all, you see,' said spokesman Hugh in conclusion.

'That doesn't follow from the data,' said Balbus, as he rose from the easy chair, where he had been dozing over *The Little Mendip Gazette*. 'They may be all single rooms. However, we may as well see them. I shall be glad to stretch my legs a bit.'

An unprejudiced bystander might have objected that the operation was needless, and that this long, lank creature would have been all the better with even shorter legs: but no such thought occurred to his loving pupils. One on each side, they did their best to keep up with his gigantic strides, while Hugh repeated the sentence in their father's letter, just received from abroad, over which he and Lambert had been puzzling. 'He says a friend of his, the Governor of—— *what* was that name again, Lambert?' ('Kgovjni,' said Lambert.) 'Well, yes. The Governor of—— what-you-may-call-it – wants to give a *very* small dinner-party, and he means to ask his father's brother-in-law, his brother's father-in-law, his father-in-law's brother, and his brother-in-law's father: and we're to guess how many guests there will be.'

There was an anxious pause. '*How* large did he say the pudding was to be?' Balbus said at last. 'Take its cubical contents, divide by the cubical contents of what each man can eat, and the quotient—'

'He didn't say anything about pudding,' said Hugh, '– and here's the Square,' as they turned a corner and come into sight of the 'eligible apartments.'

i

Problem 1. 'The Governor of Kgovjni wants to give a very small dinner party, and invites his father's brother-in-law, his brother's father-in-law, his father-in-law's brother, and his brother-in-law's father. Find the number of guests.'

Answer. 'One.'

Solution.
In this genealogy, males are denoted by capitals, and females by small letters.
    The Governor is E and his guest is C.

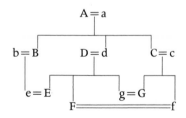

Ten answers have been received. Of these, one is wrong, GALANTHUS NIVALIS MAJOR, who insists on inviting *two* guests, one being the Governor's *wife's brother's father*. If she had taken his *sister's husband's father* instead, she would have found it possible to reduce the guests to *one*.

Of the nine who send right answers, SEA-BREEZE is the very faintest breath that ever bore the name! She simply states that the Governor's uncle might fulfill all the conditions 'by intermarriages'! 'Wind of the western sea,' you have had a very narrow escape! Be thankful to appear in the Class-list at all! BOG-OAK and BRADSHAW OF THE FUTURE use genealogies which require 16 people instead of 14, by inviting the Governor's *father's sister's husband* instead of his *father's wife's brother*. I cannot think this so good a solution as one that requires only 14. CAIUS and VALENTINE deserve special mention as the only two who have supplied genealogies.

ii

Problem 2. 'A Square has 20 doors on each side, which contains 21 equal parts. They are numbered all round, beginning at one corner. From which of the four, Nos. 9, 25, 52, 73, is the sum of the distances, to the other three, least?'

Answer. 'From No. 9.'

Solution.
Let A be No. 9, B No. 25, C No. 52, and D No. 73.

Then $AB = \sqrt{(12^2 + 5^2)} = \sqrt{169} = 13$;

$AC = 21$;

$AD = \sqrt{(9^2 + 8^2)} = \sqrt{145} = 12 +$
    (N.B. *i.e.* 'between 12 and 13.')

$BC = \sqrt{(16^2 + 12^2)} = \sqrt{400} = 20$;

$BD = \sqrt{(3^2 + 21^2)} = \sqrt{450} = 21 +$;

$CD = \sqrt{(9^2 + 13^2)} = \sqrt{250} = 15 +$;

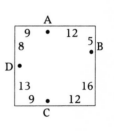

Hence sum of distances from A is between 46 and 47; from B, between 54 and 55; from C, between 56 and 57; from D, between 48 and 51. (Why not 'between 48 and 49'? Make this out for yourselves.) Hence the sum is least for A.

Twenty-five solutions have been received. Of these, 15 must be marked '0', 5 are partly right, and 5 right. Of the 15, I may dismiss ALPHABETICAL PHANTOM, BOG-OAK, DINAH MITE, FIFEE, GALANTHUS NIVALIS MAJOR (I fear the cold spring has blighted our SNOWDROP), GUY, H.M.S. PINAFORE, JANET and VALENTINE with the simple remark that they insist on the unfortunate lodgers *keeping to the pavement.* (I used the words 'crossed to Number Seventy-three' for the special purpose of showing that *short cuts* were possible.)

Knot three: 'Mad Mathesis'

'Take your places on the spring-boards!' shouted a porter.

'What are *they* for!' Clara asked in a terrified whisper.

'Merely to help us into the trains.' The elder lady spoke with the nonchalance of one quite used to the process. 'Very few people can get into a carriage without help in less than three seconds, and the trains only stop for one second.' At this moment the whistle was heard, and two trains rushed into the station. A moment's pause, and they were gone again; but in that brief interval several hundred passengers had been shot into them, each flying straight to his place with the accuracy of a Minie bullet – while an equal number were showered out upon the side-platforms.

Problem. (1) 'Two travellers, starting at the same time, went opposite ways round a circular railway. Trains start each way every 15 minutes, the easterly ones going round in 3 hours, the westerly in 2. How many trains did each meet on the way, not counting trains met at the terminus itself?' (2) 'They went round, as before, each traveller counting as "one" the train containing the other traveller. How many did each meet?'

Answers. (1) 19. (2) The easterly traveller met 12; the other 8.

Solution. The trains one way took 180 minutes, the other way 120. Let us take the L. C. M., 360, and divide the railway into 360 units. Then one set of trains went at the rate of 2 units a minute and at intervals of 30 units; the other at the rate of 3 units a minute and at intervals of 45 units. An easterly train starting has 45 units between it and the first train it will meet: it does 2–5ths of this while the other does 3–5ths, and thus meets it at the end of 18 units, and so all the way round. A westerly train starting has 30 units between it and the first train it will meet: it does 3–5ths of this while the other does 2–5ths, and thus meets it at the end of 18 units, and so all the way round. Hence if the railway be divided, by 19 posts, into 20 parts, each containing 18 units, trains meet at every post, and, in (1), each traveller passes 19 posts in going round, and so meets 19 trains. But, in (2), the easterly traveller only begins to count after traversing 2–5ths of the journey, *i.e.*, on reaching the 8th post, and so counts 12 posts: similarly the other counts 8. They meet at the end of 2–5ths of 3 hours, or 3–5ths of 2 hours, *i.e.*, 72 minutes.

Bo-Peep rightly says that the easterly traveller met all trains which started during the 3 hours of her trip, as well as all which started during the previous 2 hours, *i.e.*, all which started at the commencements of 20 periods of 15 minutes each; and she is right in striking out the one she met at the moment of starting; but wrong in striking out the *last* train, for she did not meet this at the terminus, but 15 minutes before she got there.

Knot four: 'The dead reckoning'

'What have they got in those sacks, Captain?' he inquired, as that great being passed them in his never ending parade to and fro on the deck.

The Captain paused in his march, and towered over the travellers – tall, grave, and serenely self-satisfied.

'Fishermen,' he explained, 'are often passengers in My ship. These five are from Mhruxi – the place we last touched at – and that's the way they carry their money. The money of this island is heavy, gentlemen, but it costs little, as you may guess. We buy it from them by weight – about five shillings a pound. I fancy a ten pound-note would buy all those sacks.'

Problem. 'There are 5 sacks, of which Nos. 1, 2, weigh 12 lbs.; Nos. 2, 3, $13\frac{1}{2}$ lbs.; Nos. 3, 4, $11\frac{1}{2}$ lbs.; Nos. 4, 5, 8 lbs.; Nos. 1, 3, 5, 16 lbs. Required the weight of each sack.'

Answer. '$5\frac{1}{2}$, $6\frac{1}{2}$, 7, $4\frac{1}{2}$, $3\frac{1}{2}$.'

Solution. The sum of all the weighings, 61 lbs., includes sack No. 3 *thrice* and each other *twice*. Deducting twice the sum of the 1st and 4th weighings, we get 21 lbs. for *thrice* No. 3, *i.e.*, 7 lbs. for No. 3. Hence, the 2nd and 3rd weighings give $6\frac{1}{2}$ lbs., $4\frac{1}{2}$ lbs. for Nos. 2, 4; and hence again, the 1st and 4th weighings give $5\frac{1}{2}$ lbs., $3\frac{1}{2}$ lbs., for Nos. 1, 5.

Ninety-seven answers have been received. Of these, 15 are beyond the reach of discussion, as they give no working. I can but enumerate their names, and I take this opportunity of saying that this is the last time I shall put on record the names of competitors who give no sort of clue to the process by which their answers were obtained. In guessing a conundrum, or in catching a flea, we do not expect the breathless victor to give us afterwards, in cold blood, a history of the mental or muscular efforts by which he achieved success; but a mathematical calculation is another thing. The names of this 'mute inglorious' band are COMMON SENSE, D. E. R., DOUGLAS, E. L., ELLEN, I. M. T., J. M. C., JOSEPH, KNOT I, LUCY, MEEK, M. F. C., PYRAMUS, SHAH, VERITAS. The problem is of course (as any Algebraist sees at once) a case of 'simultaneous simple equations'. It is, however, easily soluble by Arithmetic only; and, when this is the case, I hold that it is bad workmanship to use the more complex method. I have not, this time, given more credit to arithmetical solutions; but in future problems I shall (other things being equal) give the highest marks to those who use the simplest machinery.

Knot five: 'Oughts and crosses'

Clara brightened up. 'I should like to try again, very much,' she said. 'I'll take more care this time. How are we to play?'

To this question Mad Mathesis made no reply: she was busy drawing lines down the margins of the catalogue. 'See,' she said after a minute, 'I've drawn three columns against the names of the pictures in the long room, and I want you to fill them with oughts and crosses – crosses for good marks and oughts for bad. The first column is for choice of subject, the second for arrangement, the third for colouring. And these are the conditions of the match. You must give three crosses to two or three pictures. You must give two crosses to four or five—'

'Do you mean *only* two crosses?' said Clara. 'Or may I count the three-cross pictures among the two-cross pictures?'

'Of course you may,' said her aunt. 'Any one, that has *three* eyes, may be said to have *two* eyes, I suppose?'

Problem. To mark pictures, giving 3 × 's to 2 or 3, 2 to 4 or 5, and 1 to 9 or 10; also giving 3 O's to 1 or 2, 2 to 3 or 4 and 1 to 8 or 9; so as to mark the smallest possible number of pictures, and to give them the largest possible number of marks.

Answer. 10 pictures; 29 marks; arranged thus:

```
×  ×  ×  ×  ×  ×  ×  ×  ×  O
×  ×  ×  ×  ×        O  O  O  O
×  ×  O  O  O  O  O  O  O  O
```

Solution. By giving all the × 's possible, putting into brackets the optional ones, we get 10 pictures marked thus:

```
×  ×  ×  ×  ×  ×  ×  ×  ×  (×)
×  ×  ×  ×  (×)
×  ×  (×)
```

By then assigning O's in the same way, beginning at the other end, we get 9 pictures marked thus:

```
                              (O)  O
                         (O)  O    O  O
(O)  O   O   O   O   O   O    O     O
```

All we have now to do is to run these two wedges as close together as they will go, so as to get the minimum number of pictures – erasing optional marks where by so doing we can run them closer, but otherwise letting them stand. There are 10 necessary marks in the 1st row, and in the 3rd; but only 7 in the 2nd. Hence we erase all optional marks in the 1st and 3rd rows, but let them stand in the 2nd.

I. E. A. (I am happy to say that none of these bloodless phantoms appear this time in the class-list. Is it IDEA with the 'D' left out?) gives 2 × 's to 6 pictures. She then takes me to task for using the word 'ought' instead of 'nought'. No doubt, to one who thus rebels against the rules laid down for her guidance, the word must be distasteful. But does not I. E. A. remember the parallel case of 'adder'? That creature was originally 'a nadder': then the two words took to bandying the poor 'n' backwards and forwards like a shuttlecock, the final state of the game being 'an adder'. May not 'a nought' have similarly become 'an ought'? Anyhow, 'oughts and crosses' is a very old game. I don't think I ever heard it called 'noughts and crosses'.

Knot six: 'Her Radiancy'

i

The Governor smiled proudly. 'In your honour,' he said, 'Her Radiancy has ordered up ten thousand additional peacocks. She will, no doubt, decorate you, before you go, with the usual Star and Feathers.'

'It'll be Star without the S!' faltered one of his hearers.

'Come, come! Don't lose heart!' said the other. 'All this is full of charm for me.'

'You are young, Norman,' sighed his father; 'young and light-hearted. For me, it is Charm without the C.'

'The old one is sad,' the Governor remarked with some anxiety. 'He has, without doubt, effected some fearful crime?'

'But I haven't!' the poor old gentleman hastily exclaimed. 'Tell him I haven't, Norman!'

'He has not, as yet,' Norman gently explained. And the Governor repeated, in a satisfied tone, 'Not as yet.'

'Yours is a wondrous country!' the Governor resumed, after a pause. 'Now here is a letter from a friend of mine, a merchant in London. He and his brother went there a year ago, with a thousand pounds apiece; and on New-Year's day they had sixty thousand pounds between them!'

'How did they do it?' Norman eagerly exclaimed. Even the elder traveller looked excited.

The Governor handed him the open letter. 'Anybody can do it, when once they know how,' so ran this oracular document. 'We borrowed nought: we stole nought. We began the year with only a thousand pounds apiece: and last New-Year's day we had sixty thousand pounds between us – sixty thousand golden sovereigns!'

Norman looked grave and thoughtful as he handed back the letter. His father hazarded one guess. 'Was it by gambling?'

'A Kgovjnian never gambles,' said the Governor gravely, as he ushered them through the palace gates.

Problem 1. A and *B* began the year with only 1,000*l.* a-piece. They borrowed nought; they stole nought. On the New-Year's Day they had 60,000*l.* between them. How did they do it?

Solution. They went that day to the Bank of England. *A* stood in front of it, while *B* went round and stood behind it.

Two answers have been received, both worthy of much honour. ADDLEPATE makes them borrow '0' and steal '0', and use both cyphers by putting them at the right-hand end of the 1,000*l.*, thus producing 100,000*l.*, which is well over the mark. But (or to express it in Latin) AT SPES INFRACTA has solved it even more ingeniously: with the first cypher she turns the '1' of the 1,000*l.* into a '9', and adds the result to the original sum, thus getting 10,000*l.*: and in this, by means of the other '0', she turns the '1' into a '6', thus hitting the exact 60,000*l.*

ii

'It is well,' said the Governor, and translated this into Kgovjnian. 'I am now to tell you' he proceeded, 'what Her Radiancy requires of you before you go. The yearly competition for the post of Imperial Scarf-maker is just ended; you are the judges. You will take account of the rate of work, the lightness of the scarves, and their warmth. Usually the competitors differ in one point only. Thus, last year, Fifi and Gogo made the same number of scarves in the trial-week, and they were equally light; but Fifi's were twice as warm as Gogo's and she was pronounced twice as good. But this year, woe is me, who can judge it? Three competitors are here, and they differ in all points! While you settle their claims, you shall be lodged, Her Radiancy bids me say, free of expense – in the best dungeon, and abundantly fed on the best bread and water.'

Problem 2. L makes 5 scarves, while *M* makes 2: *Z* makes 4 while *L* makes 3. Five scarves of *Z*'s weigh one of *L*'s; 5 of *M*'s weigh 3 of *Z*'s. One of *M*'s is as warm as 4 of *Z*'s: and one of *L*'s as warm as 3 of *M*'s. Which is best, giving equal weight in the result to rapidity of work, lightness, and warmth?

Answer. The order is *M, L, Z.*

Solution. As to rapidity (other things being constant) *L*'s merit is to *M*'s in the ratio of 5 to 2: *Z*'s to *L*'s in the ratio of 4 to 3. In order to get one set of 3 numbers fulfilling these conditions, it is perhaps simplest to take the one that occurs *twice* as unity, and reduce the others to fractions: this gives, for *L, M,* and *Z,* the marks 1, $\frac{2}{5}$, $\frac{4}{3}$. In estimating for *lightness,* we observe that the greater the weight, the less the merit, so that *Z*'s merit is to *L*'s as 5 to 1. Thus the marks for *lightness* are $\frac{1}{5}$, $\frac{3}{5}$, 1. And similarly, the marks for warmth are 3, 1, $\frac{1}{4}$. To get the total result, we must *multiply L*'s marks together, and do the same for *M* and for *Z.* The final numbers are $1 \times \frac{1}{5} \times 3$, $\frac{2}{5} \times \frac{3}{5} \times 1$, $\frac{4}{3} \times 1 \times \frac{1}{4}$; *i.e.* $\frac{3}{5}$, $\frac{2}{5}$, $\frac{1}{3}$; *i.e.* multiplying throughout by 15 (which will not alter the proportion), 9, 10, 5; showing the order of merit to be *M, L, Z.*

Twenty-nine answers have been received, of which five are right, and twenty-four wrong. These hapless ones have all (with three exceptions) fallen into the error of *adding* the proportional numbers together, for each candidate, instead of *multiplying*. *Why* the latter is right, rather than the former, is fully proved in text-books, so I will not occupy space by stating it here: but it can be *illustrated* very easily by the case of length, breadth, and depth. Suppose *A* and *B* are rival diggers of rectangular tanks: the amount of work done is evidently measured by the number of *cubical feet* dug out. Let *A* dig a tank 10 feet long, 10 wide, 2 deep: let *B* dig one 6 feet long, 5 wide, 10 deep. The cubical contents are 200, 300; *i.e. B* is best digger in the ratio of 3 to 2. Now try marking for length, width, and depth, separately; giving a maximum mark of 10 to the best in each contest, and then *adding* the results!

Of the five winners I put BALBUS and THE ELDER TRAVELLER slightly below the other three – BALBUS for defective reasoning, the other for scanty working. BALBUS gives two reasons for saying that *addition* of marks is *not* the right method, and then adds 'it follows that the decision must be made by *multiplying* the marks together.' This is hardly more logical than to say 'This is not Spring: *therefore* it must be Autumn.'

Knot seven: 'Petty cash'

'Here's the place,' she said at last, 'and here we have yesterday's luncheon duly entered. *One glass lemonade* (Why can't you drink water, like me?) *three sandwiches* (They never put in half mustard enough. I told the young woman so, to her face; and she tossed her head – like her impudence!) *and seven biscuits. Total one-and-two-pence.* Well, now for to-day's?'

'One glass of lemonade—' Clara was beginning to say, when suddenly the cab drew up, and a courteous railway-porter was handing out the bewildered girl before she had had time to finish her sentence.

Her aunt pocketed the tablets instantly. 'Business first,' she said: 'petty cash – which is a form of pleasure, whatever *you* may think – afterwards.' And she proceeded to pay the driver, and to give voluminous orders about the luggage, quite deaf to the entreaties of her unhappy niece that she would enter the rest of the luncheon account.

Problem. Given that one glass of lemonade, 3 sandwiches, and 7 biscuits, cost 1s. 2d.; and that one glass of lemonade, 4 sandwiches, and 10 biscuits, cost 1s. 5d.: find the cost of (1) a glass of lemonade, a sandwich, and a biscuit; and (2) 2 glasses of lemonade, 3 sandwiches, and 5 biscuits.

Answer. (1) 8d.; (2) 1s. 7d.

Solution. This is best treated algebraically. Let $x =$ the cost (in pence) of a glass of lemonade, y of a sandwich, and z of a biscuit. Then we have $x + 3y +$

$7z = 14$, and $x + 4y + 10z = 17$. And we require the values of $x + y + z$, and of $2x + 3y + 5z$. Now, from *two* equations only, we cannot find, *separately*, the values of *three* unknowns: certain *combinations* of them may, however, be found. Also we know that we can, by the help of the given equations, eliminate 2 of the 3 unknowns from the quantity whose value is required, which will then contain one only. If, then, the required value is ascertainable at all, it can only be by the 3rd unknown vanishing of itself: otherwise the problem is impossible.

Let us then eliminate lemonade and sandwiches, and reduce everything to biscuits – a state of things even more depressing than 'if all the world were apple-pie' – by subtracting the 1st equation from the 2nd, which eliminates lemonade, and gives $y + 3z = 3$, or $y = 3 - 3z$; and then substituting this value of y in the 1st, which gives $x - 2z = 5$, *i.e.* $x = 5 + 2z$. Now if we substitute these values of x, y, in the quantities whose values are required, the first becomes $(5 + 2z) + (3 - 3z) + z$, *i.e.* 8: and the second becomes $2(5 + 2z) + 3(3 - 3z) + 5z$, *i.e.* 19. Hence the answers are (1) 8*d.*, (2) 1*s.* 7*d.*

STILETTO identifies sandwiches and biscuits, as 'articles'. Is the word ever used by confectioners? I fancied 'What is the next article, Ma'am?' was limited to linendrapers. TWO SISTERS first assume that biscuits are 4 a penny, and then that they are 2 a penny, adding that 'the answer will of course be the same in both cases.' It is a dreamy remark, making one feel something like Macbeth grasping at the spectral dagger. 'Is this a statement that I see before me?' If you were to say 'we both walked the same way this morning,' and *I* were to say '*one* of you walked the same way, but the other didn't,' which of the three would be the most hopelessly confused?

Knot eight: 'De omnibus rebus'

'By Her Radiancy's express command,' said the Governor, as he conducted the travellers, for the last time, from the Imperial presence, 'I shall now have the ecstasy of escorting you as far as the outer gate of the Military Quarter, where the agony of parting – if indeed Nature can survive the shock – must be endured! From that gate grurmstipths start every quarter of an hour, both ways—'

'Would you mind repeating that word?' said Norman. 'Grurm—?'

'Grurmstipths,' the Governor repeated. 'You call them omnibuses in England. They run both ways, and you can travel by one of them all the way down to the harbour.'

The old man breathed a sigh of relief; four hours of courtly ceremony had wearied him, and he had been in constant terror lest something should call into use the ten thousand additional bamboos.

In another minute they were crossing a large quadrangle, paved with marble, and tastefully decorated with a pigsty in each corner. Soldiers, carrying pigs, were marching in all directions: and in the middle stood a gigantic officer giving orders in a voice of thunder, which made itself heard above all the uproar of the pigs.

i

Problem 1. Place twenty-four pigs in four sties so that, as you go round and round, you may always find the number in each sty nearer to ten than the number in the last.

Answer. Place 8 pigs in the first sty, 10 in the second, nothing in the third, and 6 in the fourth: 10 is nearer ten than 8; nothing is nearer ten than 10; 6 is nearer ten than nothing; and 8 is nearer ten than 6.

This problem is noticed by only two correspondents. BALBUS says 'it certainly cannot be solved mathematically, nor do I see how to solve it by any verbal quibble.' NOLENS VOLENS makes Her Radiancy change the direction of going round; and even then is obliged to add 'the pigs must be carried in front of her'!

ii

Problem 2. Omnibuses start from a certain point, both ways, every 15 minutes. A traveller, starting on foot along with one of them, meets one in $12\frac{1}{2}$ minutes: when will he be overtaken by one?

Answer. In $6\frac{1}{4}$ minutes.

Solution. Let 'a' be the distance an omnibus goes in 15 minutes, and 'x' the distance from the starting-point to where the traveller is overtaken. Since the omnibus met is due at the starting-point in $2\frac{1}{2}$ minutes, it goes in that time as far as the traveller walks in $12\frac{1}{2}$; *i.e.* it goes 5 times as fast. Now the overtaking omnibus is 'a' behind the traveller when he starts, and therefore goes '$a+x$' while he goes 'x'. Hence $a+x=5x$; *i.e.* $4x=a$, and $x=\frac{a}{4}$. This distance would be traversed by an omnibus in $\frac{15}{4}$ minutes, and therefore by the traveller in $5\times\frac{15}{4}$. Hence he is overtaken in $18\frac{3}{4}$ minutes after starting, *i.e.* in $6\frac{1}{4}$ minutes after meeting the omnibus.

Four answers have been received, of which two are wrong. DINAH MITE rightly states that the overtaking omnibus reached the point where they met the other omnibus 5 minutes after they left, but wrongly concludes that, going 5 times as fast, it would overtake them in another minute. The travellers are 5-minutes-walk ahead of the omnibus, and must walk 1-4th of this distance farther before the omnibus overtakes them, which will be 1-5th of the distance traversed by the omnibus in the same time: this will require $1\frac{1}{4}$ minutes more. NOLENS VOLENS tries it by a process like 'Achilles and the Tortoise'. He rightly states that, when the overtaking omnibus leaves the gate, the travellers are 1-5th of *'a'* ahead, and that it will take the omnibus 3 minutes to traverse this distance; 'during which time' the travellers, he tells us, go 1-15th of *'a'* (this should be 1-25th). The travellers being now 1-15th of *'a'* ahead, he concludes that the work remaining to be done is for the travellers to go 1-60th of *'a'*, while the omnibus goes 1-12th. The *principle* is correct, and might have been applied earlier.

Knot nine: 'A serpent with corners'

i

'Didn't Balbus say this morning that, if a body is immersed in liquid, it displaces as much liquid as is equal to its own bulk?' said Hugh.

'He said things of that sort,' Lambert vaguely replied.

'Well, just look here a minute. Here's the little bucket almost quite immersed: so the water displaced ought to be just about the same bulk. And now just look at it!' He took out the little bucket as he spoke, and handed the big one to Lambert. 'Why, there's hardly a teacupful! Do you mean to say *that* water is the same bulk as the little bucket?'

'Course it is,' said Lambert.

'Well, look here again!' cried Hugh, triumphantly, as he poured the water from the big bucket into the little one. 'Why, it doesn't half fill it!'

'That's *its* business,' said Lambert. 'If Balbus says it's the same bulk, why, it *is* the same bulk, you know.'

'Well, I don't believe it,' said Hugh.

Problem 1. Lardner states that a solid, immersed in a fluid, displaces an amount equal to itself in bulk. How can this be true of a small bucket floating in a larger one?

Solution. Lardner means, by 'displaces', 'occupies a space which might be filled with water without any change in the surroundings.' If the portion of the floating bucket, which is above the water, could be annihilated, and the rest of it transformed into water, the surrounding water would not change its position: which agrees with Lardner's statement.

Five answers have been received, none of which explains the difficulty arising from the well-known fact that a floating body is the same weight as the displaced fluid. HECLA says that 'only that portion of the smaller bucket which descends below the original level of the water can be properly said to be immersed, and only an equal bulk of water is displaced.' Hence, according to HECLA, a solid, whose weight was equal to that of an equal bulk of water, would not float till the whole of it was below 'the original level' of the water: but, as a matter of fact, it would float as soon as it was all under water. MAGPIE says the fallacy is 'the assumption that one body can displace another from a place where it isn't,' and that Lardner's assertion is incorrect, except when the containing vessel 'was originally full to the brim.' But the question of floating depends on the present state of things, not on past history. OLD KING COLE takes the same view as HECLA. TYMPANUM and VINDEX assume that 'displaced' means 'raised above its original level,' and merely explain how it comes to pass that the water, so raised, is less in bulk than the immersed portion of bucket, and thus land themselves – or rather set themselves floating – in the same boat as HECLA.

ii

'A friend of mine has a flower-garden – a very pretty one, though no great size—'

'How big is it?' said Hugh.

'That's what *you* have to find out!' Balbus gaily replied. 'All *I* tell you is that it is oblong in shape – just half a yard longer than its width – and that a gravel-walk, one yard wide, begins at one corner and runs all around it.'

'Joining into itself?' said Hugh.

'*Not* joining into itself, young man. Just before doing *that*, it turns a corner, and runs round the garden again, alongside of the first portion, and then inside that again, winding in and in, and each lap touching the last one, till it has used up the whole of the area.'

'Like a serpent with corners?' said Lambert.

'Exactly so.'

Problem 2. An oblong garden, half a yard longer than wide, consists entirely of a gravel-walk, spirally arranged, a yard wide and 3,630 yards long. Find the dimensions of the garden.

Answer. 60, $60\frac{1}{2}$.

Solution. The number of yards and fractions of a yard traversed in walking along a straight piece of walk, is evidently the same as the number of square-yards and fractions of a square-yard, contained in that piece of walk: and the distance, traversed in passing through a square-yard at a corner, is evidently a yard. Hence the area of the garden is 3,630 square-yards: *i.e.*, if x be the width, $x(x+\frac{1}{2})=3,630$. Solving this Quadratic, we find $x=60$. Hence the dimensions are 60, $60\frac{1}{2}$.

TYMPANUM says that, by extracting the square-root of 3,630, we get 60 yards with a remainder of $\frac{30}{60}$, or half-a-yard, which we add so as to make the oblong $60\times60\frac{1}{2}$. This is very terrible: but worse remains behind. TYMPANUM proceeds thus: 'But why should there be the half-yard at all? Because without it there would be no space at all for flowers. By means of it, we find reserved in the very centre a small plot of ground, two yards long by half-a-yard wide, the only space not occupied by walk.' But Balbus expressly said that the walk 'used up the whole of the area.' Oh, TYMPANUM! My tympa is exhausted: my brain is num! I can say no more.

Knot nine: 'A serpent with corners'

iii

'To fix our thoughts,' he murmured to himself, as, with hands deep-buried in his pockets, he paced up and down the room, 'we will take a cylindrical glass jar, with a scale of inches marked up the side, and fill it with water up to the 10-inch mark: and we will assume that every inch depth of jar contains a pint of water. We will now take a solid cylinder, such that every inch of it is equal in bulk to *half* a pint of water, and plunge 4 inches of it into the water, so that the end of the cylinder comes down to the 6-inch mark. Well, that displaces 2 pints of water. What becomes of them? Why, if there were no more cylinder, they would lie comfortably on the top, and fill the jar up to the 12-inch mark. But unfortunately there *is* more cylinder, occupying half the space between the 10-inch and the 12-inch marks, so that only *one* pint of water can be accommodated there. What becomes of the other pint? Why, if there were no more cylinder, it would lie on the top, and fill the jar up to the 13-inch mark. But unfortunately – Shade of Newton!' he exclaimed, in sudden accents of terror. 'When *does* the water stop rising?'

Problem 3. Balbus states that if a certain solid be immersed in a certain vessel of water, the water will rise through a series of distances, two inches, one inch, half an inch, &c., which series has no end. He concludes that the water will rise without limit. Is this true?

Solution. No. This series can never reach 4 inches, since, however many terms we take, we are always short of 4 inches by an amount equal to the last term taken.

Three answers have been received – but only two seem to me worthy of honours.

TYMPANUM says that the statement about the stick 'is merely a blind, to which the old answer may well be applied, *solvitur ambulando,* or rather *mergendo.*' I trust TYMPANUM will not test this in his own person, by taking the place of the man in Balbus' Essay! He would infallibly be drowned.

OLD KING COLE rightly points out that the series, 2, 1, &c., is a decreasing Geometrical Progression: while VINDEX rightly identifies the fallacy as that of 'Achilles and the Tortoise'.

Knot ten: 'Chelsea buns'

'Did you notice that very old one, with a red face, who was drawing a map in the dust with his wooden leg, and all the others watching? I *think* it was a plan of battle—'

'The battle of Trafalgar, no doubt,' her aunt interrupted, briskly.

'Hardly that, I think,' Clara ventured to say. 'You see, in that case, he couldn't well be alive—'

'Couldn't well be alive!' the old lady contemptuously repeated. 'He's as lively as you and me put together! Why, if drawing a map in the dust – with one's wooden leg – doesn't prove one to be alive, perhaps you'll kindly mention what *does* prove it!'

Clara did not see her way out of it. Logic had never been her *forte*.

Problem 1. If 70 per cent. have lost an eye, 75 per cent. an ear, 80 per cent. an arm, 85 per cent. a leg: what percentage, *at least*, must have lost all four?

Answer. Ten.

Solution. (I adopt that of POLAR STAR, as being better than my own). Adding the wounds together, we get $70 + 75 + 80 + 85 = 310$, among 100 men; which gives 3 to each, and 4 to 10 men. Therefore the least percentage is 10.

DELTA makes some most amazing assumptions: 'let every one who has not lost an eye have lost an ear,' 'let every one who has not lost both eyes and ears have lost an arm.' Her ideas of a battle-field are grim indeed. Fancy a warrior who would continue fighting after losing both eyes, both ears, and both arms! This is a case which she (or 'it?') evidently considers *possible*.

Next come eight writers who have made the unwarrantable assumption that, because 70 per cent. have lost an eye, *therefore* 30 per cent. have *not* lost one, so that they have *both* eyes. This is illogical. If you give me a bag containing 100 sovereigns, and if in an hour I come to you (my face *not* beaming with gratitude nearly so much as when I received the bag) to say 'I am sorry to tell you that 70 of these sovereigns are bad,' do I thereby guarantee the other 30 to be good? Perhaps I have not tested them yet. The sides of this illogical octagon are as follows, in alphabetical order:– ALGERNON BRAY, DINAH MITE, G. S. C., JANE E., J. D. W., MAGPIE (who makes the delightful remark 'therefore 90 per cent. have two of something,' recalling to one's memory that fortunate monarch, with whom Xerxes was so much pleased that 'he gave him ten of everything!'), S. S. G., and TOKIO.

'Sister, daughter, sons – and Balbus—,' the old man began, so nervously, that Balbus put in a gentle 'Hear, hear!' while Hugh drummed on the table with his fists. This disconcerted the unpractised orator. 'Sister—' he began again, then paused a moment, moved the bag to the other side, and went on with a rush, 'I mean – this being – a critical occasion – more or less – being the year when one of my sons comes of age—' he paused again in some confusion, having evidently got into the middle of his speech sooner than he intended: but it was too late to go back. 'Hear, hear!' cried Balbus. 'Quite so,' said the old gentleman, recovering his self-possession a little: 'when first I began this annual custom – my friend Balbus will correct me if I am wrong—' (Hugh whispered 'with a strap!' but nobody heard him except Lambert, who only frowned and shook his head at him) '—this annual custom of giving each of my sons as many guineas as would represent his age – it was a critical time – so Balbus informed me – as the ages of two of you were together equal to that of the third – so on that occasion I made a speech—' He paused so long that Balbus thought it well to come to the rescue with the words 'It was a most—' but the old man checked him with a warning look: 'yes, made a speech,' he repeated. 'A few years after that, Balbus pointed out – I say pointed out—' ('Hear, Hear'! cried Balbus. 'Quite so,' said the grateful old man.) '—that it was *another* critical occasion. The ages of two of you were together *double* that of the third. So I made another speech – another speech. And now again it's a critical occasion – so Balbus says – and I am making—' (Here Mad Mathesis pointedly referred to her watch) 'all the haste I can!' the old man cried, with wonderful presence of mind. 'Indeed, sister, I'm coming to the point now! The number of years that have passed since that first occasion is just two-thirds of the number of guineas I then gave you. Now, my boys, calculate your ages from the *data*, and you shall have the money!'

'But we *know* our ages!' cried Hugh.

'Silence, sir!' thundered the old man, rising to his full height (he was exactly five-foot five) in his indignation. 'I say you must use the *data* only! You mustn't even assume *which* it is that comes of age!'

Problem 2. At first, two of the ages are together equal to the third. A few years afterwards, two of them are together double of the third. When the number of years since the first occasion is two-thirds of the sum of the ages on that occasion, one age is 21. What are the other two?

Answer. 15 and 18.

Solution. Let the ages at first be x, y, $(x+y)$. Now, if $a+b=2c$, then $(a-n)+(b-n)=2(c-n)$, whatever be the value of n. Hence the second relationship, if *ever* true, was *always* true. Hence it was true at first. But it cannot be true that x and y are together double of $(x+y)$. Hence it must be true of $(x+y)$, together with x or y; and it does not matter which we take. We assume, then, $(x+y)+x=2y$; *i.e.* $y=2x$. Hence the three ages were, at first, x, $2x$, $3x$; and the number of years, since that time is two-thirds of $6x$, *i.e.* is $4x$. Hence the present ages are $5x$, $6x$, $7x$. The ages are clearly *integers*, since this is only 'the year when one of my sons comes of age.' Hence $7x=21$, $x=3$, and the other ages are 15, 18.

Among those who have earned the highest honours, ALGERNON BRAY solves the problem quite correctly, but adds that there is nothing to exclude the supposition that all the ages were *fractional*. This would make the number of answers infinite. Let me meekly protest that I *never* intended my readers to devote the rest of their lives to writing out answers! E. M. RIX points out that, if fractional ages be admissible, any one of the three sons might be the one 'come of age'; but she rightly rejects this supposition on the ground that it would make the problem indeterminate. WHITE SUGAR is the only one who has detected an oversight of mine: I had forgotten the possibility (which of course ought to be allowed for) that the son, who came of age that *year*, need not have done so by that *day*, so that he *might* be only 20. This gives a second solution, viz., 20, 24, 28. Well said, pure Crystal! Verily, thy 'fair discourse hath been as sugar'!

I take this opportunity of thanking those who have sent, along with their answers to the Tenth Knot, regrets that there are no more Knots to come, or petitions that I should recall my resolution to bring them to an end. I am most grateful for their kind words; but I think it wisest to end what, at best, was but a lame attempt. 'The stretched metre of an antique song' is beyond my compass; and my puppets were neither distinctly *in* my life (like those I now address), nor yet (like Alice and the Mock Turtle) distinctly *out* of it. Yet let me at least fancy, as I lay down the pen, that I carry with me into my silent life, dear reader, a farewell smile from your unseen face, and a kindly farewell pressure from your unfelt hand! And so, good night! Parting is such sweet sorrow, that I shall say 'good night!' till it be morrow.

The Game of Logic

'I know what you're thinking about,' said Tweedledum; 'but it isn't so, nohow.'
    'Contrariwise,' continued Tweedledee, 'if it was so, it might be; and if it were so, it would be; but as it isn't, it ain't. That's logic.'

Through the Looking-Glass

The Game of Logic, first published privately by Carroll in 1886, was his attempt to sweeten the pill of formal deductive logic for a kindergarten audience: in his own words, 'besides being an endless source of amusement (the number of arguments, that may be worked by it, being infinite), it will give the Players a little instruction as well. But is there any great harm in *that*, so long as you get plenty of amusement?' That the game as a game for children is a failure was best shown by author Marghanita Laski, who, in putting it through its paces with her own children to provide a consumer report for her friend Derek Hudson's study of Carroll, had to admit frankly that 'after page thirteen there was no pretending that this was a game for children any more – at least, Mr.

Carroll could go on pretending, but we couldn't. . . . I think – I hope – that the other seventy-five pages of the book were meant for post-graduate university students, for I gave them up when my children did.' But if the Swiss mathematician Leonhard Euler, who first introduced the scheme developed by Carroll in 1761, would himself have been amazed at Carroll's attempts to spread his doctrine at nursery level, neither he nor Laski could deny that the examples Carroll devised to test the method were often quaint, tantalising and bitter sweet in the best Wonderland manner, making the game at least a pleasant diversion even for the post-graduate in logic who would have found no great technical originality in what Carroll had to say.

The specific object of the game itself was to deduce a conclusion from a pair of premises which shared one attribute or 'middle term'. Initially included with the book was an envelope containing a board on which were printed the two grids reproduced opposite, plus four red counters (to specify 'yes') and five grey (to specify 'no'):

See, the Sun is overhead,
Shining on us, FULL and

RED !

Now the Sun is gone away,
And the EMPTY sky is

GREY!

The purpose of the top diagram was to illustrate the conditions of the two stated premises, while the one at the bottom of the page was used to deduce the subsequent conclusion. In only a fraction of the space

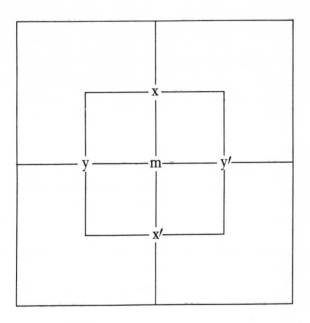

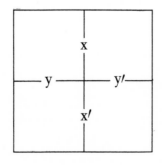

Carroll allowed himself, there is only one way in which to convey the practical gist of his instructions and that is to guide the reader through the workings of some typical examples, clearing appropriate hurdles along the way. Carroll described the top diagram as his 'Universe of Things', capable as it was of expressing all three attributes and their opposites as contained or implied in the premises.

Given, for example, the pair:

> Some new cakes are unwholesome
> No nice cakes are unwholesome

one must first find one's middle term, in this case 'wholesome' – expressed by m; its negative, 'unwholesome', by m'. Sometimes the middle term will be expressed positively in one premise, negatively in the other. The other two attributes are then assigned letters: so 'new' = x; 'nice' = y. In the grid everything inside the smaller middle square is taken for m or 'wholesome', everything outside m' or 'unwholesome'; everything inside the left vertical rectangle y or 'nice', everything in the right vertical rectangle y' or 'not nice'; everything inside the top horizontal rectangle x or 'new', everything in the lower horizontal rectangle x' or 'not new'.

In laying out counters for any one problem one gives priority to negative premises – the ones beginning with 'no' – 'because *grey* counters can always be placed with *certainty*, and will then help to fix the position of the red counters, which are sometimes a little uncertain where they will be most welcome'. To express: 'No nice cakes are unwholesome' or 'no y cakes are m' cakes', one has to indicate that none of the cakes belonging to the 'y' half of the 'Universe of Cakes' belong to the m' compartments. Hence 1 and 7 are 'empty' and one places a *grey* counter in each:

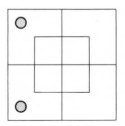

To express: 'Some new cakes are unwholesome' or 'some x cakes are m'
cakes', one has to indicate that some of the cakes in the top rectangle
also belong to the m' compartments. Thereone *one* of the two compartments 1 and 2 is occupied. No. 1 compartment we already know to be
empty; therefore a red counter must be placed in 2.

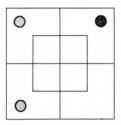

Had 1 been unoccupied one would have laid a counter along the line
dividing the two compartments.

Having laid out the premises one now transfers this information to
the smaller diagram in order to get a conclusion involving x and y and,
since it will not figure in the conclusion, omitting m.
Square 9 comprises 1 and 3 on the earlier diagram. We
know that the outer part, 1, is empty, but nothing about
the inner compartment 3. The square *may* have something
in it, but one cannot tell. So one must *not* place a counter

9	10
11	12

in 9. The same goes for compartment 11. 10 is more certain. We know
there is something in its outer portion 2. This is all one need know to
occupy 10 with a red counter. As for 12 we have no information at all,
so this must be left unoccupied. The result:

must therefore lead to the conclusion that some x are y', namely that
some new cakes are not-nice. One can now write out the completed
syllogism:

> Some new Cakes are unwholesome; ⎱
> No nice Cakes are unwholesome.   ⎰
> ∴. Some new Cakes are not-nice.

Before proceeding to a more complicated example, some further basic information should be absorbed. In expressing a 'Universal Proposition' – one beginning with 'all' – one has first to break it down to two propositions; and so 'All new cakes are nice' becomes 'Some new cakes are nice' and 'No new cakes are not-nice.'

If we take Carroll's second example:

> All Dragons are uncanny;
> All Scotchmen are canny.

'canny' now becomes the middle term, m, in a 'Universe of Animals'; x will stand for 'Dragons'; and y for 'Scotchmen'. Since both premises are universal, one must break them both down as follows:

> Some Dragons are uncanny
> No Dragons are canny
> Some Scotchmen are canny
> No Scotchmen are uncanny

or

> Some x are m'
> No x are m
> Some y are m
> No y are m'

Again the negatives must be dealt with first. 'No x are m' means that compartments 3 and 4 are empty:

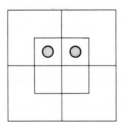

'No y are m'' means that 1 and 7 are empty:

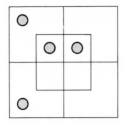

'Some x are m'' gives:

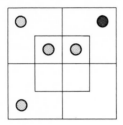

'Some y are m' gives the final result:

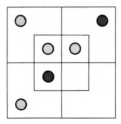

And now to transfer this information to the smaller diagram. One can see that 9 is completely empty and can therefore be marked with a grey counter; 10 is occupied, so can be marked with a red; likewise 11. Since there is no information for 12, one must leave it blank.

It is now easy to read off the final conclusions, namely that

> No x are y
> Some x are y'
> Some y are x'

from which it is possible to deduce two final universal conclusions, namely that 'All x are y' ' and 'All y are x' '. And so to the final syllogism:

> All Dragons are uncanny;⎱
> All Scotchmen are canny.⎰
> ∴ ⎰All Dragons are not-Scotchmen;
>   ⎱All Scotchmen are not-Dragons.

Remember, I don't guarantee the Premises to be *facts*. In the first place, I never even saw a Dragon: and, in the second place, it isn't of the slightest consequence to us, as *Logicians*, whether our Premises are true or false: all *we* have to do is to make out whether they *lead logically to the Conclusion*, so that, if *they* were true, *it* would be true also.

The examples and solutions which follow are taken from the chapters of the book entitled 'Cross Questions' and 'Crooked Answers' respectively.

CROSS QUESTIONS

1. No exciting books suit feverish patients;⎱
   Unexciting books make one drowsy.   ⎰

2. Some, who deserve the fair, get their deserts;⎱
   None but the brave deserve the fair.   ⎰

3. No children are patient;   ⎱
   No impatient person can sit still.⎰

4. All pigs are fat;   ⎱
   No skeletons are fat.⎰

5. No monkeys are soldiers;   ⎱
   All monkeys are mischievous.⎰

6. None of my cousins are just;⎱
   No judges are unjust. ⎰

7. All medicine is nasty;⎱
   Senna is a medicine. ⎰

8. Some Jews are rich; ⎱
   All Patagonians are Gentiles.⎰

9. All teetotalers like sugar; ⎱
   No nightingale drinks wine.⎰

10. No muffins are wholesome;⎱
    All buns are unwholesome. ⎰

11. Sugar is sweet; ⎱
    Salt is not sweet.⎰

12. Some eggs are hard-boiled;⎱
    No eggs are uncrackable. ⎰

CROOKED ANSWERS

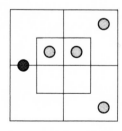 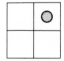

1. Let 'books' be Universe; m = 'exciting',
   x = 'that suit feverish patients'; y = 'that make one drowsy'.

   No m are x; ⎱
   All m' are y.⎰ ∴ No y' are x.

   i.e. No books suit feverish patients, except such as make one drowsy.

171

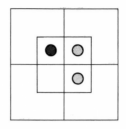

2. Let 'persons' be Universe; m='that deserve the fair';
   x='that get their deserts'; y='brave'.

   Some m are x;
   No y' are m. $\left.\right\}$ ∴ Some y are x.

                                    i.e. Some brave persons get their deserts.

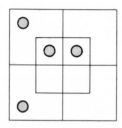
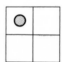

3. Let 'persons' be Universe; m='patient';
   x='children'; y='that can sit still'.

   No x are m;
   No m' are y. $\left.\right\}$ ∴ No x are y.   i.e. No children can sit still.

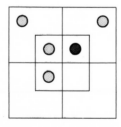

4. Let 'things' be Universe; m='fat'; x='pigs';
   y='skeletons'.

   All x are m;
   No y are m. $\left.\right\}$ ∴ All x are y' i.e. All pigs are not-skeletons.

172

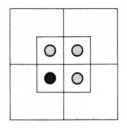
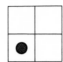

5. Let 'creatures' be Universe; m = 'monkeys';
    x = 'soldiers'; y = 'mischievous'.

> No m are x;⎫
> All m are y.⎭ ∴ Some y are x'.

> > i.e. Some mischievous creatures are not soldiers.

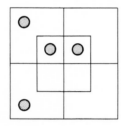

6. Let 'persons' be Universe; m = 'just';
    x = 'my cousins'; y = 'judges'.

> No x are m;⎫
> No y are m'.⎭ ∴ No x are y.   i.e. None of my cousins are judges.

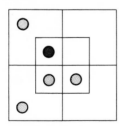
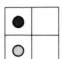

7. Let 'things' be Universe; m = 'medicine';
    x = 'nasty'; y = 'senna'.

> All m are x;⎫
> All y are m.⎭ ∴ All y are x.   i.e. Senna is nasty.

173

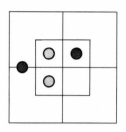

8. Let 'persons' be Universe; $m=$ 'Jews';
   $x=$ 'rich'; $y=$ 'Patagonians'.

   Some m are x;⎫
   All y are m'. ⎬ ∴ Some x are y'.

   i.e. Some rich persons are not Patagonians.

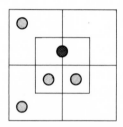

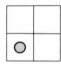

9. Let 'creatures' be Universe; $m=$ 'teetotalers';
   $x=$ 'that like sugar'; $y=$ 'nightingales'.

   All m are x;⎫
   No y are m'.⎬ ∴ No y are x'.   i.e. No nightingales dislike sugar.

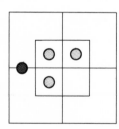

10. Let 'food' be Universe; $m=$ 'wholesome';
    $x=$ 'muffins'; $y=$ 'buns'.

    No x are m;⎫   There is 'no information' for the smaller Diagram;
    All y are m.⎬   so no Conclusion can be drawn.

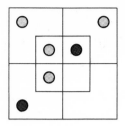

11. Let 'food' be Universe; m = 'sweet';
    x = 'sugar'; y = 'salt'.

$$\left.\begin{array}{l}\text{All } x \text{ are } m; \\ \text{All } y \text{ are } m' \end{array}\right\} \quad \therefore \quad \left\{\begin{array}{l}\text{All } x \text{ are } y'. \\ \text{All } y \text{ are } x' \end{array}\right. \quad \text{i.e.} \quad \left\{\begin{array}{l}\text{Sugar is not salt.} \\ \text{Salt is not sugar.} \end{array}\right.$$

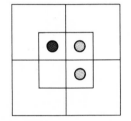
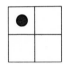

12. Let 'Things' be Universe; m = 'eggs';
    x = 'hard-boiled'; y = 'crackable'.

$$\left.\begin{array}{l}\text{Some } m \text{ are } x; \\ \text{No } m \text{ are } y'. \end{array}\right\} \quad \therefore \text{ Some } x \text{ are } y.$$

i.e. Some hard-boiled things can be cracked.

Ten years later Carroll developed the theme at length for a more adult readership in his *Symbolic Logic: Part 1, Elementary*, his last book to appear in his own lifetime. The more serious approach, far from frightening off readers, sent the work to four editions in a year. But Carroll was torn. He still considered logic a game and, significantly, *Symbolic Logic*, like *The Game of Logic*, appeared under the authorship of Lewis Carroll, not C. L. Dogdson. One has, therefore, no reservations in skimming the cream of its still playful problems without attempting an explanation of Carroll's involved and expanded methods. Certainly those who had grasped the methods of the earlier work would have been well rewarded by going straight to the examples in the new volume, even more whimsical than before and including up to ten premises all craving a final conclusion. It is enough for us to know that even these can be solved on the smaller diagrams by taking any pair of premises from the series with a middle term and drawing a conclusion from them; this result is then combined with another premise from the series with a term in common to produce another conclusion. The process continues until there are only two premises left. These will themselves yield the final desired conclusion. Whichever two premises are taken first, the chain (or Sorites, to give it its technical term) will always lead to the same result! The problems become even more fun, if more demanding, if we cover up Carroll's hints and disentangle the universal and middle terms and various other attributes for ourselves.

1.

1. There are no pencils of mine in this box;
2. No sugar-plums of mine are cigars;
3. The whole of my property, that is not in this box, consists of cigars.
   Univ. 'things of mine'; $a=$cigars; $b=$in this box; $c=$pencils; $d=$ sugar-plums.

2.

1. No one takes in *The Times*, unless he is well-educated;
2. No hedge-hogs can read;
3. Those who cannot read are not well-educated.
   Univ. 'creatures'; $a=$able to read; $b=$hedge-hogs; $c=$taking in *The Times*; $d=$well-educated.

3.

1. All members of the House of Commons have perfect self-command;
2. No M.P., who wears a coronet, should ride in a donkey-race;
3. All members of the House of Lords wear coronets.
   Univ. 'M.P.'s'; $a=$belonging to the House of Commons; $b=$having perfect self-command; $c=$one who may ride in a donkey-race; $d=$ wearing a coronet.

4.

1. No acrobatic feats, that are not announced in the bills of a circus, are ever attempted there;
2. No acrobatic feat is possible, if it involves turning a quadruple somersault;
3. No impossible acrobatic feat is ever announced in a circus bill.
   Univ. 'acrobatic feats'; a = announced in the bills of a circus; b = attempted in a circus; c = involving the turning of a quadruple somersault; d = possible.

5.

1. Nobody, who really appreciates Beethoven, fails to keep silence while the Moonlight-Sonata is being played;
2. Guinea-pigs are hopelessly ignorant of music;
3. No one, who is hopelessly ignorant of music, ever keeps silence while the Moonlight-Sonata is being played.
   Univ. 'creatures'; a = guinea-pigs; b = hopelessly ignorant of music; c = keeping silence while the Moonlight-Sonata is being played; d = really appreciating Beethoven.

6.

1. No birds, except ostriches, are 9 feet high;
2. There are no birds in this aviary that belong to any one but *me*;
3. No ostrich lives on mince-pies;
4. I have no birds less than 9 feet high.
   Univ. 'birds'; a = in this aviary; b = living on mince-pies; c = my; d = 9 feet high; e = ostriches.

7.

1. A plum-pudding, that is not really solid, is mere porridge;
2. Every plum-pudding, served at my table, has been boiled in a cloth;
3. A plum-pudding that is mere porridge is indistinguishable from soup;
4. No plum-puddings are really solid, except what are served at *my* table.
   Univ. 'plum-puddings'; a = boiled in a cloth; b = distinguishable from soup; c = mere porridge; d = really solid; e = served at my table.

8.

1. No interesting poems are unpopular among people of real taste;
2. No modern poetry is free from affectation;
3. All *your* poems are on the subject of soap-bubbles;
4. No affected poetry is popular among people of real taste;
5. No ancient poem is on the subject of soap-bubbles.
   Univ. 'poems'; a = affected; b = ancient; c = interesting; d = on the subject of soap-bubbles; e = popular among people of real taste; h = written by you.

9.

1. I despise anything that cannot be used as a bridge;
2. Everything, that is worth writing an ode to, would be a welcome gift to me;
3. A rainbow will not bear the weight of a wheel-barrow;
4. Whatever can be used as a bridge will bear the weight of a wheel-barrow;
5. I would not take, as a gift, a thing that I despise.
   Univ. 'things'; a = able to bear the weight of a wheel-barrow; b = acceptable to me; c = despised by me; d = rainbows; e = useful as a bridge; h = worth writing an ode to.

10.

1. Everything, not absolutely ugly, may be kept in a drawing-room;
2. Nothing, that is encrusted with salt, is ever quite dry;
3. Nothing should be kept in a drawing-room, unless it is free from damp;
4. Bathing-machines are always kept near the sea;
5. Nothing, that is made of mother-of-pearl, can be absolutely ugly;
6. Whatever is kept near the sea gets encrusted with salt.
   Univ. 'things'; a = absolutely ugly; b = bathing-machines; c = encrusted with salt; d = kept near the sea; e = made of mother-of-pearl; h = quite dry; k = things that may be kept in a drawing-room.

11.

1. I call no day 'unlucky', when Robinson is civil to me;
2. Wednesdays are always cloudy;
3. When people take umbrellas, the day never turns out fine;
4. The only days when Robinson is uncivil to me are Wednesdays;
5. Everybody takes his umbrella with him when it is raining;
6. My 'lucky' days always turn out fine.
   Univ. 'days'; a = called by me 'lucky'; b = cloudy; c = days when people take umbrellas; d = days when Robinson is civil to me; e = rainy; h = turning out fine; k = Wednesdays.

12.

1. No shark ever doubts that it is well fitted out;
2. A fish, that cannot dance a minuet, is contemptible;
3. No fish is quite certain that it is well fitted out, unless it has three rows of teeth;
4. All fishes, except sharks, are kind to children.
5. No heavy fish can dance a minuet;
6. A fish with three rows of teeth is not to be despised.
   Univ. 'fishes'; a = able to dance a minuet; b = certain that he is well fitted out; c = contemptible; d = having 3 rows of teeth; e = heavy; h = kind to children; k = sharks.

13.

1. All the human race, except my footmen, have a certain amount of common-sense;
2. No one, who lives on barley-sugar, can be anything but a mere baby;
3. None but a hop-scotch player knows what real happiness is;
4. No mere baby has a grain of common sense;
5. No engine-driver ever plays hop-scotch;
6. No footman of mine is ignorant of what true happiness is.
   Univ. 'human beings'; a=engine-drivers; b=having common sense; c=hop-scotch players; d=knowing what real happiness is; e=living on barley-sugar; h=mere babies; k=my footmen.

14.

1. Animals are always mortally offended if I fail to notice them;
2. The only animals that belong to *me* are in that field;
3. No animal can guess a conundrum, unless it has been properly trained in a Board-School;
4. None of the animals in that field are badgers;
5. When an animal is mortally offended, it always rushes about wildly and howls;
6. I never notice any animal, unless it belongs to me;
7. No animal, that has been properly trained in a Board-School, ever rushes about wildly and howls.
   Univ. 'animals'; a=able to guess a conundrum; b=badgers; c=in that field; d=mortally offended if I fail to notice them; e=my; h=noticed by me; k=properly trained in a Board-School; l=rushing about wildly and howling.

15.

1. I never put a cheque, received by me, on that file, unless I am anxious about it;
2. All the cheques received by me, that are not marked with a cross, are payable to bearer;
3. None of them are ever brought back to me, unless they have been dishonoured at the Bank;
4. All of them, that are marked with a cross, are for amounts of over £100;
5. All of them, that are not on that file, are marked 'not negotiable';
6. No cheque of yours, received by me, has ever been dishonoured;
7. I am never anxious about a cheque, received by me, unless it should happen to be brought back to me;
8. None of the cheques received by me, that are marked 'not negotiable,' are for amounts of over £100.
   Univ. 'cheques received by me'; a=brought back to me; b=cheques that I am anxious about; c=honoured; d=marked with a cross; e=marked 'not negotiable'; h=on that file; k=over £100; l=payable to bearer; m=your.

16.

1. All the dated letters in this room are written on blue paper;
2. None of them are in black ink, except those that are written in the third person;
3. I have not filed any of them that I can read;
4. None of them, that are written on one sheet, are undated;
5. All of them, that are not crossed, are in black ink;
6. All of them, written by Brown, begin with 'Dear Sir';
7. All of them, written on blue paper, are filed;
8. None of them, written on more than one sheet, are crossed;
9. None of them, that begin with 'Dear Sir,' are written in the third person.
    Univ. 'letters in this room'; a = beginning with 'Dear Sir'; b = crossed; c = dated; d = filed; e = in black ink; h = in third person; k = letters that I can read; l = on blue paper; m = on one sheet; n = written by Brown.

17.

1. The only animals in this house are cats;
2. Every animal is suitable for a pet, that loves to gaze at the moon;
3. When I detest an animal, I avoid it;
4. No animals are carnivorous, unless they prowl at night;
5. No cat fails to kill mice;
6. No animals ever take to me, except what are in this house;
7. Kangaroos are not suitable for pets;
8. None but carnivora kill mice;
9. I detest animals that do not take to me;
10. Animals, that prowl at night, always love to gaze at the moon.
    Univ. 'animals'; a = avoided by me; b = carnivora; c = cats; d = detested by me; e = in this house; h = kangaroos; k = killing mice; l = loving to gaze at the moon; m = prowling at night; n = suitable for pets; r = taking to me.

ANSWERS:

1. No pencils of mine are sugar-plums.
2. No hedge-hog takes in *The Times*.
3. No M.P. should ride in a donkey-race, unless he has perfect self-command.
4. No acrobatic feat, which involves turning a quadruple somersault, is ever attempted in a circus.
5. Guinea-pigs never really appreciate Beethoven.
6. No bird in this aviary lives on mince-pies.
7. No plum-pudding, that has not been boiled in a cloth, can be distinguished from soup.

8. All *your* poems are uninteresting.
9. Rainbows are not worth writing odes to.
10. Bathing-machines are never made of mother-of-pearl.
11. Rainy days are always cloudy.
12. No heavy fish is unkind to children.
13. No engine-driver lives on barley-sugar.
14. No badger can guess a conundrum.
15. No cheque of yours, received by me, is payable to order.
16. I cannot read any of Brown's letters.
17. I always avoid a kangaroo.

A day for any date

'Which reminds me—' the White Queen said, looking down and nervously clasping and unclasping her hands, 'we had *such* a thunder-storm last Tuesday – I mean one of the last set of Tuesdays, you know.'

Alice was puzzled. 'In *our* country,' she remarked, 'there's only one day at a time.'

Through the Looking-Glass

Carroll entered his discovery of a rule for finding the day of the week for any given date in his diary on March 8, 1887 and published it three weeks later on March 31 in the magazine *Nature*:

Having hit upon the following method of mentally computing the day of the week for any given date, I send it you in the hope that it may interest some of your readers. I am not a rapid computer myself, and as I find my average time for doing any such question is about 20 seconds, I have little doubt that a rapid computer would not need 15.

Take the given date in 4 portions, viz. the number of centuries, the number of years over, the month, the day of the month.

Compute the following 4 items, adding each, when found, to the total of the previous items. When an item or total exceeds 7, divide by 7, and keep the remainder only.

The Century-Item.—For Old Style (which ended September 2, 1752) subtract from 18. For New Style (which began September 14) divide by 4, take overplus from 3, multiply remainder by 2.

The Year-Item.—Add together the number of dozens, the overplus, and the number of 4s in the overplus.

The Month-Item.—If it begins or ends with a vowel, subtract the number, denoting its place in the year, from 10. This, plus its number of days, gives the item for the following month. The item for January is '0'; for February or March (the 3rd month), '3'; for December (the 12th month), '12'.

The Day-Item is the day of the month.

The total, thus reached, must be corrected, by deducting '1' (first adding 7, if the total be '0'), if the date be January or February in a Leap Year: remembering that every year, divisible by 4, is a Leap Year, excepting only the century-years, in New Style, when the number of centuries is *not* so divisible (*e.g.* 1800).

The final result gives the day of the week, '0' meaning Sunday, '1' Monday, and so on.

EXAMPLES

1783, September 18

17, divided by 4, leaves '1' over; 1 from 3 gives '2'; twice 2 is '4'.

83 is 6 dozen and 11, giving 17; plus 2 gives 19, *i.e.* (dividing by 7) '5'. Total 9, *i.e.* '2'.

The item for August is '8 from 10,' *i.e.* '2'; so, for September, it is '2 plus 3', *i.e.* '5'. Total 7, *i.e.* '0', which goes out.

18 gives '4'. Answer, '*Thursday*'.

1676, February 23

16 from 18 gives '2'.

76 is 6 dozen and 4, giving 10; plus 1 gives 11, *i.e.* '4'. Total '6'.

The item for February is '3'. Total 9, *i.e.* '2'.

23 gives '2'. Total '4'.

Correction for Leap Year gives '3'. Answer, '*Wednesday*'.

The one shortcoming in Carroll's method would appear to be the clumsy means of obtaining the 'Month-Item'. It would be surprising if he did not eventually come round to formulating a relevant chart as follows to be committed to memory through a specific mnemonic:

Month		Month	
January	0	July	6
February	3	August	2
March	3	September	5
April	6	October	0
May	8	November	3
June	4	December	12

The eleven days from September 3 to 13, 1752, were lost when a changeover was made from the old British Julian calendar to the Gregorian system. Hence Carroll's differentiation between 'Old Style' and 'New Style'. The Gregorian calendar stipulates that a year ending in two zeros, while evenly divisible by four, is a leap year only if it is evenly divisible by 400. Hence 2000 will be, while 1800 and 1900 didn't qualify.

Finally, a last example: the day, July 4, as described by W. H. Auden, 'as memorable a day in the history of literature as it is in American history'; the year, 1862:

> 18, divided by 4, leaves '2' over; 2 from 3 gives '1'; twice 1 is '2'.
> 62 is 5 dozen plus 2, giving '7'. Total 9, i.e. '2'.
> The item for July is '6'. Total 8, i.e. '1'.
> '4'; Total '5'. Answer 'Friday'.

In other words it was a Friday when, during that 'golden afternoon', Carroll took the three Liddell sisters on a rowing expedition up the Thames from Folly Bridge to Godstow and first told 'the fairy-tale of Alice's adventures underground. . . .'

Isa's ghost

> The same day, Isa saw a curious book of pictures of ghosts. If you look hard at one for a minute, and then look at the ceiling, you see another ghost there – only, when you have a black one in the book, it is a *white* one on the ceiling – when it is green in the book, it is *pink* on the ceiling.
>
> *Isa's Visit to Oxford*

Even more uncanny than Isa Bowman's experiences as detailed by Carroll in the journal he compiled to commemorate her visit to Oxford in July, 1888, is the related phenomenon known as 'Meyer's Experiment'. In this a strip of light grey paper when placed on a large sheet of green and stared at for about a minute, takes on the appearance of pink. Take the grey and place it on a sheet of bright blue and after a short while the grey will appear orange-yellow. Similarly grey on bright yellow appears blue, and, as Isa might have guessed, grey on red green. The colour which you see on the ceiling or in the grey paper in these experiments is not accidental, being the complementary colour of the one at which you have been looking. With the Meyer version you can induce this complementary colour even sooner by covering both coloured and grey paper with a transparent sheet of wax or tracing paper.

Handkerchief mouse

'Perhaps it doesn't understand English,' thought Alice. 'I daresay it's a French mouse, come over with William the Conqueror.' (For, with all her knowledge of history, Alice had no very clear notion how long ago anything had happened.) So she began again 'Où est ma chatte?' which was the first sentence in her French lesson-book. The Mouse gave a sudden leap out of the water, and seemed to quiver all over with fright.

Alice's Adventures in Wonderland

In her own account of Carroll, Isa Bowman recalls how he would interrupt their walks to Beachy Head to show her 'the most wonderful things made out of a handkerchief. Everyone when a child has, I suppose, seen the trick in which a handkerchief is rolled up to look like a mouse, then made to jump about by a movement of the hand. He did this better than any one I ever saw, and the trick was a never-failing joy.' In the following instructions the steps needed to complete the mouse coincide numerically with the relevant illustrations:

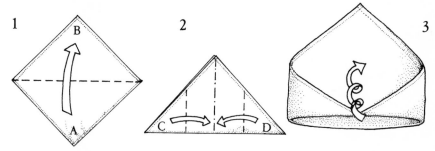

1. First fold a large white handkerchief from corner A to corner B.
2. Fold in the lower corners C and D to the centre.
3. Roll up tightly from the bottom to just past half-way.

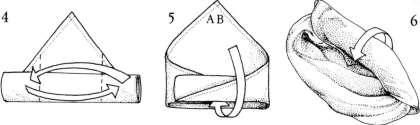

4. Fold the ends to the centre, just overlapping.
5/6. Take the top corners A and B and tuck them into the lower edge of the rolled portion.

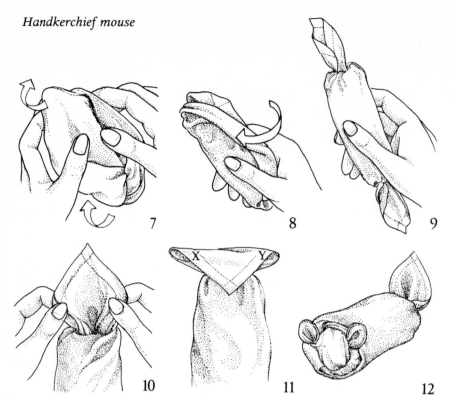

6. Keep tucking in with the fingers and you will arrive at the doughnut-shaped object as shown.

7/8. Now carefully begin to roll the doughnut inside out, unrolling the left side around the right, which the fingers keep intact until . . .

9. . . . two free ends appear.

10. Open out one of these ends.

11. Fold the corner down as shown, tying X and Y into a tight knot . . .

12. . . . to give the complete mouse.

To animate the mouse, give it a sharp flip with the fingers in the direction of your elbow. Retrieve it and keep repeating until the mouse decides to leap upon your shoulder, all a combination of the most dedicated make-believe and letting your fingers run riot with a mouse-like mind of their own.

Bert Allerton, a Chicago night-club magician of the thirties, made a great speciality of an even simpler fold, so simple in fact that it is hard to believe Allerton himself was the originator – so it may have been in the repertoire Isa was privileged to see. Certainly its motif – a white rabbit – is quite as applicable to Carroll as the mouse:

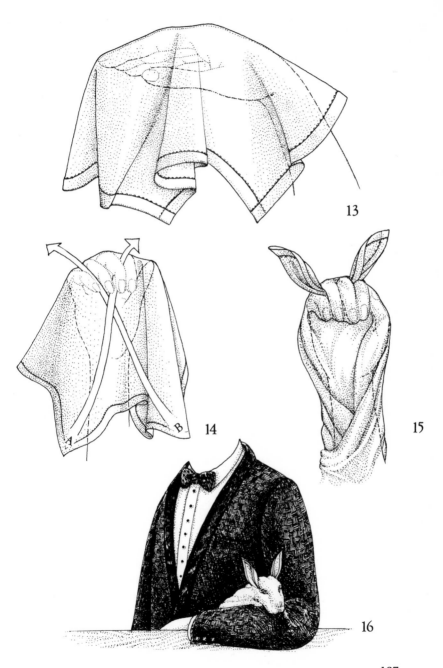

13

14

15

16

13. Drape a handkerchief over the right hand as shown.

14. With the left hand bring the front corners A and B up between the index and second fingers, and the third and little fingers respectively. These form the ears.

15. The corners are pulled taut beneath the second and third fingers of the right hand, tightening the cloth covering those fingers to form the rabbit's nose.

16. By holding the figure inside the left sleeve and moving the second and third fingers, the rabbit will appear to be nibbling and can actually be made to bite at a biscuit or crunch at a sugar cube!

The mystery of the Cheshire Cat's grin

'Did you say "pig," or "fig?"' said the Cat.
'I said "pig",' replied Alice; 'and I wish you wouldn't keep appearing and vanishing so suddenly: you make one quite giddy!'
'All right,' said the Cat; and this time it vanished quite slowly, beginning with the end of the tail, and ending with the grin, which remained some time after the rest of it had gone.
'Well! I've often seen a cat without a grin,' thought Alice; 'but a grin without a cat! It's the most curious thing I ever saw in all my life!'

Alice's Adventures in Wonderland

The Cheshire Cat's grin has been a potent source of inspiration to subsequent puzzlists. Carroll himself saw its adaptability when devising his 'Wonderland Postage-Stamp Case', the idea of which came to him on October 29, 1888. This consisted of a cardboard sleeve, approximately $4\frac{5}{8}$ by $3\frac{1}{2}$ inches, into which slipped the canvas-backed case itself, folded and comprising twelve small sewn pockets for holding stamps in value from a halfpenny to a shilling. The case was decorated with two 'Surprises': on one side of the sleeve the picture of Alice holding the Duchess's baby 'turned into' Alice holding the pig on the outside of the case

The mystery of the Cheshire Cat's grin

proper; and similarly on the other side the Cheshire Cat, full and fat, 'turned into' the lingering grin. In his *Eight or Nine Wise Words about Letter-Writing* which accompanied the case, Carroll wrote playfully:

> Some American writer has said 'the snakes in this district may be divided into one species – the venomous.'
> The same principle applies here. Postage-Stamp-Cases may be divided into one species, the 'Wonderland.' Imitations of it will soon appear, no doubt; but they cannot include the two Pictorial Surprises, which are copyright.
> You don't see why I call them 'Surprises'? Well, take the Case in your left hand, and regard it attentively. You see Alice nursing the Duchess's Baby? (An entirely new combination, by the way: it doesn't occur in the book.) Now, with your right thumb and forefinger, lay hold of the little book, and suddenly pull it out. *The Baby has turned into a Pig!* If *that* doesn't surprise you, why, I suppose you wouldn't be surprised if your own Mother-in-law suddenly turned into a Gyroscope!

At their best the 'Surprises' were a superior form of practical joke. But Carroll regarded his invention highly enough to have it entered at Stationers' Hall. It was actually manufactured by Emberlin and Son, 4, Magdalen Street, later of the Turl, Oxford.

Sam Loyd, calling into play an hypnotic letter formation as mesmeric as the Cat's grin itself, reiterated Alice's own doubts with the following puzzle. In how many different ways can one read Alice's question, 'Was it a cat I saw?', starting at any of the W's, spelling by moving up or down, left or right, to adjacent letters until you reach the C, and then back to the border again?

In his solution, Loyd underlined the error of those who reasoned that since there were 24 starting-points and the same number of endings, the number of different ways would be the square of 24, namely 576. This overlooks the branch routes, numbering some 252 ways of reaching the C at the centre. Since there are as many ways of getting back, the square of 252, or 63,504 different ways, is the answer required.

More recently, in today's age of computers and genetic engineering, the Cheshire Cat's grin has taken on a meaning Carroll could never have intended. This follows the development of the game 'Life' by Cambridge mathematician John Horton Conway, as detailed in *The Sunday Times* for June 13, 1971. In the game, which, for all its frightening implications,

could not be more aptly named, abstract mathematical concepts assume tangible 'living' shape, whether played through a computer or more simply on a chequered grid with counters or tiddlywinks. The latter represent cells, the building-blocks of life, the amino-acid equivalent, which according to specific laws will combine with other cells (live) or disintegrate (die). The laws invented after much experimentation by Conway in a virtual God-like capacity take into account the eight squares adjacent to any one counter:

> Birth: Each empty square with exactly three adjacent counters will give birth.
> Survival: Each counter with two or three adjacent counters will survive.
> Death: Each counter on its own or with only one neighbour will die of isolation; each counter with four or more adjacent counters will die of over-population.

Births and deaths occur simultaneously, so that newborn cells can play no part in killing members of the generation in which they are born.

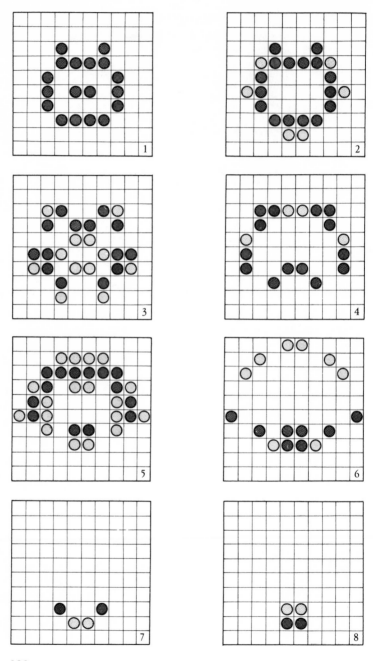

To ensure this it is suggested counters of two colours are used, say – in true Carrollian tradition – red and grey. Lay out the first pattern in red; then identify those counters which will 'die' by placing another red on top of each of them. Then identify with grey the empty squares destined to give birth. Only then discard the 'dead' red counters and replace the newborn grey with red.

With this information it is possible to track the fate of any object or pattern committed to the grid. The Cheshire Cat formation, discovered by C. R. Tompkins of California, is uncanny in its predictability. At the seventh stage the face, having taken on a life of its own separate from a body, vanishes completely to leave the mere vestige of a grin, which itself fades until only a paw print (?) remains with any sense of permanence.

What Carroll could only have imagined as fantasy would now appear to have established its own more than fleeting claim to reality. According to its inventor, the game grew out of a proposition put forward forty years ago by the Austrian mathematician Gödel, concerning the possible limits of any system of mathematical logic. It is enough to understand the rudiments of the game without having to grapple in depth with its own complicated history. And yet it is reassuring that if anyone would have come to grips with this unprecedented application of logic, it would have been Carroll himself.

Circular billiards

A Billiard-marker, whose skill was immense,
  Might perhaps have won more than his share –
But a Banker, engaged at enormous expense,
  Had the whole of their cash in his care.

. . . .

. . . .

The maker of Bonnets ferociously planned
  A novel arrangement of bows:
While the Billiard-marker with quivering hand
  Was chalking the tip of his nose.

The Hunting of the Snark

It isn't surprising that Carroll, with his flair for mathematical play, should have been enthusiastic about a game like billiards, with the scope it offers for the precise calculation of incidence and rebound of ball against baize. His fascination, however, extended far beyond the regular game. Two problems unearthed by Warren Weaver among Carroll's papers and quoted by him in an article entitled 'The Mathematical Manuscripts of Lewis Carroll' published in *The Proceedings of the American Philosophical Society* for October, 1954, reveal his eccentric preoccupation with the game: 'Can a billiard ball on a four-sided but not rectangular table travel so as to touch all four sides and continue forever on the same path? Can a billiard ball travel inside a cube in such a way that it touches all faces, continue forever on the same path, and all portions of the path be equal?' In his edition of *The Diaries* Roger Lancelyn Green quotes an amusing reminiscence by an old pupil, Watkins H. Williams, of his first tutorial with Carroll in the early sixties: 'He took me last, and, glancing at a problem of Euclid which I had written out, he placed his finger on an omission. "I deny you right to assert that." I supplied what was wanting. "Why did you not say so before? What is a corollary?" Silence. "Do you ever play billiards?" "Sometimes." "If you attempted a cannon, missed, and holed your own and the red ball, what would you call it?" "A fluke." "Exactly. A corollary is a fluke in Euclid. Good morning."'

In 1889 he invented 'Circular Billiards', an idiosyncratic notion played on a circular table without pockets which he had specially built for the purpose. The rules were published the following year:

CIRCULAR BILLIARDS
(*A Game for two players*)

The Table is circular, with a cushion all round it, and has neither pockets nor spots.

Rules

1. One Player takes the 3 balls (red, white, and spot-white) in his hand, turns his back on the Table, and rolls them on. The other Player begins.

2. A 'miss' counts 1 to the adversary.

3. If the ball in play strikes one ball, and nothing else, it counts nothing.

4. A cannon counts 2, and gives the right of playing again.

5. Striking the cushion counts 1 for every ball struck afterwards. Thus, a 'plain' cushion (struck before striking one ball) counts 1, and two such count 2: a 'sandwich' cushion (struck during a cannon) counts 1, and two such count 2: a 'previous' cushion (struck previous to a cannon) counts 2, and two such count 4. Three or more consecutive cushions are reckoned as two only.

6 Game is 50 or 100.

Remarks

The circular Table will be found to yield an interesting variety of Billiard-playing, as the rebounds from the cushion are totally different from those of the ordinary game.

To illustrate the great variety of play in this game, the 11 possible modes of scoring are here appended. (N.B. 'B' stands for 'Ball', 'c' for cushion', 's' for 'sandwich-cushion', and 'p' for 'previous cushion'.)

All scores below the line give the right of playing again.

c B		scores	1
cc B		,,	2
B	B	,,	2
B	s B	,,	3
B	ss B	,,	4
p B	B	,,	4
p B	s B	,,	5
p B	ss B	,,	6
pp B	B	,,	6
pp B	s B	,,	7
pp B	ss B	,,	8

Since Carroll's day billiards has also seen an oval table which, according to the eleventh edition of *Encyclopaedia Britannica*, was 'introduced in England by way of a change in 1907'! More recently, according to Gardner, in July, 1964, a design patent was issued to Edwin E. Robinson of Pacifica, California, for a circular table with four pockets. That same year an elliptical billiard table appeared on the market in the United States, heralded by a full page advertisement in *The New York Times* of July 1, 1964, and a publicity campaign that availed itself of the services of film stars Joanne Woodward and Paul Newman. Called 'Elliptipool', this version was patented by Arthur Frigo of Torrington, Connecticut. As yet no one has come up with a version that would bear out the following lines from *The Mikado*:

> On a cloth untrue
> With a twisted cue,
> And elliptical billiard balls!

Or, as James Joyce corrected Gilbert in *A Portrait of the Artist as a Young Man*, with 'ellipsoidal' billiard balls!

Origami

All this time the Guard was looking at her, first through a telescope, then through a microscope, and then through an opera-glass. At last he said 'You're travelling the wrong way,' and shut up the window, and went away.

'So young a child,' said the gentleman sitting opposite to her, (he was dressed in white paper), 'ought to know which way she's going, even if she doesn't know her own name!'

Through the Looking-Glass

The ancient Japanese art of paper-folding was a favourite activity of Lewis Carroll. Its soothing complexity and geometric overtones both appealed to his mathematical instincts. His diary records his delight when at Hastings on October 8, 1890 he was taught by Francis Epiphanius, the son of Coventry Patmore, how to fold a paper 'pistol' which went off with a crack when swished through the air. A year later, according to his diary entry for November 16, 1891, 'a remarkable day', he himself conveyed this same 'sharpshooting' lesson to the children of the Duchess of Albany in his rooms. To make the pistol one needs a rectangle of thin, crisp paper about twelve inches by eight. The numbered steps below correspond with the illustrations:

1. Crease the paper lengthwise down the middle; then fold the corners A, B, C and D to the points X and Y as shown.
2. Fold A over to B and crease the edge.
3. Fold A to B, crease and unfold; fold A and B along the dotted lines to a point off the paper at X.
4. Turn this stage over.
5. Fold A down to B and crease.
6. Grasp the corners X and Y.
7. Bring your hand down sharply and decisively from an outstretched position and the pistol will crack.
8. To reset, merely push back the flap X.

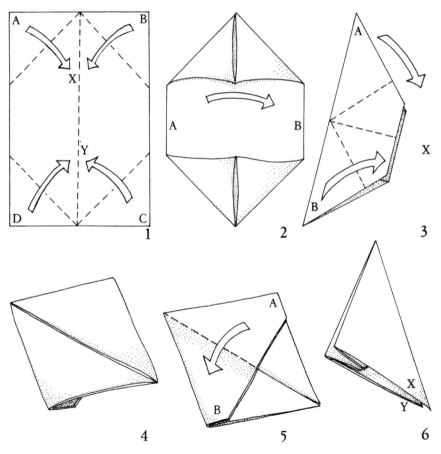

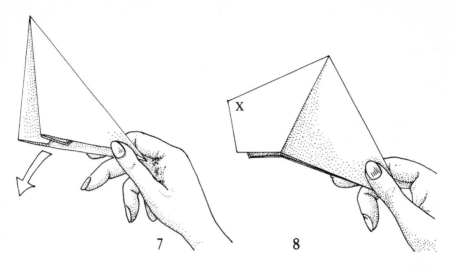

In *The Life and Letters of Lewis Carroll*, Collingwood quotes a child-friend, Freda Bremer: 'Our acquaintance began in a somewhat singular manner. We were playing on the Fort at Margate, and a gentleman on a seat near asked us if we could make a paper boat, with a seat at each end, and a basket in the middle for fish! We were, of course, enchanted with the idea, and our new friend – after achieving the feat – gave us his card, which we at once carried to our mother'. If one allows Carroll a degree of poetic licence in his choice of words, this would appear to approximate to the model more commonly known today as the Chinese Junk. Required is a square sheet of paper, preferably coloured on one side only:

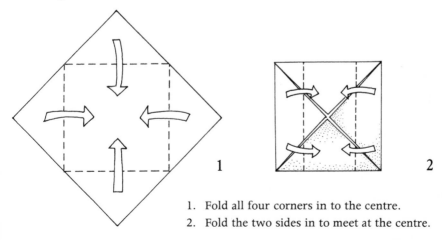

1. Fold all four corners in to the centre.
2. Fold the two sides in to meet at the centre.

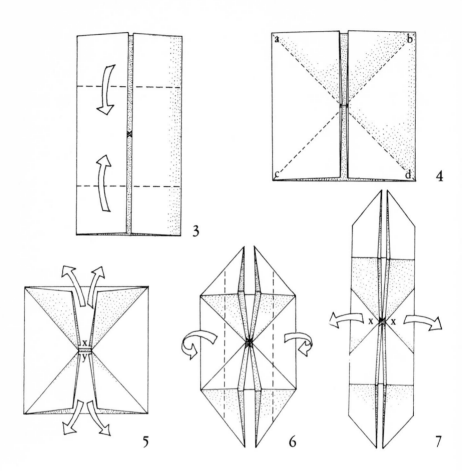

3. Fold in the top and bottom ends to meet.

4. Crease the diagonals as shown, by folding A to D and unfolding, and then repeating with B to C. The creases are to facilitate the next move where you . . .

5. . . . pull out the two points marked X and the two marked Y at the centre in the direction of the arrows as shown.

6. Fold the two sides behind the model along the dotted lines.

7. Pull out points XX at the centre and simultaneously squash flat the two points which were immediately below XX (let's designate them X'X') so that they now lie as shown to give the shape at 8.

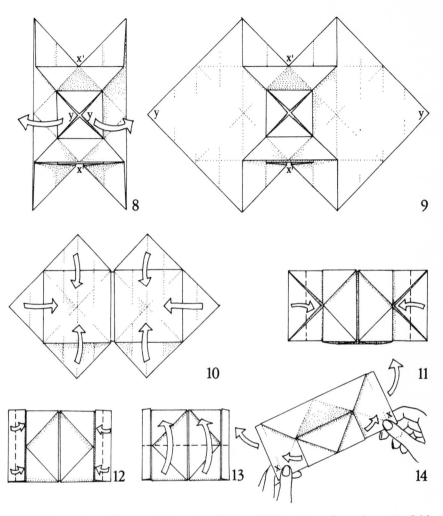

8. Again pull out centre points Y Y, unfolding them from the main fold to give 9.

9. Turn this stage over.

10. Fold all six corners in as shown.

11. Fold the ends in along the dotted lines.

12. Fold those ends over upon themselves as shown.

13. Fold the model across itself.

14. Holding firmly between thumbs and forefingers at X and X, pull out and upwards as shown.

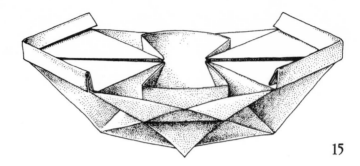

15

15. Now merely raise the ends at bow and stern to their required height to give Carroll's fishing boat, complete with basket in the middle and seats at either end.

It is significant that the boxlike paper hat worn by the Carpenter in Tenniel's illustrations, while no longer worn by carpenters, has been appropriated by the operators of newspaper printing presses who fold them from blank news sheets and wear them to prevent ink getting into their hair. Here are the folds the Carpenter handed down. Start with one double sheet of newspaper with the folded edge along the top:

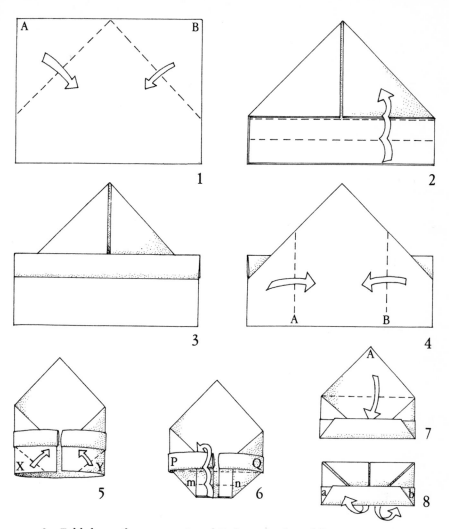

1. Fold down the corners A and B along the dotted lines.
2. Fold the top layer of the bottom edge in twice as shown.
3. Turn this stage over.
4. Fold the ends in along the dotted lines at A and B, ensuring that the distance AB coincides with your head measurement.
5. Fold the corners X and Y inwards.
6. Fold flap over twice as shown, tucking MN in beneath PQ.
7. Fold point A inwards beneath PQ.
8. Insert thumbs into the bottom opening and open out until . . .

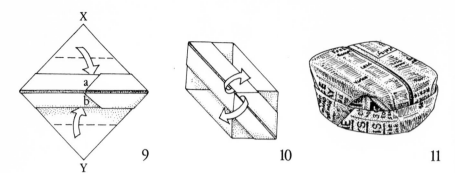

9

10

11

9. . . . A and B meet. Fold in the tips X and Y beneath A and B.

10/11. Finally open out again and prevent the sawdust from getting in your hair!

Since we opened this section with the gentleman in the paper suit, it is worth remembering by way of conclusion another old fold which would have been familiar to Carroll. This time you will need not one but two equal squares of paper:

1. Fold AB to DC, crease and unfold; fold AD to BC, crease and unfold; turn paper over.

2. Fold C to A, crease and unfold; fold D to B, crease and unfold.

3. Fold all four corners to the centre.

4. Turn stage 3 over and again fold all corners to the centre.

5. Once again turn the model over and once again fold the four corners to the centre.

6. Turn the model over; open out and press down at AB and CD.

7. Hold corner X' and open point X outwards bringing CD and AB temporarily close to each other to facilitate this.

8. Bring point X down behind . . .

9. . . . in the direction of the arrows.

10. Now repeat with point X' still under your left thumb. This completes the jacket and body. To form the trousers and legs fold another model to this stage and then fold A up to B.

11. This gives the finished trousers which are then slotted into the jacket to produce . . .

12. . . . the complete suit. One can easily add a small tube of paper for a face and a miniature hat if required to produce one's own three-dimensional facsimile of Carroll's papyrus-clad character.

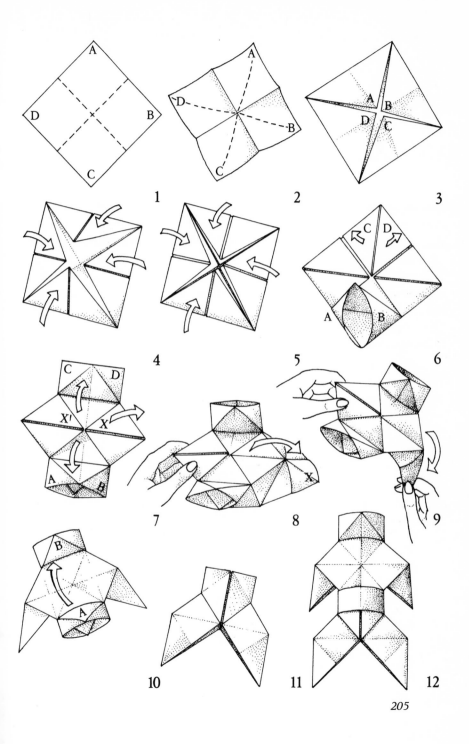

1

2

3

4

5

6

7

8

9

10

11

12

A postal problem

He thought he saw an Albatross
    That fluttered round the lamp:
He looked again, and found it was
    A Penny-Postage-Stamp.
'You'd best be getting home,' he said:
    'The nights are very damp!'

Sylvie and Bruno

Lewis Carroll was an inveterate correspondent, always numbering his letters and keeping a register of them, which on his death detailed no less than 98,721 entries from the time he was 29. He was also a cousin of the then Postmaster-General, Henry Cecil Raikes. It isn't surprising, therefore that he went out of his way to rationalise the shortcomings he found in the postal services. Among suggestions to charge all Sunday letters double postage, thoughts on the registration of parcels (he was quoted by the Postmaster-General in an official report on this subject in 1890), and plans for simplifying money orders by making the sender complete two duplicate papers, one to be handed to the postmaster containing a key number which the receiver must supply in order to obtain his money, the following questionnaire based on the official rule for commissions chargeable on overdue postal orders has received the greatest attention. The ambiguity of the Post Office Guide in this respect

led in Carroll's own words to 'a very curious verbal puzzle', which he had printed anonymously in pamphlet form in June, 1891 to send to friends and interested parties for completion; the Supplement followed later the same month.

The Rule, for Commissions chargeable on overdue Postal Orders, is given in the 'Post Office Guide' in these words, (it is here divided, for convenience of reference, into 3 clauses):

a. After the expiration of 3 months from the last day of the month of issue, a Postal Order will be payable only on payment of a Commission, equal to the amount of the original poundage;

b. with the addition (if more than 3 months have elapsed since the said expiration) of the amount of the original poundage for every further period of 3 months which has so elapsed;

c. and for every portion of any such period of 3 months over and above every complete period.

You are requested to answer the following questions, in reference to a Postal Order for 10/- (on which the 'original poundage' would be 1d.) issued during the month of January, so that the 1st 'period' would consist of the months February, March, April; the 2nd would consist of the months May, June, July; and the 3rd would consist of the months August, September, October.

1. Supposing the Rule to consist of clause a. only, on what day would a 'Commission' begin to be chargeable? (   )

2. What would be its amount? (   )

3. Supposing the Rule to consist of clauses a. and b., on what day would the lowest 'Commission' begin to be chargeable? (   )

4. What would be its amount? (   )

5. On what day would a larger 'Commission' (being the sum of 2 'Commissions') begin to be chargeable? (   )

6. What would be its amount? (   )

7. On what day would a yet larger 'Commission' begin to be chargeable? (   )

8. What would be its amount? (   )

9. Taking the Rule as consisting of all 3 clauses, in *which* of the above-named 3 'periods' does clause (c) first begin to take effect? (   )

10. *Which* day, of any 'period', is the earliest on which it can be said that a 'portion' of the 'period' has elapsed? (   )

11. On what day would the lowest 'Commission' begin to be chargeable? (   )

12. What would be its amount? (   )

13. On what day would a larger 'Commission' begin to be chargeable?
( )
14. What would be its amount? ( )
15. On what day would a yet larger 'Commission' begin to be chargeable?
( )
16. What would be its amount? ( )

Signature....................
Date....................

SUPPLEMENT

The Rule is given, below, in a form which exhibits its grammatical construction:

a.1. After the expiration of 3 months
from the last day of the month of
issue, a Postal Order will be
payable only on payment

of
a.2. a Commission, equal to the
amount of the original poundage

b.1. with the addition (if more than
3 months have elapsed since the said
expiration)
of
the amount of the original
poundage

for
b.2. every further period
of 3 months which has so
elapsed

and for
c. every portion of any
such period of 3 months
over and above every complete period.

Syzygies

December 12, 1879:
Invented a new way of working one word into another. I think of calling
the puzzle 'syzygies'.

The Diaries

That 'Syzygies' was a more complicated proposition than 'Doublets' can
be seen from the reaction of *Vanity Fair*, to whom Carroll submitted the
puzzle twelve years later on April 14, 1891. Their rejection resulted in
its publication in *The Lady* on July 30, the same year. As in 'Doublets'
two words are given, the idea being to link them by a series of intermediate words which have groups of letters in common. The following
example was found by Warren Weaver among Carroll's mathematical
papers. Incidentally, the second 'link' is itself dubious, as we shall see.

CONSERVATIVE
LIBERAL

CONSERVATIVE
(servati)
re servations
(ation)
deliberation
(libera)
LIBERAL

The shared letters themselves constitute the 'syzygy' or 'yoke'; the
whole set of four (or whatever) words represents a 'chain'; all but the
end-words are called 'links'.

The usual restrictions are laid down regarding permissible words.
More thoughtful are specifically forbidden syzygies. Thus when two
words begin with the same set of one or more letters, or would do so if
certain prefixes (e.g. un-; in-) were removed, each letter in the one set
is 'barred' with relation to the corresponding letter in the other set. In
the following these 'barred' letters are underlined:

DOG	CARRIAGE	UNDONE	UNDONE
DOOR	CARCASE	DOOR	INDOORS

There is, though, nothing to prevent the yoke of the first 'ca' in 'carriage' to the second 'ca' in 'carcase'. When two words end similarly, or would do so if certain suffixes (e.g. -ed; -ing; -s; -es) were removed, a similar restriction applies:

ONION	SINKING	SINKING	PLUNGES
MOON	LINK	LINKS	CHANGING

One must also ensure that one of two consecutive syzygies does not contain the other. When that does happen, one must in scoring erase the intermediate link and the longer syzygy, namely the one containing the other. So with this chain:

MEETING

(ting)

TINGE

(ing)

LOVING

one erases 'tinge' and the first syzygy, giving the unlawful (anyhow) syzygy:

MEETING

(ing)

LOVING

By allowing Carroll his own fantastical head one obtains a far clearer idea of what he had in mind than from his rather forbidding rules and statistics. In a pamphlet published privately in 1893 he provided his 'hints on making chains':

> I have tried to embody some useful hints on this subject in the form of a soliloquy, supposed to be indulged in by the possessor of what Tennyson would call 'a second-rate sensitive mind', while solving the problem '*Turn* CAMEL *into* DROMEDARY'.
> 'No use trying the whole Camel. Let's try four letters. "Came". That must be something ending in "cament", I fancy. That gives "predicament", and

"medicament"; I can't think of any others: and either of these would lead to "mental" or "mention". Then "amel". That gives "tamely" and "lamely". "Samely" is hardly an "ordinary" word: and I'm afraid "gamely" is slang! Well, we've got *four* Links, at any rate. Let's put them down:

CAMEL $\begin{cases} \text{(came)} \\ \text{(amel)} \end{cases}$ $\begin{cases} \text{predicament (ment)} \\ \text{medicament} \end{cases}$ $\begin{cases} \text{mental} \\ \text{mention} \end{cases}$
$\begin{cases} \text{tamely} \\ \text{lamely} \end{cases}$

'Now for DROMEDARY. No 5-letter Syzygy, that *I* can see. Let's try the 4s. "Drom". There's "loxodrome", but that's quite a *specialist's* word. And there's "palindrome" – no, *that* won't do: "palin" is a prefix. "Rome". That gives "chrome", which is *not* very hopeful to go on with. "Omed". That'll give us all the participles ending in "omed": "domed", "doomed", "groomed"; not very suggestive: however, there's "comedy": *that* sounds hopeful. "Meda". Well, there's "medal", and "medalist", and – and – that's all, I think; but "medalist" leads to "listen", or "listless". "Edar". That leads to "cedar", and words beginning with "re", such as "re-darn this stocking" – no, I'm afraid that would have a hyphen! However, "cedar", leads to "dared", or any participle ending in "-ced". "Dary". There's "daring": that might lead to something, such as "fringe", or "syringe". Well, let's tabulate again:

DROMEDARY $\left\{ \begin{array}{l} \text{(omed)} \quad \begin{cases} \text{domed, \&c.} \\ \text{comedy} \end{cases} \\ \\ \text{(meda)} \quad \begin{cases} \text{medal} \\ \text{medalist} \end{cases} \text{(list)} \begin{cases} \text{listen} \\ \text{listless} \end{cases} \\ \\ \text{(edar) cedar} \quad \begin{cases} \text{(dar) dared} \\ \text{(ced) . . . ced} \end{cases} \\ \\ \text{(dary) daring (ring)} \begin{cases} \text{fringe} \\ \text{syringe} \end{cases} \end{array} \right.$

'Now, can we link any of these ragged ends together? "Predicament". That'll link on to "dared", though it's only a 3-letter Syzygy. That gives the Chain "Camel (came) predicament (red) dared (dar) cedar (edar) dromedary". But there's something wrong there! "Edar" contains "dar". We must write it "Camel (came) predicament (red) dared (dar) dromedary". That'll score 17. Let's try another Chain. "Predicament" and "cedar" can be linked by putting in "enticed". How will *that* work? "Camel (came) predicament (ent) enticed (ced) cedar (edar) dromedary". *That* scores only 16! Try again. "Medicament". Why that links straight on to "comedy", with a 4-letter Syzygy! That's the best chance we've had yet. "Camel (came) medicament (medi) comedy (omed) dromedary". And what does *that* score, I wonder? Why it actually scores 31! Bravo!'

If any of my readers should fail, in attempting a similar soliloquy, let her say to herself, 'It is not that my mind is not *sensitive*: it is that it is not *second-rate!*' *Then* she will feel consoled!

Once one had completed the chain, the task in hand was only half over. The score still has to be reckoned, an amalgam of no less than six separate figures. To calculate, write down in turn:

1. The greatest No. of letters in an end-Syzygy, *plus* twice the least.
2. The least No. of letters in a Syzygy.
3. The sum of (1) *plus* the product of the two numbers next above (2).
4. The No. of Links.
5. The No. of waste letters.
6. The sum of twice (4) *plus* (5).
7. The remainder left after deducting (6) from (3). If (6) be greater than (3), the remainder is written as '0'.

No (7) is entered as the Score of the Chain.

Example

The figures on the right indicate the Nos. of waste letters.

WALRUS	..	..	..	..	3
(rus)					
peruse	..	..	..	..	1
(per)					
harper	..	..	..	..	1
(arpe)					
CARPENTER	..	..	..	..	3

As the greatest No. of letters is an end-Syzygy is '4', and the least is '3', No. (1) is '10'. Also (No. 2) is '3'. Hence No. (3) is the sum of '10' *plus* '4 times 5', *i.e.* it is '30'. Also there are 2 Links and 8 waste letters. Hence No. (4) is '2', No. (5) is '8'; and No. (6) is the sum of 'twice 2' *plus* '8'; *i.e.*, it is '12'. Hence No. (7) is the remainder after deducting '12' from '30'; *i.e.*, it is '18'; which is the Score for the Chain.

The result may be conveniently recorded thus:

10, 3, 30; 2, 8, 12; 18.

All this to ensure that positive credit is given for shared letters, negative credit for letters which are not shared, or, as Carroll describes them, 'waste'. The one exception when un-yoked words are not considered 'waste' is when the end-words contain more than seven letters. Then the extra ones are not counted. The following problems were all published in *The Lady* on the dates shown. The scores given are the highest then achieved:

SOLUTIONS OF THE PROBLEMS

The appended dates refer to the numbers
of *The Lady* in which these solutions appeared.

1. March 24, 1892.

OH 0
  (oh)
cohere 1
  (ere)
reredos 2
  (do)
DO 0
Score: 6, 2, 18; 2, 3, 7: 11.

2. March 3, 1892.

INDULGE 4
  (ndu)
unduly 1
  (duly)
incredulity 3
  (incr)
IDIOSYNCRASY 3
Score: 10, 3, 30; 2, 11, 15: 15.

3. March 17, 1892.

LEAD 1
  (lea)
plea 0
  (ple)
sample 0
  (sam)
jetsam 1
  (ets)
BULLETS 4
Score: 9, 3, 29; 3, 6, 12: 17.

4. October 1, 1891.

DOG 0
  (dog)
endogen 2
  (gen)
gentry 0
  (ntry)
intricate 2
  (cat)
CAT 0
Score: 9, 3, 29; 3, 4, 10: 19.

5. May 5, 1892.

COOK 1
  (coo)
scooping 2
  (pin)
pinned 1
  (inne)
DINNER 2
Score: 10, 3, 30; 2, 6, 10: 20.

6. March 10, 1892.

KNIFE 1
  (nife)
manifest 2
  (man)
workman 1
  (ork)
FORK 1
Score: 10, 3, 30; 2, 5, 9: 21.

7.   May 26, 1892.

CONVERSE	3
(erse)	
persevering	3
(erin)	
merino	1
(meri)	
perfumery	1
(erfu)	
CHEERFULLY	3

Score: 12, 4, 42; 3, 11, 17: 25.

8.   May 12, 1892.

SPREAD..	2
(read)	
readiness	1
(ines)	
shines	0
(shin)	
vanquishing	3
(anqu)	
BANQUET	3

Score: 12, 4, 42; 3, 9, 15: 27.

9.   April 14, 1892.

WEDNESDAY	2
(ednes)	
blessedness	3
(esse)	
finesse	1
(iness)	
craftiness	1
(raft)	
rafter	0
(after)	
AFTERNOON	2

Score: 15, 4, 45; 4, 9, 17: 28.

10.   March 31, 1892.

DEMAND	2
(eman)	
gentleman	1
(gent)	
tangent	1
(ange)	
orange	0
(oran)	
CORMORANT	3

Score: 12, 4, 42; 3, 7, 13: 29.

The Nyctograph

'I engage with the Snark – every night after dark –
In a dreamy delirious fight:
I serve it with greens in those shadowy scenes,
And I use it for striking a light.'

The Hunting of the Snark

Carroll's insomnia led to his own protracted struggle against the dark, solved in part towards the end of his life by the invention of the 'Typhlograph', subsequently changed at the suggestion of a student to 'Nyctograph'. This was a grating of sixteen squares, cut out in cardboard along stencil lines, to facilitate writing notes unseen. The instructions were published in the edition of *The Lady* for October 29, 1891.

. . . I think of calling the mechanical appliance which my system requires, in addition to an ordinary 'indelible' memorandum-book, the 'Nyctograph'. I invented it September 24th, 1891, but I do not intend to patent it. Anyone who chooses is welcome to make and sell the article.

Any one who has tried, as I have often done, the process of getting out of bed at 2 a.m. in a winter night, lighting a candle, and recording some happy thought which would probably be otherwise forgotten, will agree with me it entails much discomfort. All I have now to do, if I wake and think of something I wish to record, is to draw from under the pillow a small memorandum book, containing my Nyctograph, write a few lines, or even a few pages, without even putting the hands outside the bed-clothes, replace the book, and go to sleep again.

There is an ingenious machine already made and sold (I bought mine from Messrs. Elliot, 101, St. Martin's Lane), where you write a line of MS. inside a narrow oblong opening, then turn a handle till you hear a click; this shifts the paper upwards and gives a fresh surface for another line of MS. I tried to put this into a more portable shape, by cutting a series of oblong apertures in a piece of pasteboard the size of a page of a small memorandum book; but the writing is apt to be illegible, as it is difficult to know where you are, and you constantly come against the edge of the aperture when you wish to go further in order to make the loop of an 'h' or the tail of a 'y'. Then I tried rows of square holes, each to hold one letter (quarter of an inch square I found a very convenient size), and this proved a much better plan than the former; but the letters were still apt to be illegible. Then I said to myself 'Why not invent a square alphabet, using only dots at the corners, and lines along the sides?' I soon found that, to make the writing easy to read, it was necessary to know where each square began. This I secured by the rule that *every* square-letter should contain a large black dot in the N.W. corner. Also I found that it would cause confusion to have any symbol which used only the W. side of the square. These limitations reduced the number of available symbols to 31, of which I selected 26 for the letters of the alphabet, and succeeded in getting 23 of them to have a distinct resemblance to the letters they were to represent.

Think of the number of lonely hours a blind man often spends doing nothing, when he would gladly record his thoughts, and you will realise what a blessing you can confer on him by giving him a small 'indelible' memorandum-book, with a piece of paste-board containing rows of square holes, and teaching him the square-alphabet. The crowning blessing would be that, instead of having to dictate letters to his attendant, he could write them himself, and no one need see them except those to whom they were written. In the following list, I call the N.E. corner '2', the S.W. corner '3', and the S.E. corner '4'. Also I have bracketed letters whose symbols run in pairs, each being the reverse of the other. Every symbol is assumed to have a large dot in its N.W. corner.

	Corners	Sides	Resemblance to letters, &c.
A	4	none	right-hand side of 'A'
B	2, 4	W	vertical line of 'B', with dots to stand for the semicircles

	Corners	Sides	Resemblance to letters, &c.
⎰C	none	N, W, S	obvious
⎱D	none	N, E, S	obvious; also reverse of preceding symbol
E	none	N	top of 'E'; taken as simplest symbol for commonest letter
⎧F	4	N, W	obvious; dot stands for cross-piece which has fallen off
⎨G	2	W, S	analagous to symbol for 'C'; also reverse of preceding symbol
H	none	W, E	obvious
I	none	S	like 'i', vertical line having fallen down
J	none	E, S	like 'j', dot having slipped to one side
K	4	W	vertical line, and foot, of 'K'
L	none	W, S	obvious
⎰M	none	N, W, E	like 'm', with central vertical erased
⎱N	none	W, E, S	reverse of preceding symbol
O	none	N, W, E, S	obvious
⎧P	2	W	vertical line of 'p', with dot to stand for the semicircle
⎨Q	none	E	vertical line of 'q', with dot to stand for the semicircle; also reverse of preceding symbol
R	3	N, E	lower part of 'R'
⎰S	none	N, W	like old-fashioned 's'
⎱T	none	N, E	left-hand part of 'T'; also reverse of preceding symbol
U	2	none	tops of 'U'
V	2, 4	none	corners of 'V'
W	2	S	like 2 'V' symbols, with lower corners connected by a line
⎰X	3	N	no likeness claimed
⎱Y	4	N	ditto, but is reverse of preceding symbol
Z	none	N, S	upper and lower lines of 'Z'
'figures'	2, 3	none	corners of 'F'; means 'symbols will now represent figures'
'date'	2, 3, 4	none	corners of a square 'D'; means 'next 6 symbols will represent date, 2 standing for day of month, 2 for month, and 2 for year of century (e.g. '070305' would represent '7th of March, 1805')
'letters'	3, 4	none	corners of 'L'; means 'symbols will now represent letters again'
'and'	3	E	symbol for 'A' put upright; and right-hand portions of symbols for 'N' and 'D'
'the'	3, 4	N	upper portion of symbol for 'T'; feet of symbol for 'H'; and symbol for 'E'

When the symbols are to represent figures, they should be the symbols for 10 of the letters, as follows:

	Letters	Reasons for Selection
1	B	first consonant
2	D	initial of 'duo' and 'deux'
3	T	initial of 'three'
4	F	initial of 'four'
5	L	means '50'
6	S	initial of 'six'
7	M	final of 'septem'
8	H	initial of 'huit'; also resembles '8'
9	N	initial of 'nine'
0	Z	initial of 'zero'

These 10 letters are a portion of my 'Memoria Technica', in which (by assigning 2 consonants to each digit, and assigning no meanings to vowels and 'Y') I can always represent any date, or other number, by a *real* word: the others 10 consonants being as follows: '1, C; 2, W; 3, J; 4, Q; 5, V; 6, X; 7, P; 8, K; 9, G; 0, R.' There are reasons for selection in all these pairs, except '3, J', which had to pair off as the sole survivors.

Rab – Ymra – ?

June 30, 1892:
Invented what I think is a *new* kind of riddle: 'A Russian had three sons. The first, named Rab, became a lawyer; the second, Ymra, became a soldier. The third became a sailor: what was his name?'

The Diaries

The answer to this may not be immediately apparent – until one spots that Rab, spelt backwards, reads bar; likewise Ymra, army. Not illogically, therefore, the sailor's name was Yvan! The word 'semordnilap' (palindromes spelt backwards) has been proposed for such a word that spells another in reverse. Other worthy examples are DELIVER, DEVIL, and LAMINA. Nabokov has ventured REPAID, while another of Carroll's favourite word play discoveries falls into the same category. This was placed on the lips of Bruno in *Sylvie and Bruno Concluded*:

> Sylvie was arranging some letters on a board – E - V - I - L. 'Now, Bruno,' she said, 'what does *that spell?*'
> Bruno looked at it, in solemn silence, for a minute. 'I know what it *doesn't* spell!' he said at last.
> 'That's no good,' said Sylvie. 'What *does* it spell?'
> Bruno took another look at the mysterious letters. 'Why, it's "LIVE", backwards!' he exclaimed. (I thought it was, indeed.)
> 'How *did* you manage to see that?' said Sylvie.
> 'I just twiddled my eyes,' said Bruno, 'and then I saw it directly.'

The simplest and most famous example, however, is that instanced by James Joyce in *Ulysses*: namely DOG spells GOD. Joyce's *Finnegan's Wake* abounds in Carrollian word play and references to the Alice books, not the least significant of which is the teasingly irreverent reference to Carroll himself as 'Dodgfather, Dodgson & Coo'. In the mathematical section Joyce writes: 'One of the most murmurable loose carollaries ever Ellis threw his cookingclass'. Twenty-four pages earlier one meets 'Though Wonderlawn's lost us for ever. Alis, alas, she broke the glass! Liddell lokker through the leafery . . .'

To revert to EVIL spells LIVE, Dudeney seized upon the even more prolific anagrammatic nature of the word(s) and linking this to a chess-board theme, arrived at the following problem:

		V	E	I	L		
		I	L	V	E		
I	V					L	E
L	E					I	V
V	I					E	L
E	L					V	I
		E	V	L	I		
		L	I	E	V		

Study the illustration and you will see that no two similar letters share any one vertical, horizontal, or diagonal line. The puzzle is to find a similar arrangement of eight Es, eight Vs, eight Is and eight Ls, that gives the largest possible number of four letter words (VEIL, VILE, LEVI, as well as EVIL and LIVE, all qualify) reading upwards, downwards, backwards, forwards or diagonally. A word may be repeated as many times as required. Dudeney's solution, which gives twenty readings of the five words, six horizontal, six vertical, and eight diagonal, will be found at the end of this volume. Remember that every LIVE or EVIL counts as two words.

Pillow-problems

'Oh, don't go on like that!' cried the poor Queen, wringing her hands in despair. 'Consider what a great girl you are. Consider what a long way you've come to-day. Consider what o'clock it is. Consider anything, only don't cry!'

Alice could not help laughing at this, even in the midst of her tears. 'Can *you* keep from crying by considering things?' she asked.

'That's the way it's done,' the Queen said with great decision: 'nobody can do two things at once, you know. Let's consider your age to begin with – how old are you?'

Through the Looking-Glass

In his introduction to the first edition of 'Pillow-Problems', published in May, 1893 as Part II of *Curiosa Mathematica*, Carroll reveals himself as a devotee of his own White Queen's advice. Almost all of the seventy-two problems were solved by him while lying awake at night between 1874 and 1891 in a quasi-therapeutic attempt to allay less wholesome thoughts, which he goes to great lengths to catalogue: 'There are sceptical thoughts, which seem for the moment to uproot the firmest faith; there are blasphemous thoughts, which dart unbidden into the most reverent souls; there are unholy thoughts, which torture, with their hateful presence, the fancy that would fain be pure.'

However complicated most of the problems may appear to the general reader, the challenge presented by them to Carroll was far more acceptable than that of having

. . . . to carry out the resolution 'I will *not* think of so-and-so.' (Witness the common trick, played on a child, of saying 'I'll give you a penny, if you'll stand in that corner for five minutes, and *not once* think of strawberry-jam.'

No human child ever yet won the tempting wager!) But it *is* possible – as I am most thankful to know – to carry out the resolution 'I *will* think of so-and-so.' Once fasten the attention upon a subject so chosen, and you will find that the worrying subject, which you desire to banish, is *practically* annulled. It may recur, from time to time – just looking in at the door, so to speak; but it will find itself so coldly received, and will get so little attention paid to it, that it will, after a while, cease to be any worry at all.

He took great pains to stress that nothing was committed to paper until the morning, each problem worked out to the very end before he drew a single line, jotted down a mere word of the solution. Moreover, characteristically of a man who was in the habit of addressing the envelope before writing the letter, when he did come to record the night's work he would generally write the answer down first, followed by the question, and then the solution.

Amid a plethora of algebra, plane geometry and trigonometry, 'Pillow-Problems' invites its reader to prove in his head that three times the sum of three squares is also the sum of four squares; to find a new expression for the chance that if an infinite number of rods be broken, at least one would break in the middle; to find the points on a plain on which three cylindrical towers of different widths have been set, from which they will all appear the same width. A recurring motif throughout the book involves the various permutations on an assortment of black and white counters used to explore probability theory. The first and last of these are included in the selection which follows, a subjective assessment of what will most appeal to the puzzle fanatic or Wonderland admirer, as distinct from Carroll's own equal in mathematics. The numeration of the puzzles coincides with the original, while the figures after the problems represent the exact or approximate dates of the sleepless nights in question.

One should note that Carroll's solution to the first counter problem can be stated far more simply. If B and W1 are used to represent the black or white counter that may be in the bag at the beginning, and W2 the white counter added, after one removes one white counter the three possible states may be denoted as follows:

1.	W1 (bag)		W2 (outside)
2.	W2 (bag)		W1 (outside)
3.	B (bag)		W2 (outside)

And so far more simply to Carroll's conclusion.

Less easy to dismiss is the final excursion into probability tiddlywinks described proudly by the author as his

> . . . . one Problem in 'Transcendental Probabilities' – a subject in which, I believe, *very* little has yet been done by even the most enterprising of mathematical explorers. To the casual reader it may seem abnormal, and even paradoxical; but I would have such a reader ask himself, candidly, the question 'Is not Life itself a Paradox?'

This problem as stated by Carroll cannot actually be solved, while in attempting the impossible he falls into the snare of fallacious reasoning, introducing an additional black counter to confuse the reader and then making the fatal assumption in concluding that since the probability of drawing a black counter is now 2/3, the only possible constitution of the bag is BBW minus the black, or one black counter and one white. A similar paradoxical conclusion can, in fact, be introduced without the addition of the third counter, the flaw still resting in the step where the probabilities of drawing a black counter in the individual cases are combined to give a single probability.

QUESTIONS:

5.

A bag contains one counter, known to be either white or black. A white counter is put in, the bag shaken, and a counter drawn out, which proves to be white. What is now the chance of drawing a white counter?   [8/9/87

8.

Some men sat in a circle, so that each had 2 neighbours; and each had a certain number of shillings. The first had 1s. more than the second, who had 1s. more than the third, and so on. The first gave 1s. to the second, who gave 2s. to the third, and so on, each giving 1s. more than he received, as long as possible. There were then 2 neighbours, one of whom had 4 times as much as the other. How many men were there? And how much had the poorest man at first?   [3/89

10.

A triangular billiard-table has 3 pockets, one in each corner, one of which will hold only one ball, while each of the others will hold two. There are 3 balls on the table, each containing a single coin. The table is tilted up, so that the balls run into one corner, it is not known which. The 'expectation', as to the contents of the pocket, is 2/6. What are the coins?   [8/90

31.

On July 1, at 8 a.m. by my watch, it was 8*h*. 4*m*. by my clock. I took the watch to Greenwich, and, when it said 'noon', the true time was 12*h*. 5*m*. That evening, when the watch said '6*h*.', the clock said '5*h*. 59*m*.'.

On July 30, at 9 a.m. by my watch, it was 8*h*. 57*m*. by my clock. At Greenwich, when the watch said '12*h*. 10*m*.', the true time was 12*h*. 5*m*. That evening, when the watch said '7*h*.' the clock said '6*h*. 58*m*.'.

My watch is only wound up for each journey, and goes uniformly during any one day: the clock is always going, and goes uniformly.

How am I to know when it is *true* noon on July 31?   [14/3/89

39.

A and *B* begin, at 6 a.m. on the same day, to walk along a road in the same direction, *B* having a start of 14 miles, and each walking from 6 a.m. to 6 p.m. daily. *A* walks 10 miles, at a uniform pace, the first day, 9 the second, 8 the third, and so on: *B* walks 2 miles, at a uniform pace, the first day, 4 the second, 6 the third, and so on. When and where are they together?

                    [16/3/78

52.

Five beggars sat down in a circle, and each piled up, in a heap before him, the pennies he had received that day: and the five heaps were equal.

Then spake the eldest and wisest of them, unfolding, as he spake, an empty sack.

'My friends, let me teach you a pretty little game! First, I name myself "Number One", my left-hand neighbour "Number Two", and so on to "Number Five". I then pour into this sack the whole of my earnings for the day, and hand it on to him who sits next but one on my left, that is, "Number Three". *His* part in the game is to take out of it, and give to his two neighbours, so many pennies as represent their names (that is, he must give four to "Number Four" and two to "Number Two"); he must then put *into* the sack half as much as it contained when he received it; and he must then hand it on just as I did, that is, he must hand it to him who sits next but one on his left – who will of course be "Number Five". *He* must proceed in the same way, and hand it on to "Number Two", from whom the sack will find its way to "Number Four", and so to me again. If any player cannot furnish, from his own heap, the whole of what he has to put into the sack, he is at liberty to draw upon any of the other heaps, *except mine!*'

The other beggars entered into the game with much enthusiasm: and in due time the sack returned to 'Number One', who put into it the two pennies he had received during the game, and carefully tied up the mouth of it with a string. Then, remarking 'it is a *very* pretty little game', he rose to his feet, and hastily quitted the spot. The other four beggars gazed at each other with rueful countenances. Not one of them had a penny left!

How much had each at first?   [16/2/89

68.

Five friends agreed to form themselves into a Wine-Company (Limited). They contributed equal amounts of wine, which had been bought at the same price. They then elected one of themselves to act as Treasurer; and another of them undertook to act as Salesman, and to sell the wine at 10% over cost-price.

The first day the Salesman drank one bottle, sold some, and handed over the receipts to the Treasurer.

The second day he drank none, but pocketed the profits on one bottle sold, and handed over the rest of the receipts to the Treasurer.

That night the Treasurer visited the Cellars, and counted the remaining wine. 'It will fetch just £11,' he muttered to himself as he left the Cellars.

The third day the Salesman drank one bottle, pocketed the profits on another, and handed over the rest of the receipts to the Treasurer.

The wine was now all gone: the Company held a Meeting, and found to their chagrin that their profits (i.e. the Treasurer's receipts, less the original value of the wine) only cleared 6d. a bottle on the whole stock. These profits had accrued in 3 equal sums on the 3 days (i.e. the Treasurer's receipts for the day, less the original value of the wine taken out during the day, had come to the same amount every time); but of course only the Salesman knew this.

(1) How much wine had they bought? (2) At what price?   [28/2/89

72.

A bag contains 2 counters, as to which nothing is known except that each is either black or white. Ascertain their colours without taking them out of the bag.   [8/9/87

ANSWERS:

5.
Two-thirds.

8.
7 men; 2 shillings.

10.
Either 2 florins and a sixpence; or else a half-crown and 2 shillings.

31.
When the clock says '12h. 2m. $29\frac{277}{288}$ sec.'

39.
They meet at end of 2d. 6h., and at end of 4d.: and the distances are 23 miles, and 34 miles.

52.
2l. 18s. 0d.

68.
(1) 5 dozen; (2) 8/4 a bottle.

72.
One is black, and the other white.

SOLUTIONS:

5.

At first sight, it would appear that, as the state of the bag, *after* the operation, is necessarily identical with its state *before* it, the chance is just what it then was, viz. $\frac{1}{2}$. This, however, is an error.

The chances, *before* the addition, that the bag contains (a) 1 white (b) 1 black, are (a) $\frac{1}{2}$ (b) $\frac{1}{2}$. Hence the chances, *after* the addition, that it contains (a) 2 white (b) 1 white, 1 black, are the same, viz. (a) $\frac{1}{2}$ (b) $\frac{1}{2}$. Now the probabilities, which these 2 states give to the observed event, of drawing a white counter, are (a) certainty (b) $\frac{1}{2}$. Hence the chances, after drawing the white counter, that the bag, before drawing, contained (a) 2 white, (b) 1 white, 1 black, are proportional to (a) $\frac{1}{2}$. 1 (b) $\frac{1}{2}$. $\frac{1}{2}$; i.e. (a) $\frac{1}{2}$ (b) $\frac{1}{4}$; i.e. (a) 2 (b) 1. Hence the chances are (a) $\frac{2}{3}$ (b) $\frac{1}{3}$. Hence, after the removal of a white counter, the chances, that the bag now contains (a) 1 white (b) 1 black, are for (a) $\frac{2}{3}$ and for (b) $\frac{1}{3}$.

Thus the chance, of now drawing a white counter, is $\frac{2}{3}$.

8.

Let $m=$ No. of men, $k=$ No. of shillings possessed by the last (i.e. the poorest) man. After one circuit, each is a shilling poorer, and the moving heap contains m shillings. Hence, after k circuits, each is k shillings poorer, the last man now having nothing, and the moving heap contains mk shillings. Hence the thing ends when the last man is again called on to hand on the heap, which then contains $(mk+m-1)$ shillings, the penultimate man now having nothing, and the first man having $(m-2)$ shillings.

It is evident that the first and last man are the only 2 neighbours whose possessions can be in the ratio '4 to 1'. Hence either

$$mk+m-1=4\,(m-2),$$

or else $\quad 4\,(mk+m-1)=m-2.$

The first equation gives $mk=3m-7$, i.e. $k=3-\dfrac{7}{m}$, which evidently gives no integral values other than $m=7$, $k=2$.

The second gives $4mk=2-3m$, which evidently gives no positive integral values.

Hence the answer is '7 men; 2 shillings'.

10.

Call them x, y, z; and let $x+y+z=s$.

The chance, that the pocket contains 2 balls, is $\frac{2}{3}$; and, if it does, the 'expectation' is the average value of

$$(y+z),\ (z+x),\ (x+y);\ \text{i.e. it is } \frac{2s}{3}.$$

Also the chance, that it contains only one, is $\frac{1}{3}$; and, if it does, the 'expectation' is $\dfrac{s}{3}$.

Hence total 'expectation' $= \dfrac{4s}{9} + \dfrac{s}{9} = \dfrac{5s}{9}$.

$$\therefore \ \dfrac{5s}{9} = 30d.; \qquad \therefore \ s = 54d. = 4/6.$$

Hence the coins must be 2 florins and a sixpence; or else a half-crown and 2 shillings.

31.

On July 1, watch gained on clock $5m$. in $10h$.; i.e. $\frac{1}{2}m$. per hour; i.e. $2m$. in $4h$. Hence, when watch said 'noon', clock said '$12h.\ 2m.$'; i.e. clock was $3m$. slow of true time, when *true* time was $12h.\ 5m$.

On July 30, watch lost on clock $1m$. in $10h$.; i.e. 6 sec. per hour; i.e. 19 *sec.* in $3h.\ 10m$. Hence when watch said '$12h.\ 10m.$', clock said '$12h.\ 7m.\ 19\ sec.$'; i.e. clock was $2m.\ 19sec.$ fast of *true* time, when true time was $12h.\ 5m$.

Hence clock gains, on *true* time, $5m.\ 19sec.$ in 29 days; i.e. $319sec.$ in

29 days; i.e. $11sec.$ per day; i.e. $\dfrac{11}{24 \times 12}$ sec. in $5m$.

Hence, while *true* time goes $5m.$, watch goes $5m.\ \frac{11}{288}sec.$

Now, when *true* time is $12h.\ 5m.$ on July 31, clock is ($2m.\ 19sec. + 11sec.$) fast of it; i.e. says '$12h.\ 7\frac{1}{2}m.$' Hence, if *true* time be put $5m.$ back, clock must be put $5m.\ \frac{11}{288}sec.$ back; i.e. must be put back to $12h.\ 2m.\ 29\frac{277}{288}sec.$

Hence, on July 31, when clock indicates this time, it is *true* noon.

39.

Let $x =$ no. of days.

Then $(2 \times 10 - \overline{x-1}).\dfrac{x}{2} = 14 + \{2 \times 2 + \overline{x-1}\ .\ 2\}.\dfrac{x}{2}$;

i.e. $\dfrac{21x}{2} - \dfrac{x^2}{2} = 14 + x + x^2$;

$\therefore \ 3x^2 - 19x + 28 = 0; \quad \therefore \ x = \dfrac{19 \pm 5}{6} = 4\ \text{or}\ \dfrac{7}{3}$.

Now the above solution has taken no account of the *discontinuity* of increase, or decrease of pace, and is the true solution only on the supposition that the increase or decrease is *continuous*, and such as to coincide with the

above data at the end of each day. Hence '4' is a correct answer; but '$\frac{7}{3}$'

only indicates that a meeting occurs *during the third day*. To find the hour of this, let $y =$ no. of hours.

Now in 2 days A has got to the end of 19 miles, B to the end of $(14+6)$, i.e. 20.

$\therefore \ 19 + y.\frac{8}{12} = 20 + y.\frac{6}{12}$

i.e. $y.\frac{2}{3} = 1 + y.\frac{1}{2}$; $\therefore \ y = 6$.

Hence they meet at end of 2*d*. 6*h*., and at end of 4*d*.: and the distances are 23 miles, and 34 miles.

52.

Let x be the number of pennies each had at first.

No. (3) received x, took out $(2+4)$, and put in $\frac{x}{2}$; so that the sack then con-

tained $(x \cdot \frac{3}{2} - 6)$. Let us write '*a*' for '$\frac{3}{2}$'.

No. (5) received $(xa-6)$, took out $(4+1)$, and put in enough to multiply, by a, its contents when he received it. The sack now contained (xa^2-6a-5).

No. (2) took out $(1+3)$, and handed on (xa^3-6a^2-5a-4).

No. (4) took out $(3+5)$, and handed on $(xa^4-6a^3-5a^2-4a-8)$.

No. (1) put in 2. The sack now contained $5x$.

Hence $xa^4-6a^3-5a^2-4a-6 = 5x$;

$$\therefore x = \frac{6a^3+5a^2+4a+6}{a^4-5} \; ;$$

$$= \frac{(6 \cdot 3^3+5 \cdot 3^2 \cdot 2+4 \cdot 3 \cdot 2^2+6 \cdot 2^3) \cdot 2}{3^4-5 \cdot 2^4} \; ;$$

$$= \frac{(162+90+48+48) \cdot 2}{81-80} = 696 = 2l. \; 18s. \; 0d.$$

68.

Let the Nos of bottles, taken out on the 3 days, be 'x, y, z'. Let each bottle have cost $10v$ pence, and therefore be sold for $11v$ pence.

Then the Treasurer's receipts, on the 3 days, were $(x-1). \; 11v, y \cdot 11v-v,$ $(z-1) \cdot 11v-v$; yielding, as profits (i.e. as remainders after deducting cost-price of bottles taken out), $xv-11v, yv-v, zv-12v$. Then these 3 quantities are equal. Hence $y = x-10$, and $z = x+1$;

$\therefore$ total No. of bottles, being $(x+y+z)$, $= 3x-9$.

Now total profits are $(x+y+z) \cdot v-24v$; i.e. $(3x-33) v$;

$\therefore$ profit, per bottle $= \frac{(3x-33) \cdot v}{3x-9}$; and this must $= 6$;

$\therefore (x-11) \cdot v = (x-3) \cdot 6.$

Also $z \cdot 11v = 11 \times 240$; i.e. $(x+1) \cdot 11v = 11 \times 240$;

$\therefore \frac{x-11}{x+1} = \frac{6 \cdot (x-3)}{240}$;

$\therefore (x+1) \cdot (x-3) = 40 \cdot (x-11)$;

$\therefore x^2-2x-3 = 40x-440$;

$\therefore \; x^2 - 42x + 437 = 0.$

Now $42^2 - 4 \times 437 = 1764 - 1748 = 16$;

$\therefore \; x = \dfrac{42 \pm 4}{2} = 23 \text{ or } 19$;

$\quad \therefore$ No. of bottles $= 60$ or 48; but it is a multiple of 5;

$\therefore$ it $= 60$.

Also $(x+1) \cdot 11v = 11 \times 240$; i.e. $24v = 240$;

$\therefore \; v = 10$;

i.e. the wine was bought @ 8/4 a bottle, and sold @ 9/2 a bottle.

72.

We know that, if a bag contained 3 counters, 2 being black and one white, the chance of drawing a black one would be $\frac{2}{3}$; and that any *other* state of things would *not* give this chance.

Now the chances, that the given bag contains (α) BB, (β) BW, (γ) WW, are respectively $\frac{1}{4}$, $\frac{1}{2}$, $\frac{1}{4}$.

Add a black counter.

Then the chances, that it contains (α) BBB, (β) BWB, (γ) WWB, are, as before, $\frac{1}{4}$, $\frac{1}{2}$, $\frac{1}{4}$.

Hence the chance, of now drawing a black one,

$$= \tfrac{1}{4} \cdot 1 + \tfrac{1}{2} \cdot \tfrac{2}{3} + \tfrac{1}{4} \cdot \tfrac{1}{3} = \tfrac{2}{3}.$$

Hence the bag now contains BBW (since any *other* state of things would *not* give this chance).

Hence, before the black counter was added, it contained BW, i.e. one black counter and one white.

As Warren Weaver has pointed out, this last solution is 'good Wonderland, but very amateurish mathematics'. One will never know whether Carroll's powers of reason did fail at the climactic moment of his book, or whether, true to the spirit of his more popular works, he intended to sign off with a 'transcendental' leg-pull, hoping all along that for 'paradoxical' his readers would need no hint to read 'non-sensical'.

The monkey and the weight

'We have applied the same process,' Mein Herr continued, not noticing Bruno's question, 'to many other purposes. We have gone on selecting *walking-sticks* – always keeping those that walked *best* – till we have obtained some, that can walk by themselves! We have gone on selecting *cotton-wool*, till we have got some lighter than air! You've no idea what a useful material it is! We call it "Imponderal".'

'What do you use it for?'

'Well, chiefly for *packing* articles, to go by Parcel-Post. It makes them weigh *less than nothing*, you know.'

'And how do the Post Office people know what you have to pay?'

'That's the beauty of the new system!' Mein Herr cried exultingly. 'They pay *us*: we don't pay *them*! I've often got as much as five shillings for sending a parcel.'

Sylvie and Bruno Concluded

Few of Carroll's puzzles perplexed his contemporaries more than that of 'The Monkey and the Weight' which, alongside 'Where does the day begin?', was one of his own two favourites. A weightless and perfectly flexible rope is hung over a weightless, frictionless pulley attached to the roof of a building. At one end of the rope is a weight which exactly counterbalances a monkey at the other end. If the monkey begins to climb, what will happen to the weight? Reading his diary entry for December 21, 1893, one can detect the delight of the master baffler:

Got Prof. Clifton's answer to the 'Monkey and Weight' problem. It is very curious, the different views taken by good mathematicians. Price says the weight goes *up*, increasing velocity. Clifton (and Harcourt) that it goes *up*, at the same rate as the monkey, while Sampson says that it goes *down*!

Six years later in *The Lewis Carroll Picture Book* Collingwood quotes the suggestion of the Rev. Arthur Brook that 'the weight remains stationary'. Warren Weaver, writing in *Scientific American* for April, 1956, underlines a possible lack of definition in the problem with regard to the monkey's own movement. Does it jerk the rope or does it begin to pull very gently? How does he sustain his pull? While valid in so far as we need to know this to have an exact detailed picture of the weight's movement, one does not need an exact definition to arrive at an answer. The correct solution is that regardless of how the monkey climbs the rope, the monkey and weight always remain opposite. There is nothing the monkey can do to get above or below it at any time, whether climbing ever so slowly or with frenetic leaps or jerks.

228

Given the now familiar conditions, it is clear that the tension on the rope must be the same on both sides of the pulley. The rope will always pull equally hard on both the weight and monkey. This coupled with the force of gravitation – similar on both monkey and weight – clinches the fact that they are partners in every move and deed. A. G. Samuelson, replying with this answer to Weaver in June, 1956, cites a more recent version of the problem which substitutes a mirror for the weight and asks, as if it were in retrospect of the correct solution, whether the monkey can escape the unsightly spectacle of his own image.

The illustration, mis-spelling included, is taken from an early publication of the American puzzle-expert Sam Loyd who himself answered the problem incorrectly by stating that as the monkey climbs the rope, so he will, in fact, fall with increasing speed. But then at no time did Carroll demonstrate that he himself really understood the mechanics of the problem!

Fortunatus's purse

'You have heard of Fortunatus's Purse, Miladi? Ah, so! Would you be surprised to hear that, with three of these leetle handkerchiefs, you shall make the Purse of Fortunatus, quite soon, quite easily?'

'Shall I indeed?' Lady Muriel eagerly replied, as she took a heap of them into her lap, and threaded her needle. '*Please* tell me how, Mein Herr! I'll make one before I touch another drop of tea!'

'You shall first,' said Mein Herr, possessing himself of two of the handkerchiefs, spreading one upon the other, and holding them up by two corners, 'you shall first join together these upper corners, the right to the right, the left to the left; and the opening between them shall be the *mouth* of the Purse.'

A very few stitches sufficed to carry out *this* direction. 'Now, if I sew the other three edges together,' she suggested, 'the bag is complete?'

'Not so, Miladi: the *lower* edges shall *first* be joined – ah, not so!' (as she was beginning to sew them together). 'Turn one of them over, and join the *right* lower corner of the one to the *left* lower corner of the other, and sew the lower edges together in what you would call *the wrong way*.'

'*I* see!' said Lady Muriel, as she deftly executed the order. 'And a very twisted, uncomfortable, uncanny-looking bag it makes! But the *moral* is a lovely one. Unlimited wealth can only be attained by doing things *in the wrong way*! And how are we to join up these mysterious – no, I mean *this* mysterious opening?' (twisting the thing round and round with a puzzled air). 'Yes, it *is* one opening. I thought it was *two*, at first.'

'You have seen the puzzle of the Paper Ring?' Mein Herr said, addressing the Earl. 'Where you take a slip of paper, and join its ends together, first twisting one, so as to join the *upper* corner of *one* end to the *lower* corner of the *other*?'

'I saw one made, only yesterday,' the Earl replied. 'Muriel, my child, were you not making one, to amuse those children you had to tea?'

'Yes, I know that Puzzle,' said Lady Muriel. 'The Ring has only *one* surface, and only *one* edge. It's very mysterious!'

'The *bag* is just like that, isn't it?' I suggested. 'Is not the *outer* surface of one side of it continuous with the *inner* surface of the other side?'

'So it is!' she exclaimed. 'Only it *isn't* a bag, just yet. How shall we fill up this opening, Mein Herr?'

'Thus!' said the old man impressively, taking the bag from her, and rising to his feet in the excitement of the explanation. 'The edge of the opening consists of *four* handkerchief edges, and you can trace it continuously, round and round the opening: down the right edge of *one* handkerchief, up the left edge of the *other*, and then down the left edge of the *one*, and up the right edge of the *other*!'

'So you can!' Lady Muriel murmured thoughtfully, leaning her head on her hand, and earnestly watching the old man. 'And that *proves* it to be only *one* opening!'

She looked so strangely like a child, puzzling over a difficult lesson, and Mein Herr had become, for the moment, so strangely like the old Professor, that I felt utterly bewildered: the 'eerie' feeling was on me in its full force, and I felt almost *impelled* to say 'Do you understand it, Sylvie?' However I checked myself by a great effort, and let the dream (if indeed it *was* a dream) go on to its end.

'Now, this *third* handkerchief,' Mein Herr proceeded, 'has *also* four edges, which you can trace continuously round and round: all you need do is to join its four edges to the four edges of the opening. The Purse is then complete, and its outer surface—'

'*I* see!' Lady Muriel eagerly interrupted. 'Its *outer* surface will be continuous with its *inner* surface! But it will take time. I'll sew it up after tea.' She laid aside the bag, and resumed her cup of tea. 'But why do you call it Fortunatus's Purse, Mein Herr?'

The dear old man beamed upon her, with a jolly smile, looking more exactly like the Professor than ever. 'Don't you see, my child – I should say Miladi? Whatever is *inside* that Purse, is *outside* it; and whatever is *outside* it, is *inside* it. So you have all the wealth of the world in that leetle Purse!'

Sylvie and Bruno Concluded

The paper ring mentioned by the German professor is known among magicians and mathematicians as the Moebius Band, after his 'fellow countryman', Augustus Ferdinand Moebius, the astronomer and topologist who first described the curiosity to the Paris Academy in the mid-nineteenth century. For some gentle baffling amusement one can easily construct the band from a long strip of paper as detailed by Carroll. It is now easy to prove the assertion that it has only one edge and surface. Take a pencil and starting at any point on the surface pull the paper beneath it, inscribing a continuous line as you do so and keeping to the middle of the strip. You eventually come back to your starting point having inscribed both 'sides' of the band without ever coming off the edge. Even more surprising, if you now cut the band in half lengthwise along that line, the cutting results not in two separate bands, but in one single band with a circumference twice the size of the original. Take another strip and make another band, this time giving *two* twists through 180 degrees before joining. Cut again down the centre and the result will now be two single bands, but linked together! Yet again, if you slip an elastic band or finger ring over the strip and then give *three* twists through 180 degrees before joining the ends, the result after cutting will once again be an extra large band, this time with the ring securely knotted to the paper!

More recent developments of Moebius' miracle include the double Moebius band, formed by placing two strips together, giving them both the conventional twist of 180 degrees as if they were one strip and then joining the ends as shown. A couple of paper-clips will keep the two strips together during this procedure.

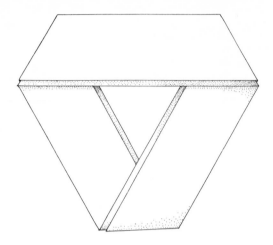

You now have two Moebius bands, 'proved' as such by placing a finger between them and running it all the way round to your starting-point. And yet separate the bands and what seemed to be two is actually one! Canadian magician and mathematician Mel Stover has taken this double model one step further. Using flexible white plastic for the 'double' band, he then inserts a red plastic strip (it is not possible to join the ends of this) 'between' the 'two' white bands. It would now appear to be more obvious than ever that the white bands are separate, since the red layer is at all points between them. The red strip, its ends over-lapped but not glued, is then slipped out and the climax heightened.

However detailed Carroll's instructions for making 'Fortunatus's Purse', they do contain one oversight: with reference to the third from last paragraph, it is impossible in our three-dimensional world to join the four edges of the single handkerchief to the four edges comprising the single edge of the 'opening' without the self-intersection of the surface. The simplest way to show self-intersection at work is to explain how to make a paper version of what is known as the Klein Bottle, after the German mathematician Felix Klein who discovered it in 1882. This is simpler than the projected 'projective plane' (the precise topological term) of the purse, but similar in so far as at once one-sided and no-

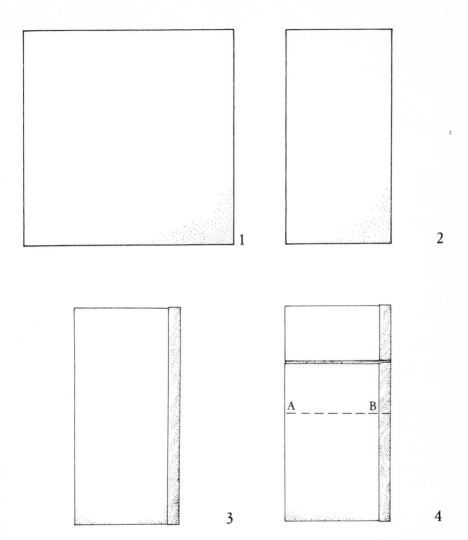

edged, with neither inside nor outside. In one of several methods discovered by Stephen Barr and described at length in his *Experiments in Topology*, you begin with a square of paper folded over into a tube, the right edges fastened with tape as shown. You then cut a slit the width of the tube in the side nearer you, about a quarter of the distance down. Fold the tube along the line AB and push the lower end up through the

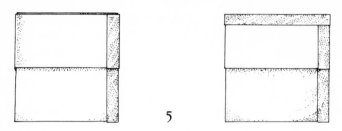

5   6

slot. The double edges at the top of the tube are now taped together all the way around to produce the 'opening' of the bottle (looking more like a purse, in fact), a bottle as comprehensive in its 'contents' as 'Fortunatus's Purse' could ever have been.

Backgammon variations

February 4, 1894:
The idea occurred to me that it might be a pleasant variation in Backgammon to throw *three* dice, and choose any two of the three numbers. The average quality of the throws would be much raised. I reckon that the chance of '6, 6' would be about two and a half what it now is. It would also furnish a means, similar to giving points in billiards, for equalising players: the weaker might use three dice, the other using two. I think of calling it 'Thirdie Backgammon'.

The Diaries

This was not the only time Carroll applied his fanciful mind to Back-gammon, a game of which, according to Isa Bowman, 'he was passionately fond and of which he could never have enough'. As early as January 6, 1868, his diary mentions a previous variation, 'Blot-backgammon', which Roger Lancelyn Green suggests may have been the one where each contestant scored his opponent's points. Then on March 6, 1894 he proclaimed to the nation the rules for 'Co-operative Backgammon' in the Personal Columns of *The Times* after a request regarding the return for exchange of sub-standard copies of the sixtieth thousand of *Through the*

Looking-Glass and the redistribution of the latter to Mechanics' Institutes, Village Reading Rooms, and other worthwhile institutions. The announcement then proceeds:

> 'Mr. Lewis Carroll . . . takes this opportunity of giving his readers the rules for *Co-operative Backgammon*, which he thinks will prove a novel and interesting variety of the game. (1) Each player throws three dice: with two he moves for himself, and with the third for his adversary. (2) If no one of the three dice is available for the adversary, a player may use any two he likes; otherwise he is bound to leave, as third dice, one which will be available for the adversary.'

A logical paradox

'For a *complete* logical argument,' Arthur began with admirable solemnity, 'we need two prim Misses—'

'Of course!' she interrupted. 'I remember that word now. And they produce—?'

'A Delusion,' said Arthur.

'Ye—es?' she said dubiously. 'I don't seem to remember that so well. But what is the *whole* argument called?'

'A Sillygism.'

'Ah, yes! I remember now. But I don't need a Sillygism, you know, to prove that mathematical axiom you mentioned.'

'Nor to prove that "all angles are equal", I suppose?'

'Why, of course not! One takes such a simple truth as that for granted!'

Here I ventured to interpose, and to offer her a plate of strawberries and cream. I felt really uneasy at the thought that she *might* detect the trick: and I contrived, unperceived by her, to shake my head reprovingly at the pseudo-philosopher. Equally unperceived by her, Arthur slightly raised his shoulders, and spread his hands abroad, as who should say 'What else can I say to her?' and moved away leaving her to discuss her strawberries by 'involution', or any other way she preferred.

Sylvie and Bruno

Of the puzzles Collingwood included in *The Lewis Carroll Picture Book*, pride of place went to the Logical Paradox, first written out by Carroll in dialogue form on May 4, 1894 for the magazine *Mind*, where it was published in July of that year. Stated briefly the paradox involves three barbers, Allen, Brown and Carr, and two premises:

1. Allen is unwell and, if he leaves the shop, Brown has to accompany him.
2. All three are unable to leave together, as then the shop would be empty.

If one now assumes that Carr goes out, then according to the second premise if Allen also goes out, Brown must stay in. The first premise, however, has already told us that if Allen goes out, Brown goes as well. And so the initial assumption that Carr goes out has led to a false conclusion. Therefore, the assumption is false and Carr can't leave the shop. And yet that is also absurd, for Carr obviously can go out without disobeying either of the restrictions embodied in the premises.

Here in Carroll's own words is the full switchback ride of a text, intended eventually, as we shall see, for the second volume of his *Symbolic Logic* and described by himself as an 'ornamental presentation' of a dispute between himself (Uncle Jim) and John Cook Wilson (Uncle Joe), a Professor of Logic at Oxford, that had begun in 1893.

'What, *nothing* to do?' said Uncle Jim. 'Then come along with me down to Allen's. And you can just take a turn while I get myself shaved.'

'All right,' said Uncle Joe. 'And the Cub had better come too, I suppose?'

The 'Cub' was *me*, as the reader will perhaps have guessed for himself. I'm turned *fifteen* – more than three months ago; but there's no sort of use in mentioning *that* to Uncle Joe; he'd only say, 'Go to your cubbicle, little boy!' or, 'Then I suppose you can do cubbic equations?' or some equally vile pun. He asked me yesterday to give him an instance of a Proposition in A. And I said, 'All uncles make vile puns.' And I don't think he liked it. However, that's neither here nor there. I was glad enough to go. I *do* love hearing those uncles of mine 'chop logic,' as they call it; and they're desperate hands at it, *I* can tell you!

'That is not a logical inference from my remark,' said Uncle Jim.

'Never said it was,' said Uncle Joe; 'it's a *Reductio ad Absurdum*.'

'An *Illicit Process of the Minor*!' chuckled Uncle Jim.

That's the sort of way they always go on, whenever *I'm* with them. As if there was any fun in calling me a Minor!

After a bit, Uncle Jim began again, just as we came in sight of the barber's. 'I only hope *Carr* will be at home,' he said. 'Brown's so clumsy. And Allen's hand has been shaky ever since he had that fever.'

'Carr's *certain* to be in,' said Uncle Joe.

'I'll bet you sixpence he *isn't*!' said I.

'Keep your bets for your betters,' said Uncle Joe. 'I mean' – he hurried on, seeing by the grin on my face what a slip he'd made – 'I mean that I can *prove* it, logically. It isn't a matter of *chance*.'

'Prove it *logically*!' sneered Uncle Jim. 'Fire away, then! I defy you to do it!'

'For the sake of argument,' Uncle Joe began, 'let us assume Carr to be *out*. And let us see what that assumption would lead to. I'm going to do this by *Reductio ad Absurdum*.'

'Of course you are!' growled Uncle Jim. 'Never knew any argument of *yours* that didn't end in some absurdity or other!'

'Unprovoked by your unmanly taunts,' said Uncle Joe in a lofty tone, 'I proceed. Carr being out, you will grant that, if Allen is *also* out, *Brown* must be at home?'

'What's the good of *his* being at home?' said Uncle Jim. 'I don't want *Brown* to shave me! He's too clumsy.'

'Patience is one of those inestimable qualities—' Uncle Joe was beginning; but Uncle Jim cut him off short.

'*Argue!*' he said. 'Don't *moralise*!'

'Well, but *do* you grant it?' Uncle Joe persisted. 'Do you grant me that, if Carr is out, it follows that if Allen is out Brown *must* be in?'

'Of course he must,' said Uncle Jim; 'or there'd be nobody to mind the shop.'

'We see, then, that the absence of Carr brings into play a certain Hypothetical, whose *protasis* is "Allen is out," and whose *apodosis* is "Brown is in." And we see that, so long as Carr remains out, this Hypothetical remains in force?'

'Well, suppose it does. What then?' said Uncle Jim.

'You will also grant me that the truth of a Hypothetical – I mean its *validity* as a logical *sequence* – does not in the least depend on its *protasis* being actually *true*, nor even on its being *possible*. The Hypothetical "If you were to run from here to London in five minutes you would surprise people,' remains true as a sequence, whether you can do it or not.'

'I can't do *it*,' said Uncle Jim.

'We have now to consider *another* Hypothetical. What was that you told me yesterday about Allen?'

'I told you,' said Uncle Jim, 'that ever since he had that fever he's been so nervous about going out alone, he always takes Brown with him.'

'Just so,' said Uncle Joe. 'Then the Hypothetical 'If Allen is out Brown is out' is *always* in force, isn't it?'

'I suppose so,' said Uncle Jim. (He seemed to be getting a little nervous himself now.)

'Then, if Carr is out, we have *two* Hypotheticals, "if Allen is out Brown is *in*," and "if Allen is out Brown is *out*," in force at once. And two *incompatible* Hypotheticals, mark you! They can't *possibly* be true together!'

'*Can't* they?' said Uncle Jim.

'How *can* they?' said Uncle Joe. 'How *can* one and the same *protasis* prove two contradictory *apodoses*? You grant that the two *apodoses*, "Brown is *in*" and "Brown is *out*", are contradictory, I suppose?'

'Yes, I grant *that*,' said Uncle Jim.

'Then I may sum up,' said Uncle Jim. 'If Carr is out, these two Hypotheticals are true together. And we know that they *cannot* be true together. Which is absurd. Therefore Carr *cannot* be out. There's a nice *Reductio ad Absurdum* for you!'

Uncle Jim looked thoroughly puzzled; but after a bit he plucked up courage, and began again. 'I don't feel at all clear about that *incompatibility*. Why shouldn't those two Hypotheticals be true together? It seems to me that would simply prove "*Allen* is in." Of course it's clear that the *apodoses* of those two Hypotheticals are incompatible – "Brown is *in*" and "Brown is *out*". But why shouldn't we put it like this? If Allen is out, Brown is *out*. If Carr and Allen are *both* out, Brown is *in*. Which is absurd. Therefore Carr and Allen can't be *both* of them out. But, so long as Allen is *in*, I don't see what's to hinder Carr from going out.'

'My dear, but most illogical brother!' said Uncle Joe. (Whenever Uncle Joe begins to 'dear' you, you may make pretty sure he's got you in a cleft stick!) 'Don't you see that you are wrongly dividing the *protasis* and the *apodosis* of that Hypothetical? Its *protasis* is simply "Carr is out"; and its *apodosis* is a sort of sub-Hypothetical, "If Allen is out, Brown is in". And a most absurd apodosis it is, being hopelessly incompatible with that other Hypothetical, that we know is *always* true, "If Allen is out, Brown is *out*". And it's simply the assumption "Carr is out" that has caused this absurdity. So there's only *one* possible conclusion – *Carr is in*!'

How long this argument *might* have lasted I haven't the least idea. I believe *either* of them could argue for six hours at a stretch. But just at this moment we arrived at the barber's shop; and, on going inside, we found—

The paradox hinges on the introduction into the argument of an assumption that does, in fact, violate one of the two premises. As long as Allen, Brown and Carr are together in the shop, nothing can stop any one of them leaving at a given time. If, however, Carr goes out first, then Allen and Brown are no longer so free in their choice of movement. Brown may go out as he pleases, but Allen is then confined to the shop. First, Brown is no longer there to help him; secondly, if Brown's help were available, it would be of no use since they could not leave the shop empty. As Alexander Morris pointed out in *Scientific American* for June, 1956, it is improper to introduce here, in Carr's absence, the assumption that Allen goes out, a course of action impossible for him under the given conditions – short of a miracle to mend his prohibitive ailment and to validate the assumption in the process.

Over the years the problem has claimed the attention of a mind no less distinguished than that of Bertrand Russell, who in a footnote to his *Principia Mathematica* states: 'The principle that false propositions imply all propositions solves Lewis Carroll's logical paradox in *Mind*. . . . The assertion made in that paradox is that, if p, q, r, be propositions, and q implies r, while p implies that q implies not-r, then p must be false, on the supposed ground that "q implies r" and "q implies not-r" are incompatible. But in virtue of our definition of negation, if q be false both these implications will hold the two together, in fact, whatever proposition r may be, are equivalent to not-q. Thus, the only inference warranted by Lewis Carroll's premises is that if p be true, q must be false, i.e. that p implies not-q; and this is the conclusion, oddly enough, which common sense would have drawn in the particular case which he discusses.' More to the point for our purposes is the remark made by R. B. Braithwaite in *The Mathematical Gazette* for July, 1932: 'Lewis Carroll was ploughing deeper than he knew. His mind was permeated by an admirable logic which he was unable to bring to full consciousness and explicit criticism. It is this that makes his *Symbolic Logic* so superficial and his casual puzzles so profound.'

A state of puzzlement

Eastbourne,
September 29, 1894

My Dear (Christian name unknown),
I find I have a duplicate ring-puzzle with me, and so beg your acceptance
of it. Don't be in too great a hurry to explain it to your friends! A state of
puzzlement is good for the young, as it leads to a spirit of enquiry. . . .

Yours affectionately,
Charles L. Dodgson

The above letter followed on from a chance meeting in a railway carriage
the day before with, according to his diary, 'a nice girl of about fifteen
(surname "Newby") who was on her way to school in Eastbourne'.
Carroll never got to know her first name, Mary, but wasted no time in
initiating her further still into his puzzle-circle, appending three amusing
quibbles to his letter:

> Make sense of this sentence: 'It was and I said not all.' Make the letters of
> this sentence into one word: 'Nor do we.' Read this (it is French)
>
> I liers
>
> G sans

All three have a catch. The reading 'G *sous* I, *sans sous liers*' can be read
more intelligibly as '*J'ai souci sans souliers*'; the nonsense sentence
ceases to be so with the studied addition of relevant punctuation: 'It was
"and", I said, not "all" '; while the anagram produced the following
stanza by way of solution:

> 'Nor do we'
> Yes, we do:
> And in 'One Word'
> I'll tell it you!

oblivious of the further anagram that can be coaxed from the same
letters, 'New Door'.

Spelling out the cards

First came ten soldiers carrying clubs; these were all shaped like the three gardeners, oblong and flat, with their hands and feet at the corners: next the ten courtiers: these were ornamented all over with diamonds, and walked two and two, as the soldiers did. After these came the royal children: there were ten of them, and the little dears came jumping merrily along, hand in hand, in couples: they were all ornamented with hearts. Next came the guests, mostly Kings and Queens, and among them Alice recognized the White Rabbit: it was talking in a hurried nervous manner, smiling at everything that was said, and went by without noticing her. Then followed the Knave of Hearts, carrying the King's crown on a crimson velvet cushion; and, last of all this grand procession, came THE KING AND THE QUEEN OF HEARTS.

Alice's Adventures in Wonderland

In his *Winter Nights Entertainments*, R. M. Abraham attributes the
following trick, in which the cards actually do assume a well regulated,
processional identity, to Carroll. Doubtless this is the trick with the pack
of cards which he performed, according to his diary, at 'Mrs. Barber's'
on October 11, 1894, together with 'the money sum (written backwards)
and the history of Mr. C and Mr. T.' To perform, you require a full pack
of fifty-two cards, in which the suits are devoid of any significance:

1. Lay down face upwards an ace, two, three, and four; and then immediately below these a two, four, six, and eight as depicted below:

   AD   2S   3H   4C

   2H   4S   6C   8D

2. On each card in the lower row place a card the pips of which equal the
   sum of that card and the one above it. So on the lower two you place
   one plus two, or a three. You will then arrive at this:

   AD   2S   3H   4C

   3S   6H   9C   QD

With regard to court cards, Jacks count as eleven, Queens twelve, and
Kings thirteen.

3. Continue placing cards on the lower row in the same way. Each card you place down is the sum of the card above and the card immediately below it in the pile. When the total exceeds thirteen, subtract thirteen and use the card equal to the remainder. So after the second addition you will arrive at this:

4. Eventually you will exhaust the cards and the final stage will look something like this:

5. Then gather together the cards, turning them face downwards as they are lifted in the following order: the King-pile below the four, the four, the King-pile below the three, the three, the King-pile below the two, the two, the final King-pile, the ace.

6. Deal out singly the first thirteen cards face downwards in a row.

7. Deal the next thirteen on top of the first thirteen, but start on the second card, miss the third, and then on the fourth, the sixth, and so on, dealing on to alternate cards, going twice round the circuit until you put the thirteenth card on the thirteenth card of the first deal.

8. Deal the next thirteen as before, except that here you begin on the third, missing out two cards each time, and going back to the beginning twice until thirteenth meets thirteenth again.

9. Finally, deal the first of the last thirteen upon the fourth and skip three each time, going four times around the circuit until the final card is placed upon the last pile.

10. You will now have thirteen packets of four cards each. Reassemble the pack, still face downwards, by taking up the thirteenth pile, then the twelfth, the eleventh, and so on, putting each packet on top of the previous one.

11. Now at last the tedium of the above is rewarded! Holding the pack face downwards spell out A-C-E, dealing face downwards into a pile a card for each letter, but turning up the card which coincides with the sound of the last letter of each value, here 'E'. The card will be an ACE! Place this aside. Continue dealing on to the pile, spelling out T-W-O, T-H-R-E-E, and so on through to K-I-N-G, always laying aside the card that coincides with the final letter of its own name. All the cards will come out in sequence.

12. Finally, spread out the pile of thirty-nine cards face upwards, when they will be seen to be arranged in full order of seniority!

Money-sum puzzle

The Hatter looked at the March Hare, who had followed him into the court, arm-in-arm with the Dormouse. 'Fourteenth of March, I *think* it was,' he said.
   'Fifteenth,' said the March Hare.
   'Sixteenth,' said the Dormouse.
   'Write that down,' the King said to the jury; and the jury eagerly wrote down all three dates on their slates, and then added them up, and reduced the answer to shillings and pence.

Alice's Adventures in Wonderland

The money sum is one of two 'numerical curiosities' believed by Collingwood to have been discovered by Carroll and included by the former in *The Lewis Carroll Picture Book*.

Put down any number of pounds not more than twelve, any number of shillings under twenty, and any number of pence under twelve. Under the

pounds put the number of pence, under the shillings the number of shillings, and under the pence the number of pounds, thus reversing the line.
    Subtract.
    Reverse the line again.
    Add.
    Answer, £12 18s. 11d., *whatever* numbers may have been selected.

One is meant to infer from 'subtract' that the smaller amount is taken from the larger, regardless of which was the initial sum written and which its reversal. More disconcerting, however, than trying to subtract, say, £9 17s. 3d. from £3 17s. 9d. is to select initially a sum with palindromic qualities, say £6 3s. 6d. or £11 11s. 11d. In this case no sooner has one subtracted than one is left with a line of noughts. Whatever his flair with numbers – and under the conditions outlined above a similar phenomenon works with three ordinary digits producing a final total of 1,089 – even Carroll couldn't double nought to produce the magic total.

Mr. C. & Mr. T.

'Cheshire Puss,' she began, rather timidly, as she did not at all know whether it would like the name: however, it only grinned a little wider. 'Come, it's pleased so far,' thought Alice, and she went on. 'Would you tell me, please, which way I ought to go from here?'
    'That depends a good deal on where you want to get to,' said the Cat.
    'I don't much care where—' said Alice.
    'Then it doesn't matter which way you go,' said the Cat.

Alice's Adventures in Wonderland

Carroll was fond of telling his young friends stories which hinged upon a 'trick drawing'. Isa Bowman recalls one which ended with the words, 'My dear, you are a Perfect Goose.' Carroll would then turn upside down his accompanying drawing of a little man and his wife with their house beside a lake to reveal none other than the 'Perfect Goose' itself. Dare one imagine an unwieldy lake for its body, a pointed roof for its beak, and matchstick men for its feet? Sadly, the tale of the goose has not been

Mr. C. & Mr. T.

handed down, but 'Mr. C. & Mr. T.', a similar phenomenon in which lines were likewise added to a drawing to illustrate each subsequent point of a story, was featured as the final appendix to Green's edition of *The Diaries*, in a version recalled by a child friend, Mary Burrows, later Mrs. Knyvett. The words are Carroll's own, as far as Mrs. Knyvett could remember them:

Mr C. (1) had a great friend called Mr T. (2) and one day Mr C. determined to go and see Mr T's new house. He was not very sure of the way, so he took a path which he knew was in the right direction, but which was very hilly and frightfully muddy. He started off alright down the hill but at the bottom he slipped badly and fell down in the mud. (3) However nothing daunted, he picked himself up and scrambled back to the path, but alas, he had only gone a few yards when down he fell again. (4) Up he scrambled again, muddier than ever, but luckily, he then came to a nice straight bit (5) but, alas, he was striding along a little too quickly and he came to another muddy bit and down he fell again (6). Very annoyed with himself, he scrambled up yet again but had hardly got on the path when he slipped again (7). Then he came to a steep hill up. However he managed that alright (8) and then, to his delight, he saw Mr T's house in front of him with the front door facing him (9). Mr T. came out to greet him and said 'Do look at the lovely flowers in my garden (10). You see how beautifully my house is built (11). My fires never smoke because I have got such good chimneys (12).' Then Mr T. took him upstairs and showed him the lovely views from his windows (13). They had a lovely tea together and much chat and Mr T. asked Mr C. which way he had come. When Mr C. told him, Mr T. said 'Oh

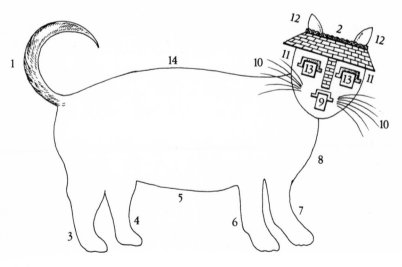

that is entirely the wrong way. I will show you the proper way home,' and when he did so Mr C. found there was a perfectly good road, absolutely straight, and not muddy at all, back to his own house. (14)

There have recently come to light two actual puzzle drawings by Carroll. The first is a modification on 'Mr. C. & Mr. T.'; the second again depicts more than at first meets the eye – an alphabetically-conscious SOW. In ink on blue-tinted paper, they were discovered by artist Graham Ovenden inside a book presented by Carroll to E. R. Baynes on November 25, 1895.

To revert to the earlier goose motif, the idea of upside-down drawing was carried to its most inventive extreme in 1903 by cartoonist Gustave Verbeek in a comic strip he drew for the Sunday edition of *The New York Herald*. One interprets the pictures in normal order, reading the captions beneath; then, having rotated the entire page through 180 degrees, you continue the story with a new set of captions, returning to the initial panel picture. Verbeek's two chief characters were called Little Lady Lovekins and Old Man Muffaroo, who through the uncanniest exploitation of split identity ever known became each other when inverted. In Verbeek's world a goblin would become a goat, a genie a bull, a bird a rhinoceros, always the appropriate facial expression being maintained.

The Snark was a Boojum

> 'It's a Snark!' was the sound that first came to their ears,
>   And seemed almost too good to be true.
> Then followed a torrent of laughter and cheers:
>   Then the ominous words, 'It's a Boo –'
>
> Then, silence. Some fancied they heard in the air
>   A weary and wandering sigh
> That sounded like '– jum!' but the others declare
>   It was only a breeze that went by.
>
> *The Hunting of the Snark*

Carroll's penchant for puzzle pictures may also be detected in Henry Holiday's ingenious penultimate illustration for *The Hunting of the Snark*, first published in 1876. This speaks for itself. Or does it? Look closely at the bottom left corner of the picture and you will see the menacing deformed claw of the Snark grappling with the Baker's wrist, while the aghast bulbous features of the Baker himself materialise in the top half. One wonders, however, how many hundreds of readers will have glanced casually at this view of a craggy landscape with no more concrete result than the remaining members of the Bellman's intrepid crew:

> They hunted till darkness came on, but they found
>   Not a button, or feather, or mark,
> By which they could tell that they stood on the ground
>   Where the Baker had met with the Snark.
>
> In the midst of the word he was trying to say,
>   In the midst of his laughter and glee,
> He had softly and suddenly vanished away –
>   For the Snark *was* a Boojum, you see.

What the Tortoise said to Achilles

'Now, Kitty, let's consider who it was that dreamed it all. This is a serious question, my dear, and you should *not* go on licking your paw like that – as if Dinah hadn't washed you this morning! You see, Kitty, it *must* have been either me or the Red King. He was part of my dream, of course – but then I was part of his dream, too! *Was* it the Red King, Kitty? You were his wife, my dear, so you ought to know.'

Alice's Adventures in Wonderland

In the same light-hearted approach to logic he applied to 'A Logical Paradox', Carroll contributed this dialogue between Achilles and the Tortoise to the December, 1894 edition of *Mind*. Here he is treading in the footsteps of the ancient Greek Sceptic, Agrippa, who argued that nothing can be proved because each proof must itself be proved valid, thus demanding a further proof and so on. The opening lines refer to the famous race which constitutes Zeno's famous second paradox, as propounded by Aristotle, involving a not unrelated infinite regress of ever-diminishing distances. In this Achilles, who runs at ten times the speed of the tortoise, gives the animal a ten-yard start. Achilles then runs those ten yards, the tortoise one; Achilles runs that yard, the tortoise a tenth of a yard; Achilles runs that tenth, the tortoise a hundredth; Achilles runs that hundredth, the tortoise a thousandth. And again ad infinitum, without the slowest ever being overtaken by the swiftest. This has become so well known that it has even stunted the reputation of his first paradox, in which Zeno argued that movement was impossible since the moving object must cover half of the distance to reach its destination, and, before reaching the half-way mark, half of the half; and before the half-way mark of the half, half of the half of the half, and so on. . . . Both assume, wrongly of course, that each segment of the distance to be covered takes the same length of time. If, however, Achilles and the tortoise are given regular uniform speeds so that half the distance is covered in half the time, a quarter of the distance in a quarter of the time and so on, Achilles will certainly overtake the tortoise.

Achilles had overtaken the Tortoise, and had seated himself comfortably on its back.

'So you've got to the end of our race-course?' said the Tortoise. 'Even though it *does* consist of an infinite series of distances? I thought some wise-acre or other had proved that the thing couldn't be done?'

'It *can* be done,' said Achilles. 'It *has* been done! *Solvitur ambulando.*

You see the distances were constantly *diminishing*: and so—'

'But if they had been constantly *increasing*?' the Tortoise interrupted. 'How then?'

'Then I shouldn't be *here*,' Achilles modestly replied; 'and *you* would have got several times round the world, by this time!'

'You flatter me – *flatten*, I mean,' said the Tortoise; 'for you *are* a heavy weight, and *no* mistake! Well now, would you like to hear of a race-course, that most people fancy they can get to the end of in two or three steps, while it *really* consists of an infinite number of distances, each one longer than the previous one?'

'Very much indeed!' said the Grecian warrior, as he drew from his helmet (few Grecian warriors possessed *pockets* in those days) an enormous note-book and a pencil. 'Proceed! And speak *slowly*, please! *Short-hand* isn't invented yet!'

'That beautiful First Proposition of Euclid!' the Tortoise murmured dreamily. 'You admire Euclid?'

'Passionately! So far, at least, as one *can* admire a treatise that won't be published for some centuries to come!'

'Well, now, let's take a little bit of the argument in that First Proposition – just *two* steps, and the conclusion drawn from them. Kindly enter them in your note-book. And in order to refer to them conveniently, let's call them *A*, *B*, and *Z*:

A. Things that are equal to the same are equal to each other.
B. The two sides of this Triangle are things that are equal to the same.
Z. The two sides of this Triangle are equal to each other.

'Readers of Euclid will grant, I suppose, that *Z* follows logically from *A* and *B*, so that any one who accepts *A* and *B* as true, *must* accept *Z* as true?'

'Undoubtedly! The youngest child in a High School – as soon as High Schools are invented, which will not be till some two thousand years later – will grant *that*.'

'And if some reader has *not* yet accepted *A* and *B* as true, he might still accept the *Sequence* as a *valid* one, I suppose?'

'No doubt such a reader might exist. He might say "I accept as true the Hypothetical Proposition that, if *A* and *B* be true, *Z* must be true; but I *don't* accept *A* and *B* as true.' Such a reader would do wisely in abandoning Euclid, and taking to football.'

'And might there not *also* be some reader who would say "I accept *A* and *B* as true, but I *don't* accept the Hypothetical"?'

'Certainly there might. *He*, also, had better take to football.'

'And *neither* of these readers,' the Tortoise continued, 'is *as yet* under any logical necessity to accept *Z* as true?'

'Quite so,' Achilles assented.

'Well, now, I want you to consider *me* as a reader of the *second* kind, and to force me, logically, to accept *Z* as true.'

'A tortoise playing football would be—' Achilles was beginning.

'—an anomaly, of course,' the Tortoise hastily interrupted. 'Don't wander from the point. Let's have *Z* first, and football afterwards!'

'I'm to force you to accept *Z*, am I?' Achilles said musingly. 'And your

present position is that you accept *A* and *B*, but you *don't* accept the Hypothetical—'

'Let's call it *C*,' said the Tortoise.

'—but you don't accept:

   C. If *A* and *B* are true, *Z* must be true.'

'That is my present position,' said the Tortoise.

'Then I must ask you to accept *C*.'

'I'll do so,' said the Tortoise, 'as soon as you've entered it in that note-
book of yours. What else have you got in it?'

'Only a few memoranda,' said Achilles, nervously fluttering the leaves:
'a few memoranda of – of the battles in which I have distinguished myself!'

'Plenty of blank leaves, I see!' the Tortoise cheerily remarked. 'We shall
need them *all*!' (Achilles shuddered.) 'Now write as I dictate:

   A.   Things that are equal to the same are equal to each other.

   B.   The two sides of this triangle are things that are equal to the same.

   C.   If *A* and *B* are true, *Z* must be true.

   Z.   The two sides of this Triangle are equal to each other.'

'You should call it *D*, not *Z*,' said Achilles. 'It comes *next* to the other three.
If you accept *A* and *B* and *C*, you *must* accept *Z*.'

'Any why *must* I?'

'Because it follows *logically* from them. If *A* and *B* and *C* are true, *Z must*
be true. You don't dispute *that*, I imagine?'

'If *A* and *B* and *C* are true, *Z must* be true,' the Tortoise thoughtfully
repeated. 'That's *another* Hypothetical, isn't it? And, if I failed to see its
truth, I might accept *A* and *B* and *C*, and *still* not accept *Z*, mightn't I?'

'You might,' the candid hero admitted; 'though such obtuseness would
certainly be phenomenal. Still, the event is *possible*. So I must ask you to
grant one more Hypothetical.'

'Very good. I'm quite willing to grant it, as soon as you've written it down.
We will call it

   D.   If *A* and *B* and *C* are true, *Z* must be true.

'Have you entered that in your note-book?'

'I *have*!' Achilles joyfully exclaimed, as he ran the pencil into its sheath.
'And at last we've got to the end of this ideal race-course! Now that you
accept *A* and *B* and *C* and *D*, *of course* you accept *Z*.'

'Do I?' said the Tortoise innocently. 'Let's make that quite clear. I accept
A and *B* and *C* and *D*. Suppose I *still* refuse to accept *Z*?'

'Then Logic would take you by the throat, and *force* you to do it!'
Achilles triumphantly replied. 'Logic would tell you "You ca'n't help
yourself. Now that you've accepted *A* and *B* and *C* and *D*, you *must* accept
Z?" So you've no choice, you see.'

'Whatever *Logic* is good enough to tell me is worth *writing down*,' said
the Tortoise. 'So enter it in your book please. We will call it

   E.   If *A* and *B* and *C* and *D* are true, *Z* must be true.

'Until I've granted *that*, of course, I needn't grant *Z*. So it's quite a
necessary step, you see?'

'I see,' said Achilles; and there was a touch of sadness in his tone.

Here the narrator, having pressing business at the Bank, was obliged to leave the happy pair, and did not again pass the spot until some months afterwards. When he did so, Achilles was still seated on the back of the much-enduring Tortoise, and was writing in his note-book, which appeared to be nearly full. The Tortoise was saying 'Have you got that last step written down? Unless I've lost count, that makes a thousand and one. There are several millions more to come. And *would* you mind, as a personal favour – considering what a lot of instruction this colloquy of ours will provide for the Logicians of the Nineteenth Century – *would* you mind adopting a pun that my cousin the Mock Turtle will then make, and allowing yourself to be re-named Taught-Us?'

'As you please!' replied the weary warrior, in the hollow tones of despair, as he buried his face in his hands. 'Provided that *you*, for *your* part, will adopt a pun the Mock Turtle never made, and allow yourself to be renamed A Kill-Ease!'

Jorge Luis Borges, in 'Avatars of the Tortoise', included in his collection of stories and essays, *Labyrinths*, cites Carroll's contribution to that 'illusory Biography of the Infinite'. He also summons Sextus Empiricus' conjecture that definitions are in vain, since in each definition one must define each of the words used, and Byron writing of Coleridge in the dedication of *Don Juan*: 'I wish he would explain his Explanation.' An old issue of *Punch* includes the following statement from a Chairman of a meeting: 'Before we put the motion: "That the motion be now put", should we not first put the motion: "That the motion: 'That the motion be now put' be now put"?' The November, 1964 edition of that same magazine depicted on its cover a magician pulling a rabbit from a hat. The rabbit itself is pulling a smaller rabbit from a smaller hat. This continues ad infinitum until the endless series of rabbits and hats has crowded itself off the edge of the page. As Martin Gardner has pointed out in *The Annotated Alice*, the quotation at the head of this chapter embodies its own form of infinite regress – Alice dreaming of the Red King, who is dreaming of Alice, who is dreaming of the King, who is. . . . One wonders if Edward Albee had Carroll in his thoughts when he wrote his play *Tiny Alice* with its Chinese Box implications of a set within a set within a set, its title character inhabiting through increasingly smaller manifestations of herself each decreasing scale model with a harrowing sense of parallelism to her full-scale life.

A magic number

'Then you keep moving round, I suppose?' said Alice.
'Exactly so,' said the Hatter: 'as the things get used up.'
'But what happens when you come to the beginning again?' Alice ventured to ask.

Alice's Adventures in Wonderland

Ethel Rowell, a former pupil of Carroll, explains in her book *Time and Time Again* how The Mad Hatter's Tea Party exactly illustrates the idea of cyclic order, the idea demonstrated more overtly by Carroll in the other 'numerical curiosity' detailed by Collingwood. This is almost certainly the 'number repeating puzzle' mentioned in his diary on January 26, 1897 as part of a lecture/performance he gave at Guildford High School, and published anonymously in *Chatterbox* two weeks later.

A cyclical number is one that repeats itself endlessly. By dividing 1 by 7, one obtains 00·142857142857142857 etc. Taking the minimum stretch of digits before repetition begins, Carroll discovers some fascinating characteristics:

A MAGIC NUMBER: 142857

285714 twice that number.
428571 thrice that number.
571428 four times that number.
714285 five times that number.
857142 six times that number.

Begin at the '1' in each line and it will be the same order of figures as the magic number up to six times that number, while seven times the magic number results in a row of 9s.

Three right-angled triangles

He thought he saw a Garden-Door
    That opened with a key:
He looked again, and found it was
    A Double Rule of Three:
"And all its mystery," he said,
    "Is clear as day to me!"

Sylvie and Bruno

The last entry but one in Carroll's published diaries mentions how on December 19, 1897 he 'sat up last night till 4 a.m., over a tempting problem, sent me from New York, "to find three equal (in area) rational-sided right-angled triangles". I found *two*, whose sides are 20, 21, 29; 12, 35, 37; but could not find three.' He was never able to present the problem to his readers to see if they could succeed where he failed; but there is, in fact, no limit to the number of right-angled triangles that can be constructed according to Carroll's stipulations. Dudeney later gave the original puzzle an Oriental slant, whereby the sole dominions of a certain Eastern monarch form a perfect square; to prevent his four sons plotting together against him, he decides to confine them to the four corners of his territory; to prevent jealousy each is to be given a triangle of equal area, beyond which they will pass at pain of death. The physical character of the land, however, prevents the four triangles being of the same shape. The puzzle is to give the three dimensions for each of the four triangles in the smallest possible numbers. For the record Dudeney's answer is as follows:

First triangle:	518	1,320	1,418
Second triangle:	280	2,442	2,458
Third triangle:	231	2,960	2,969
Fourth triangle:	111	6,160	6,161

Of more relevance is the formula he gives for finding three triangles of equal area. Given two 'generating' numbers, x and y, then x^2+y^2, x^2-y^2, and $2xy$ will constitute the three sides of a rational right-angled triangle. To form three such triangles of equal area, the following formula comes into play, where x is the larger number:

$$xy + x^2 + y^2 = a$$
$$x^2 - y^2 = b$$
$$2xy + y^2 = c$$

255

Now one has merely to find three triangles from the following pairs of 'generating' numbers:

$$a \& b$$
$$a \& c$$
$$a \& b+c$$

They will all be of equal area. The three smallest right-angled triangles which Carroll could have found (starting with the generating numbers, 1 and 2) are:

First triangle:	40	42	58
Second triangle:	24	70	74
Third triangle:	15	112	113

each with an area of 840 square units. It is ironic that had Carroll only doubled the measurements he cited in his diary, he would have arrived at the first two of these triangles. It is difficult to imagine that he would then have had to struggle so hard to locate the third.

Nose trick

> 'Oh, *please* mind what you're doing!' cried Alice, jumping up and down in an agony of terror. 'Oh, there goes his *precious* nose!' as an unusually large saucepan flew close by it, and very nearly carried it off.
>
> 'If everybody minded their own business,' the Duchess said, in a hoarse growl, 'the world would go round a deal faster than it does.'
>
> *Alice's Adventures in Wonderland*

Discovered among Carroll's effects on his death was the item known affectionately among members of his family as 'CLD's Nose Trick'. Home-made out of polished wood, this consisted of a 'V' shape comprising two arms, approximately four inches in length, with a string entering one of the ends and coming out at the other so that when the nose was held between the arms and the string pulled from side to side, it gave the illusion of penetrating the nasal passages.

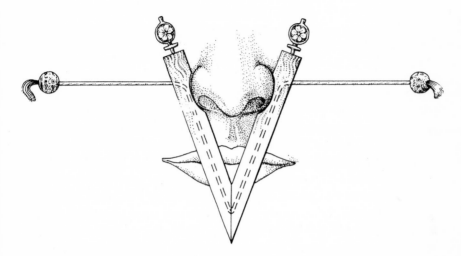

In the illustration, the dotted line indicates the path of the string inside the wood which is hollow, while the two nodules at the end of each arm, made of ivory in Carroll's version, are doubtless there to hide the drill holes. If the interior of the apex of the 'V' is hinged, it is possible to fold the two arms flush against one another, when the string will appear to pass straight through horizontally with no tell-tale gap. The performer now takes a sharp knife and thrusting the blade between the arms at the top pretends to cut the string. The 'V' is opened out and the stringless gap is its own proof that the knife has cut straight through. Closing the 'V' is all that's needed apparently to restore the string, which can of course be pulled through as before. The insertion of the nose before this point, however, disposing of the gap and effecting the restoration in its own zany way, is doubtless why the item had such a special appeal for a master of nonsense.

Brandy and water

However, this bottle was *not* marked 'poison', so Alice ventured to taste it, and, finding it very nice (it had, in fact, a sort of mixed flavour of cherry-tart, custard, pine-apple, roast turkey, toffy, and hot buttered toast), she very soon finished it off.

Alice's Adventures in Wonderland

The less exotic combination of brandy and water provided Carroll with one of his favourite after-dinner problems. According to Viscount Simon in an appendix to Derek Hudson's biography of Carroll, the puzzle in his own terms involved two glasses, one of which contained fifty spoonfuls of brandy, the other fifty spoonfuls of water. One spoonful of brandy is now taken from the first glass and added without spilling to the second. After this has been stirred, one spoonful of the new mixture is transferred back, again without spilling, to the glass of brandy. With this procedure complete, has more brandy been transferred from the first glass to the second, or more water from the second to the first?

Most people plump for the first suggestion, since a spoonful of pure brandy was placed in the second glass, while only a mixture of brandy and water was taken back. But in actual fact both suggestions are wrong. Since the glasses were originally filled to the same level, they will again be equally full after the two operations: the volume of brandy now missing from the first glass is replaced by water taken from the second; similarly the volume of water missing for this purpose from the second glass is necessarily replaced by brandy. The amounts of foreign material in both glasses are equal. You can prove this yourself by working out the following: call the respective quantities of brandy and water 10 spoonfuls each. Transfer one spoonful of brandy to the water glass and the respective mixtures become 9 parts brandy and 10 parts water plus 1 part brandy, or fractionally, $\frac{10}{11}$ water and $\frac{1}{11}$ brandy. When the spoonful of water mixture is transferred to the brandy glass you have $9\frac{1}{11}$ spoonfuls of brandy and $\frac{10}{11}$ of a spoonful of water, i.e. a ratio of $100:10$ or $10:1$, the same as the ratio of water to brandy in the other glass. If it did work out the way most people suggest, you would actually increase the total amount of brandy and decrease that of water. A profitable but impossible process!

Currency conundrum

'But what is the new Money-Act?'

The Professor brightened up again. 'The Emperor started the thing,' he said. 'He wanted to make everybody in Outland twice as rich as he was before – just to make the new Government popular. Only there wasn't nearly enough money in the Treasury to do it. So *I* suggested that he might do it by doubling the value of every coin and bank-note in Outland. It's the simplest thing possible. I wonder nobody ever thought of it before! And you never saw such universal joy. The shops are full from morning to night. Everybody's buying everything!'

Sylvie and Bruno

Another problem with which, according to Simon, Carroll would perplex his guests at the dinner table, involved a man who wanted to purchase a theatre ticket costing one shilling and sixpence. Since he had only a shilling, he went to a pawnbroker who, issuing him with a pawn-ticket for the shilling, lent him ninepence on it. He later met a friend to whom he sold the ticket itself for an additional ninepence. He now had ninepence from the pawnbroker, and ninepence from the friend, enough to purchase the theatre ticket. Who was the loser and by how much? Carroll's reply to Simon when he suggested that the friend lost sixpence, since he had to repay the loan to the pawnbroker to recover the shilling, reflects a similar credit on the naive friend who came to the theatre-goer's rescue: 'My young friend, your answer is not indeed right, but it does you the greatest credit, for it shows that you are so ignorant of the ways of pawnbrokers that you think they do their business for nothing!' The pawnbroker would not only have demanded the ninepence, but the inevitable interest charged.

A more impressive paradox along the same lines involves the exchange of currency at an international level: the governments of two neighbouring countries – say 'Wonderland' and 'Looking-glass' – had come to an agreement whereby a Wonderland pound was worth a pound in Looking-glass and vice versa. One day, however, the Wonderland government decreed that from then on the Looking-glass pound was to be worth a mere ninety pence in Wonderland. The following day, the Looking-glass government retaliated with the decree that now also the Wonderland pound was to be worth only ninety pence in Looking-glass. Armed with this news, an enterprising individual living in a village straddling the border between the two countries went into a shop on the

259

Wonderland side, bought a pen for tenpence and paid for it with a Wonderland pound. He was given a Looking-glass pound, worth ninety pence there, as change. He then crossed the border, went into a Looking-glass shop and bought a magazine for tenpence, paying for it with the Looking-glass pound. He was given a Wonderland pound worth ninety pence as change. On returning home he now had his original pound, plus his purchases. And both shopkeepers had an additional tenpence in the till! Who paid for the pen and the magazine, unless the mysterious extra twenty pence had materialised out of nowhere?

Predicting the total

'In one moment I've seen what has hitherto been
Enveloped in absolute mystery,
And without extra charge I will give you at large
A Lesson in Natural History.'

The Hunting of the Snark

In an article entitled 'Give My Love to the Children' in *The Reader's Digest* for February, 1953, Lancelot Robson, the son of one of Carroll's friends, another reverend mathematician, recalls a surprise performance by the gentleman he knew as 'Mr. Alice in Wonderland' at a children's party, during which Carroll claimed to know in advance the total of a sum not yet set: 'I am afraid you go to a very poor school. I never add up sums; I always put the answer down first and set the sum afterwards.' To demonstrate, he wrote his prediction on a piece of paper which he entrusted to the safe keeping of one of the adults present: 'That will be the answer to our sum when we have set it.' He then scribbled a four-digit number on another piece of paper and invited a small girl in the audience to put down any four figures of her own choice beneath them. He then penned another four, a small boy four more, and finally Carroll added a fifth line – something like this:

1,066   Lewis Carroll
2,961   Child
7,038   Lewis Carroll
5,017   Child
4,982   Lewis Carroll

Needless to say, the total, 21,064, tallied with Carroll's prediction!

The deception hinged on the fact that whatever the children wrote, Carroll added in both cases a number that made the total of those two lines 9999. Therefore, the total of the complete sum would always be twice 9999, plus whatever number he wrote at the top of the column, or that top number plus 20,000, minus 2. If your prediction is to be, say, 23,791, simply remove the first digit and add it to the remaining number to arrive at the initial line of the sum, in this case 3,793:

$$
\begin{array}{l}
3,793 \\
\left.\begin{array}{l} 4,162 \\ 5,837 \end{array}\right\} \quad 9,999 \\
\left.\begin{array}{l} 8,814 \\ 1,185 \end{array}\right\} \quad 9,999 \\
\overline{} \\
23,791
\end{array}
$$

This assumes that the first digit of the prediction will be a 2. If it is a 3, then *three* pairs of numbers each totalling 9999 are required, making seven numbers in all to be added. And so on up and down the numerical scale. Always, however, the first number to be listed is obtained by removing the first digit from the total and adding it to whatever remains.

Numerical roundabout

'Taking Three as the subject to reason about –
A convenient number to state –
We add Seven, and Ten, and then multiply out
By One Thousand diminished by Eight.

'The result we proceed to divide, as you see,
By Nine Hundred and Ninety and Two:
Then subtract Seventeen, and the answer must be
Exactly and perfectly true.'

The Hunting of the Snark

According to Robson, the same tea party produced a second miracle by way of an encore. Asking a small boy to write down the number 12,345,679, Carroll rebuked him jokingly for not forming his figures clearly and by way of correction sprung the following surprise, in which the reader himself may participate. First write down the number and then either assess which figure is the least legible or choose one of the eight digits at random. Multiply the 12,345,679 by this digit, and then multiply that result by nine. You'll find yourself getting practice at forming the mis-shaped digit in the most unexpected fashion!

A mechanical Humpty Dumpty

'Don't stand chattering to yourself like that,' Humpty Dumpty said, looking at her for the first time, 'but tell me your name and your business.'
    'My *name* is Alice, but—'
    'It's a stupid name enough!' Humpty Dumpty interrupted impatiently. 'What does it mean?'
    '*Must* a name mean something?' Alice asked doubtfully.
    'Of course it must,' Humpty Dumpty said with a short laugh: '*my* name means the shape I am – and a good handsome shape it is, too. With a name like yours, you might be any shape, almost.'

Through the Looking-Glass

In *The Life and Letters of Lewis Carroll* Collingwood reproduces the following letter from Walter Lindsay of Philadelphia. There is certainly no doubt that the puppet representation of Humpty Dumpty detailed therein would have had far greater appeal to the child-loving, sometime

marionette enthusiast Lewis Carroll than the subsequent portrayal by the legendary child-hating comedian W. C. Fields in the Paramount film version of *Alice* in 1933.

PHILA, *September* 12, 1898.

Dear Sir,—I shall be very glad to furnish what information I can with respect to the 'Mechanical Humpty Dumpty' which I constructed a few years ago, but I must begin by ackowledging that, in one sense at least, I did not 'invent' the figure. The idea was first put into my head by an article in the *Cosmopolitan,* somewhere about 1891, I suppose, describing a similar contrivance. As a devoted admirer of the 'Alice' books, I determined to build a Humpty Dumpty of my own; but I left the model set by the author of the article mentioned, and constructed the figure on entirely different lines. In the first place, the figure as described in the magazine had very few movements, and not very satisfactory ones at that; and in the second place, no attempt whatever was made to reproduce, even in a general way, the well-known appearance of Tenniel's drawing.

Humpty, when completed, was about two feet and a half high. His face, of course, was white; the lower half of the egg was dressed in brilliant blue. His stockings were grey, and the famous cravat orange, with a zigzag pattern in blue. I am sorry to say that the photograph hardly does him justice; but he had travelled to so many different places during his career, that he began to be decidedly out of shape before he sat for his portrait.

263

When Humpty was about to perform, a short 'talk' was usually given before the curtain rose, explaining the way in which the Sheep put the egg on the shelf at the back of the little shop, and how Alice went groping along to it. And then, just as the explanation had reached the opening of the chapter on Humpty Dumpty, the curtain rose, and Humpty was discovered, sitting on the wall, and gazing into vacancy. As soon as the audience had had time to recover, Alice entered, and the conversation was carried on just as it is in the book. Humpty Dumpty gesticulated with his arms, rolled his eyes, raised his eyebrows, frowned, turned up his nose in scorn at Alice's ignorance, and smiled from ear to ear when he shook hands with her. Besides this, his mouth kept time with his words all through the dialogue, which added very greatly to his life-like appearance.

The effect of his huge face, as it changed from one expression to another, was ludicrous in the extreme, and we were often obliged to repeat sentences in the conversation (to 'go back to the last remark but one') because the audience laughed so loudly over Humpty Dumpty's expression of face that they drowned what he was trying to say. The funniest effect was the change from the look of self-satisfied complacency with which he accompanied the words: 'The king has promised me—' to that of towering rage when Alice innocently betrays her knowledge of the secret. At the close of the scene, when Alice has vainly endeavoured to draw him into further conversation, and at last walks away in disgust, Humpty loses his balance on the wall, recovers himself, totters again, and then falls off backwards; at the same time a box full of broken glass is dropped on the floor behind the scenes, to represent the 'heavy crash,' which 'shook the forest from end to end'; – and the curtain falls.

Now, as to how it was all done. Humpty was made of barrel hoops, and covered with stiff paper and muslin. His eyes were round balls of rags, covered with muslin, drawn smoothly, and with the pupil and iris marked on the front. These eyes were pivoted to a board, fastened just behind the eye-openings in the face. To the eyeballs were sewed strong pieces of tape, which passed through screw-eyes on the edges of the board, and so down to a row of levers which were hinged in the lower part of the figure. One lever raised both eyes upward, another moved them both to the left, and so on. The eyebrows were of worsted and india-rubber knitted together. They were fastened at the ends, and raised and lowered by fine white threads passing through small holes in the face, and also operated by levers. The arms projected into the interior of the machine, and the gestures were made by moving the short ends inside. The right hand contained a spring clothes-pin, by which he was enabled to hold the notebook in which Alice set down the celebrated problem:

$$\frac{365}{1} = 364$$

The movement of the mouth, in talking, was produced by a long tape, running down to a pedal, which was controlled by the foot of the performer.

And the smile consisted of long strips of red tape, which were drawn out through slits at the corners of the mouth by means of threads which passed through holes in the sides of the head. The performer – who was always your humble servant – stood on a box behind the wall, his head just reaching the top of the egg, which was open all the way up the back. At the lower end of the figure, convenient to the hands of the performer, was the row of levers, like a little keyboard; and by striking different chords on the keys, any desired expression could be produced on the face.

Of course, a performance of this kind without a good Alice would be unutterably flat; but the little girl who played opposite to Humpty, Miss Nellie K——, was so exactly the counterpart of Alice, both in appearance and disposition, that most children thought she was the original, right out of the book.

Humpty still exists, but he has not seen active life for some years. His own popularity was the cause of his retirement; for having given a number of performances (for Charity, of course), and delighted many thousands of children of all ages, the demands upon his time, from Sunday-schools and other institutions, became so numerous that the performers were obliged to withdraw him in self-defence. He was a great deal of trouble to build, but the success he met with and the pleasure he gave more than repaid me for the bother; and I am sure that any one else who tries it will reach the same conclusion.

Yours sincerely,

WALTER LINDSAY

This same letter was included seventy years later in the official catalogue for 'Play Orbit', an exhibition of original toys and games by selected artists held at the Institute of Contemporary Arts, London during Christmas, 1969. It would be interesting to know what Carroll, with his 'Off with her head!' penchant for black humour at a nursery level, would have thought of the juvenile decapitation kits and deformity-ridden dolls jostling side by side with his own Humpty Dumpty in those glossy pages.

The Crocodile and the Baby

'How doth the little crocodile
    Improve his shining tail,
And pour the waters of the Nile
    On every golden scale!

'How cheerfully he seems to grin,
    How neatly spreads his claws,
And welcomes little fishes in,
    With gently smiling jaws!'

Alice's Adventures in Wonderland

The most exciting happening in Carrollian scholarship in recent years has been the gradual discovery by W. W. Bartley III, professor of philosophy at Pittsburgh University, of the complete manuscript and galley proofs of Carroll's sequel to *Symbolic Logic: Part 1, Elementary*. The full extent of the light thrown by the find upon Carroll's status as a logician will not be revealed until the publication of Bartley's critical edition of the completed work. However, a preview of what lies in store was given in an article, 'Lewis Carroll's Lost Book on Logic', in the July, 1972 edition of *Scientific American*. Bartley's article, in addition to suggesting a newly discovered originality in Carroll's work as a logician, poised as it was between the traditional Aristotelian school and the new logic espoused by Bertrand Russell, also confirmed not only his expertise as a propounder of puzzles and paradoxes, but also that in this field aspects of Wonderland still persisted in the whimsical hinterland of his imagination. Many of the characters who have their own specific points to make in the new book would not apparently have been out of place along Alice's curious path: the Sympathetic Friend and the Small Girl glad she doesn't like asparagus, because if she did, she would have to eat it – 'and I can't bear it'; the Pork-Chop-eating Logician and the Gambler; Achilles and the Tortoise, and the Three Barbers, in the form we have already met them; the Crocodile and the Baby; the Liar, reported most concisely of all: 'If a man says "I am telling a lie", and speaks truly, he *is* telling a lie, and therefore speaks falsely; but if he speaks falsely, he is *not* telling a lie, and therefore speaks truly.'

The majority of the puzzles in the volume date back to classical times, but there is no mistaking the new identity his presentation gives the characters concerned, enhanced by memories of their counterparts in the earlier works. Thus it is hard not to believe that the Crocodile, for all its Stoic origins, hasn't been grinning and gleaming, walking 'on the top of its tail, and along its back, all the way to its head', ever since it claimed Carroll's attention in a logical context. In this, the most colourful of the problems, Carroll, exploiting that ambiguous limboland between statement of intention and actual deed, asks his readers to imagine a conversation between the crocodile and the mother of a baby born on the banks of the Nile. The crocodile has abducted the baby and the mother, anxious for its safety, pleads for its return. The crocodile, whose good word is implicit, then specifies that if the mother can predict accurately the fate it intends for the child – whether to devour it or return it home – the child will be handed back to her. However, if she fails to state the true outcome of its intention, the baby will be gobbled down. The mother asserts that the crocodile will devour the child, whereupon the crocodile replies that now he cannot restore the baby, as, if he restores it, she will have predicted falsely, the fate for which was the baby's death. The mother, however, for all her grief, proves a match for the wily reptile, because, as she claims, if he does devour the baby, she will have spoken truly and the promise in that case was that the baby would be returned!

'It *were* proud of its new tail! Oo never saw a Crocodile so proud! Why it could go round and walk on the top of its tail, and along its back, all the way to its head!' *(Sylvie and Bruno)*

Pepper's Ghost

'I've caught a cold,' the Thing replies,
'Out there upon the landing.'
I turned to look in some surprise,
And there, before my very eyes,
A little Ghost was standing!

Phantasmagoria

'Pepper's Ghost' was the brainchild of two men: Henry Dircks (1806–1873), a civil engineer to whom the project owed its basic technical details, and Professor John Henry Pepper (1821–1900), a lecturer in chemistry and optics at the Royal Polytechnic Institution in Regent Street where he became honorary director in 1852. It was Pepper who injected the life-blood of showmanship into the idea and worked out the necessary modifications required for a stage presentation which would preserve its essential mystery.

Dircks had lodged the details of his apparatus for producing 'spectral optical illusions' with the British Association in September, 1858, but not until December 24, 1862 did Pepper first present the idea before the public, as an illustration of Charles Dickens's *The Haunted Man*. By means of the device live actors and ghosts could appear together on a fully lit stage, a development emphasised in the provisional patent specification filed on February 5, 1863:

> The object of our said Invention is by a peculiar arrangement of apparatus to associate on the same stage a phantom or phantoms with a living actor or actors, so that the two may act in concert, but which is only an optical illusion as respects the one or more phantoms so introduced.
>
> The arrangement of the theatre requires in addition to the ordinary stage a second stage at a lower level than the ordinary one, hidden from the audience as far as direct vision is concerned; this hidden stage is to be strongly illuminated by artificial light, and is capable of being rendered dark instantaneously whilst the ordinary stage and the theatre remain illuminated by ordinary lighting. A large glass screen is placed on the ordinary stage and in front of the hidden one.
>
> The spectators will not observe the glass screen, but will see the actors on the ordinary stage through it as if it were not there; nevertheless the glass will serve to reflect to them an image of the actors on the hidden stage when these are illuminated, but this image will be made immediately to disappear by darkening the hidden stage. The glass screen is set in a frame so that it can readily be moved to the place required, and it is to be set at an inclination to enable the spectators, whether in the pit, boxes, or gallery, to see the reflected image.

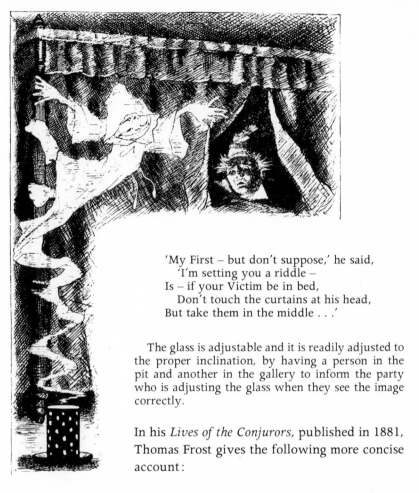

'My First – but don't suppose,' he said,
  'I'm setting you a riddle –
Is – if your Victim be in bed,
  Don't touch the curtains at his head,
But take them in the middle . . .'

The glass is adjustable and it is readily adjusted to
the proper inclination, by having a person in the
pit and another in the gallery to inform the party
who is adjusting the glass when they see the image
correctly.

In his *Lives of the Conjurors,* published in 1881,
Thomas Frost gives the following more concise
account:

In the production of this illusion in a theatre or music-hall, the figure to be
reproduced is placed below the level of the stage, and strongly illuminated
by the oxy-hydrogen or other powerful light. A large sheet of plate-glass
is placed on the front of the stage, at an angle regulated by the distance
between the figure below and the spectator, so that the reflected image
shall appear to the audience to be behind the glass, at a distance which will
permit an actor on the stage to apparently walk through the phantom,
pierce it with a sword, etc. As the actor cannot see the ghosts, these movements require very nice management. The floor of the stage is marked for
certain positions, and the mechanical arrangements must allow the person
who represents the ghost to see the actors on the stage, and also his own

reflection. The auditorium is darkened, and the glass cannot, if properly arranged, be detected by the spectators.

The reproduction of the ghost image was essentially the same as a normal mirror reflection, the image apparently reproduced behind the glass at the same distance as the figure is in front of it. That a plain unsilvered sheet of plate glass can serve as a mirror should not puzzle people who when plunged into a tunnel during a train journey have suddenly found themselves staring out of the window at their own double. Whether it was this full-scale version of the phenomenon which Pepper presented at Cheltenham in April, 1863 or merely the 'Miniature Ghost of a danseuse' mentioned in *The True History of the Ghost*, Pepper's own account of the involved legal tangles which came increasingly to surround his project, it is hard to imagine that his ingeniously practical portrayal of straightforward action in what amounted to a mirror-reversed world would not have triggered off a response in Carroll's own fantastic imagination. And whether or not Carroll ever visualised Alice as standing behind Pepper's invisible glass barrier and the denizens of Looking-Glass land in the secret well of some weathered stage, not least the Red Queen who did vanish with 'no way of guessing', he would not have failed to register the 'modus vivendi' which this Pepper, not Pig's partner, had unconsciously volunteered to make his Cheshire Cat a reality, appearing and disappearing gradually or in its entirety in full view of its special audience of one. It is worth noting that neither the Cheshire Cat nor the 'Pig and Pepper' episode figured in the earliest version of *Alice's Adventures in Wonderland* as told on the trip to God-stow in 1862. They did not appear until the full publication of the book in 1865, where the word 'Pepper' is accorded a status in the chapter title which it would have been more appropriate to allow the cat itself – unless Carroll was attaching a more than superficial alliterative import-ance to the word!

Until one can prove inconclusively that by 'Herr Dobler' Carroll did mean Pepper, one is prepared to accept charges of being far-fetched; the ghost of Pepper himself, one trusts, as ready to be considered with a proverbial grain of salt. If, however, one is reassured at all it is by Carroll himself, or at least by the Red Queen just prior to vanishing: 'You may call it "nonsense" if you like,' she said, 'but *I've* heard non-sense, compared with which that would be as sensible as a dictionary!'

Solutions

The three squares

page 59

Tangrams

page 99

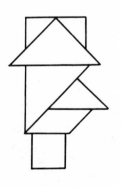

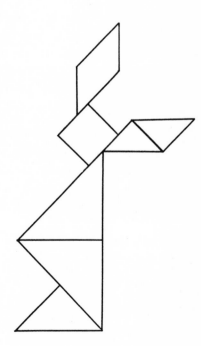

Tangrams (*continued*)

page 99

Dudeney, in his *Amusements in Mathematics*, resolves the paradox as follows:

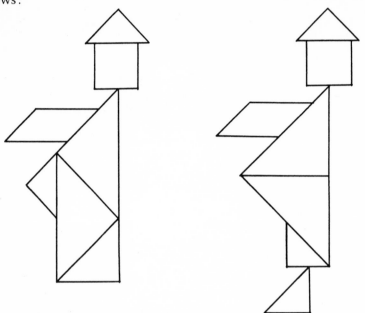

The square window

pages 105–6

A brief comparison of the two illustrations will immediately quell any 'awful effects' such as intimated by Carroll:

The third illustration reveals a window measuring one foot on each side, with eight triangular lights six inches on each side:

At no point does Dudeney specify that window or lights must be square!

Rab–Ymra–?

page 217

There are two ways in fact of getting the maximum of twenty readings. One has only to exchange the Vs with the Is, and the Ls with the Es to arrive at the other.

		I	V	E	L		
E	V	L			I		
L			I			V	E
I		V	E				L
	E			L	V		I
	L			I		E	V
V		E	L			I	
	I			V	E	L	

Afterword

This volume has been an attempt to bring forward some of the magic and fun of Lewis Carroll smothered by the spate of serious criticism and analysis of the author and his work that has gushed forth in recent years. Academics, often earnestly seizing upon the *Alice* books as a coat-hanger for their own fantasies, have variously interpreted Carroll's representation of Alice Liddell as pastoral swain and phallic symbol, as Jungian anima and the first acid-head in children's literature; have laid bare the books themselves as allegories of philosophical systems and Darwinian evolution, of the Oxford Movement and Victorian toilet training. Carroll's own character has itself been scrupulously toothcombed in the often wearisome cause of these theories. Had the Oxford don, who according to his diary used to entertain children by showing them how to produce intriguing designs by blotting their names in creased paper, realised that his two masterpieces would one day achieve combined notoriety as the fashionable Rorschach ink-blot of criticism, it is hard not to believe that *Alice* would have been lost to the world, the manuscripts torn into the shreds he often threatened when projects went amiss.

A book seen originally as light relief amid a heavy hodge-podge of scholarship and pretension, ingenuity and wishful thinking, must reflect the whole panorama of light relief as seen through *Carroll's* eyes. It is for this reason that nursery tricks here jostle side by side with complex mathematical games and joky word play with involved logical paradox. Carroll's own sense of playfulness transcended the normal idea to the extent that it alone has assured him recognition as mathematician and logician. His straightforward work in both these fields was disappointing, although, as we have seen, recent literary discoveries may cause some reassessment of his reputation in the latter. He had no qualms, however, about using both as escape routes, as playthings of their own. And, ironically, it was in so doing that he then justifiably found himself in the spiritual company of mathematicians as distinguished as Leibnitz and Newton, Abel and Pascal, obsessed with probability and methods of scoring, paradox and ciphers, new games and newer versions of old ones. His logical problems and paradoxes became worthy of later consideration by philosophical names as eminent as Russell and Whitehead, Eddington and Millikan.

It is unlikely that Carroll himself would have been aware of how important his sense of fun and escapism would subsequently be to his reputation in those fields other than nonsense literature. If this had been so, his modesty, his hypersensitivity, his sense of propriety all suggest he would have been embarrassed into other avenues of escape, no longer the White Knight, but his own White Rabbit, scurrying away agitated in the realisation that it was too late.

J.F.

Bibliography

Abbott, Edwin Abbott: *Flatland*. London: Seeley; 1884

Abraham, R. M.: *Winter Nights Entertainments*. London: Constable; 1932

Albee, Edward: *Tiny Alice*. New York: Atheneum; 1965

Atherton, James S.: *The Books at the Wake*. New York: Viking; 1960

Auden, W. H.: 'The Man who Wrote "Alice" '; *New York Times Book Review*, February 28, 1954

——: 'Today's "Wonder-World" Needs Alice'; *New York Times Magazine*, July 1, 1962

Barr, Stephen: *Experiments in Topology*. New York: Crowell; 1964

Barry, John: 'The Game of Life: is it just a game?' *The Sunday Times*, June 13, 1971

Bartley, W. W.: 'Lewis Carroll's Lost Book on Logic'; *Scientific American*, July, 1972

Bombaugh, C. C.: *Oddities and Curiosities of Words and Literature*. New York: Dover; 1961

Borges, Jorge Luis: *Labyrinths*. New York: New Directions; 1964

Borgmann, Dmitri A.: *Language on Vacation*. New York: Charles Scribner's Sons; 1965

——: *Beyond Language*. New York: Charles Scribner's Sons; 1967

Bowman, Isa: *The Story of Lewis Carroll*. London: Dent; 1899

Braithwaite, R. B.: 'Lewis Carroll as Logician'; *The Mathematical Gazette*, July, 1932

Carroll, Lewis: *Explication of the Enigma*. Oxford: private circulation; 1866

——: *Circular Billiards*. Oxford: private circulation; 1890

——: *Some Rare Carrolliana* (with notes by Sidney Herbert Williams). London: private circulation; 1924

——: *The Collected Verse of Lewis Carroll*. London: Macmillan; 1932

——: *The Rectory Umbrella and Mischmasch*. London: Cassell; 1932

——: *The Diaries of Lewis Carroll* (edited by Roger Lancelyn Green). London: Cassell; 1953

——: *Useful and Instructive Poetry*. London: Geoffrey Bles; 1954

——: *Pillow-Problems and A Tangled Tale*. New York: Dover; 1958

——: *Symbolic Logic and the Game of Logic*. New York: Dover; 1958

——: *The Works of Lewis Carroll* (edited by Roger Lancelyn Green). London: Hamlyn; 1965

Christopher, Milbourne: *Panorama of Magic*. New York: Dover; 1962

Collingwood, Stuart Dodgson, ed.: *The Lewis Carroll Picture Book*. London: T. Fisher Unwin: 1899 (reissued as *Diversions and Digressions of Lewis Carroll*. New York: Dover; 1961)

——: *The Life and Letters of Lewis Carroll*. London: T. Fisher Unwin; 1898

Corinda: *Thirteen Steps to Mentalism*. London: Corinda's Magic Studio; 1958

Coxeter, H. S. M.: 'The Four Colour Map Problem, 1840-1890', *Mathematics Teacher*, April, 1959

Cremer Jnr., W. H., ed.: *The Secret Out*. London: Chatto & Windus; c. 1871

——, ed.: *The Magician's Own Book*. Edinburgh: John Grant; 1871

——, ed.: *Magic no Mystery*. Edinburgh: John Grant; 1876

Crutch, Denis, & R. B. Shaberman: *Under the Quizzing Glass*. London: Magpie Press; 1972

Curry, Paul: *Magician's Magic*. London: Whiting & Wheaton; 1966

Davies, Rev. Ivor Ll.: 'Looking-Glass Chess', *The Anglo-Welsh Review*, Autumn, 1970

De La Mare, Walter: *Lewis Carroll*. London: Faber & Faber; 1932

De Vries, Leonard: *The Book of Experiments*. London: John Murray; 1958

——: *The Second Book of Experiments*. London: John Murray; 1963

——: *The Third Book of Experiments*. London: John Murray; 1965

Dudeney, Henry Ernest: *Amusements in Mathematics*. London: Thomas Nelson; 1917

——: *The Canterbury Puzzles*. London: Thomas Nelson; 1919

——: *The World's Best Word Puzzles*. London: Daily News; 1925

Eddington, Arthur Stanley: *Space, Time and Gravitation*. Cambridge: University Press; 1920

Elliott, Bruce: *Classic Secrets of Magic*. London: Faber & Faber; 1953

Eperson, D. B.: 'Lewis Carroll, Mathematician', *The Mathematical Gazette*, May, 1933

Frost, Thomas: *The Lives of the Conjurors*. London: Chatto & Windus; 1881

Gamow, George, & Marvin Stern: *Puzzle-Math*. London: Macmillan; 1958

Gardner, Martin: *Mathematics, Magic and Mystery*. New York: Dover; 1956

——, ed.: *The Annotated Alice*. New York: Clarkson N. Potter; 1960

——: 'The Games and Puzzles of Lewis Carroll', *Scientific American*, March, 1960

——: *Mathematical Puzzles and Diversions*. London: Bell; 1961

——, ed.: *The Annotated Snark*. New York: Bramhall House; 1962

——: *More Mathematical Puzzles and Diversions*. London: Bell; 1963

——: *The Ambidextrous Universe*. London: Allen Lane, The Penguin Press; 1967

——: 'Can Time Go Backward?', *Scientific American*, January, 1967

——: *New Mathematical Diversions*. London: George Allen & Unwin; 1969

——: *Further Mathematical Diversions*. London: George Allen & Unwin; 1970

——: *Sixth Book of Mathematical Games*. San Francisco: Freeman; 1971

Gernsheim, Helmut: *Lewis Carroll, Photographer*. London: Max Parrish; 1949

Green, Roger Lancelyn, ed.: *The Diaries of Lewis Carroll*, 2 volumes. London: Cassell; 1953

——: 'Lewis Carroll's Fugitive Pieces', *Times Literary Supplement*, July 31, 1953

——, ed.: *The Lewis Carroll Handbook* (see Sidney Herbert Williams and Falconer Madan). London: Oxford University Press; 1962

——, ed.: *The Works of Lewis Carroll*. London: Hamlyn; 1965

——: 'Looking-Glass Reflections', *Jabberwocky*, Autumn, 1971

——: 'Haigha Hunting', *Jabberwocky*, Spring, 1972

Harbin, Robert: *Paper Magic*. London: Oldbourne; 1956

——: *Party Lines*. London: Oldbourne; 1963

——: *Origami: the Art of Paper-Folding*. London: Hodder; 1969

Hatch, Evelyn M.: *A selection from the Letters of Lewis Carroll to his child-friends*. London: Macmillan; 1933

Hay, Henry, ed.: *Cyclopedia of Magic*. Philadelphia: McKay; 1949

Heath, Royal Vale: *Math e Magic*. New York: Dover; 1953

Hindman, Darwin A.: *1,800 Riddles, Enigmas and Conundrums*. New York: Dover; 1963

Hoffmann, Professor Louis (Angelo Lewis): *Modern Magic*; London: Routledge; 1886

———: *More Magic*. London: Routledge; 1890

———: *Later Magic*. London: Routledge; 1904

Hudson, Derek: *Lewis Carroll*. London: Constable; 1954

James, William: *Principles of Psychology*. New York: Holt; 1890

Jourdain, Philip E. B.: *The Philosophy of Mr. B*rtr*nd R*ss*ll*. London: George Allen & Unwin; 1918

Joyce, James: *Finnegan's Wake*. London: Faber & Faber; 1939

Koestler, Arthur: *The Roots of Coincidence*. London: Hutchinson; 1972

Lee, Wallace: *Math Miracles*. Durham, North Carolina: Lee's Magic Studio; 1960

Lennon, Florence Becker: *Victoria Through the Looking-Glass*. New York: Simon & Schuster; 1945

———: *The Life of Lewis Carroll*. New York: Collier; 1962

Levin, Harry: 'Wonderland Revisited', *Kenyon Review*, Vol. 27, 1965

Loyd, Sam: *Cyclopedia of Puzzles*. New York: Loyd, Jnr.; 1914

———: *The Mathematical Puzzles of Sam Loyd*, 2 volumes. New York: Dover; 1959 & 1960

MacDonald, Greville: *George MacDonald and his Wife*. London: George Allen & Unwin; 1924

Madan, Falconer, ed.: *The Lewis Carroll Centenary Catalogue*. London: J. & E. Bumpus; 1932

———, & Sidney Herbert Williams: *The Lewis Carroll Handbook* (revised by Roger Lancelyn Green). London: Oxford University Press; 1962 (reissued London: Dawson; 1970)

Milner, Florence: 'Mathematics and Fun', *St. Nicholas Magazine* (New York), November, 1927

Nabokov, Vladimir: *Pale Fire*. London: Weidenfeld & Nicolson; 1962

———: *The Defence*. London: Weidenfeld & Nicolson; 1964

———: *Speak Memory*. London: Weidenfeld & Nicolson; 1967

Neil, C. Lang: *The Modern Conjuror*. London: C. Arthur Pearson; 1903

Newman, James R., ed.: *The World of Mathematics*. New York: Simon & Schuster; 1956

Northrop, Eugene P.: *Riddles in Mathematics*. London: English Universities Press; 1945

O'Beirne, T. H.: *Puzzles and Paradoxes*. London: Oxford University Press; 1965

Ovenden, Graham, ed,: *The Illustrators of Alice*. London: Academy Editions; 1972

Parrish, Robert, ed.: *Bert Allerton's The Close-up Magician*. Chicago: Ireland Magic Company; 1958

Pedoe, Dan: *The Gentle Art of Mathematics*. London: English Universities Press; 1958

Pepper, Professor John Henry: *The True History of the Ghost*. London: Cassell; 1890

Read, Ronald C.: *Tangrams*. New York: Dover; 1965

Reed, Langford: *The Life of Lewis Carroll*. London: Foyle; 1932

Reichardt, Jasia, ed.: *Play Orbit*. London: Studio International; 1969

Robson, Lancelot: 'Give My Love to the Children', *The Reader's Digest*, February, 1953

Rowell, Ethel: *Time and Time Again*. London: George Allen & Unwin; 1941

Royce, Josiah: *The World and the Individual*. New York: Macmillan; 1899

Russell, A. S.: 'Lewis Carroll, Tutor and Mathematician', *The Listener*, January 13, 1932

Russell, Bertrand: *Principia Mathematica*. London: George Allen & Unwin; 1937

Russell, L. J.: 'A Problem of Lewis Carroll', *Mind*, July, 1951

Scarne, John: *Scarne's Magic Tricks*. London: Constable; 1953

Sewell, Elizabeth: *The Field of Nonsense*. London: Chatto & Windus; 1952

Shaberman, R. B., & Denis Crutch: *Under the Quizzing Glass*. London: Magpie Press; 1972

Shepherd, Walter: *Mazes and Labyrinths*. New York: Dover; 1961

Smith, John Maynard: 'The Limits of Molecular Evolution', *The Scientist Speculates* (ed. I. J. Good). London: Heinemann; 1962

Stern, Marvin, & George Gamow: *Puzzle-Math*. London: Macmillan; 1958

Taylor, Alexander L.: *The White Knight: A Study of C. L. Dodgson*. Edinburgh: Oliver & Boyd; 1952

——: Talk given to the Lewis Carroll Society, London, on October 6, 1971, *Jabberwocky*, Winter, 1971

Verbeek, Gustave: *The Incredible Upside-Downs of Gustave Verbeek*. Summit, N. J.: The Rajah Press; 1963

Watson, James D.: *The Double Helix*. London: Weidenfeld & Nicolson; 1968

Weaver, Warren: 'Lewis Carroll and a Geometrical Paradox', *American Mathematical Monthly*, April, 1938

——: 'The Mathematical Manuscripts of Lewis Carroll', *Proceedings of the American Philosophical Society*, October, 1954

——: 'Lewis Carroll: Mathematician', *Scientific American*, April, 1956

Wiener, Norbert: *Cybernetics*. New York: John Wiley; 1948

Willane: *Willane's Wizardry*. London: Arcas; 1947

Williams, Sidney Herbert, & Falconer Madan: *The Lewis Carroll Handbook* (revised by Roger Lancelyn Green). London: Oxford University Press; 1962 (reissued London: Dawson; 1970)

Winkfield, Trevor, ed.: *Juillard*, Spring, 1972. Leeds: private circulation

Woolf, Virginia: 'Lewis Carroll', *The Moment, and other Essays*. London: Hogarth Press; 1947

Acknowledgements

One has to extend thanks in many directions for help given in compiling this volume. Special mention must be made of the courtesy shown by Philip Jaques, the great-nephew of C. L. Dodgson, and Mrs. Georgina Christie, his great-niece; of the enthusiasm and kindness of Anne Clark of The Lewis Carroll Society, based at the County Hall, London; and of the tireless work by Bill West and Peter Eldin, Honorary Librarians of The International Brotherhood of Magicians (British Ring). Other individuals to whom I am indebted for their patience, interest and generosity include W. H. Auden, Stephen Barr, John Horton Conway, Ivor Ll. Davies, Richard Drewett and all my BBC colleagues, Selwyn Goodacre, Roger Lancelyn Green, Patricia Houlihan, Jonathan Miller, Patrick Moore, Thomas O'Beirne, Graham Ovenden, Michael Parkinson, Alexander L. Taylor, Terry Wright and Warren Weaver.

Research was facilitated by the staffs of the Bodleian Library, Oxford; the British Museum; the University Library, Cambridge; and the Guildford Muniment Room. A detailed bibliography is appended to the text.

I am indebted to all the authors listed, but the work in the field of Carrollian scholarship by Roger Lancelyn Green and in that of recreational mathematics by Martin Gardner should be underlined for special mention; while Gardner's own contribution to Carrollian lore, *The Annotated Alice*, is the one work guaranteed to convince the most resolute sceptic that the work of Lewis Carroll has an appeal far beyond nursery level.

Grateful thanks are extended to the Executors of the Rev. C. L. Dodgson and to A. P. Watt and Son for permission to reproduce on pages 20, 55, 57 and 63 facsimile material first published in *Some Rare Carrolliana*; the facsimile of the charade beginning "The air is bright with hues of light"; the double acrostic beginning "I sing a place wherein agree" first published in *The Lewis Carroll Centenary Catalogue*; the poem "Facts" first published in *The Collected Verse of Lewis Carroll*. Also, in addition to the above two parties, to Roger Lancelyn Green for permission to reproduce the full texts of "Arithmetical Croquet" and "Mr. C. & Mr. T." from *The Diaries of Lewis Carroll*; "The Anagrammatic Sonnet" and the charade beginning "They both make a roaring" from *The Lewis Carroll Handbook*.

The illustrations from *A Tangled Tale* (page 146) and *Phantasmagoria* (pages 184 and 269) by Arthur B. Frost, from *Sylvie and Bruno* (page 267)

280

by Harry Furniss, and from *The Hunting of the Snark* (page 249) by Henry Holiday are all reproduced by kind permission of Macmillan and Company. The picture-puzzles of Sam Loyd are reproduced from the two-volume Dover edition of his puzzles, edited by Martin Gardner, while the original drawings by Carroll of the cat and the sow on page 247 are from the collection of artist Graham Ovenden.

Every effort has been made to acknowledge the copyright of material used in this volume and apologies are made for any omissions that may have occurred, omissions which will be corrected in subsequent editions.

J.F.

Index